COMMITTED
JOURNALISM

EDMUND B. LAMBETH

COMMITTED JOURNALISM

An Ethic for the Profession

Indiana University Press

BLOOMINGTON

Manufactured in the United States of America

Library of Congress Cataloging in Publication Data

Lambeth, Edmund B.
  Committed journalism.

  Bibliography: p.
  Includes index.
  1. Journalistic ethics. I. Title.
PN4756.L33   1986   174'.9097   85-42847
ISBN 0-253-31392-9
ISBN 0-253-20364-3 (pbk.)
1 2 3 4 5   90 89 87 86

Contents

PREFACE

Many American journalists believe, as do I, that the American press, overall, is the freest and probably the best in the world; yet that position has not been particularly persuasive with the public. A 1984 poll by the National Opinion Research Center (NORC) of the University of Chicago reports that only 16.7 percent of the American public had "a great deal of confidence" in the American press. In only one other year since 1973 has the rating been lower: 13.4 percent in 1983.

Reacting to the public, journalists themselves have become introspective. They are holding conferences and chartering surveys on news media credibility. Journalism professors are demonstrating their propensity—once disparaged by the late H. L. Mencken—for writing articles and books on ethics of the field they have allegedly forsaken. The news media themselves are reporting openly on the dismal state of their own public relations.

For perspective, it is helpful to list the relative ratings for other institutions included in the 1984 NORC poll. The press ranked tenth, above television but just below the executive branch of the federal government. Here are the ratings:

Medicine	50.4%
Scientific community	44.0
Military	35.5
U.S. Supreme Court	32.8
Banks and financial institutions	31.3
Organized religion	30.7
Major companies	30.4
Education	27.8
Executive Branch	18.3
Press	16.7
Television	13.0
Congress	12.4
Organized labor	8.5

Clearly it is a time of declining faith in all institutions. For journalism, this circumstance seems linked to an increasing awareness by the public of the news media's power over people's lives. Researchers also have shown that bad news affects personal moods. Bad news hurts, upsets, and, in an increasingly complex world, it can disorient. And if the world is more complicated with its new technology and its painful and mysterious new global economy, it also is unsteady in matters of morals. Church, school, family, and marriage are seen by many to be losing their once steadying grip on the hearts of people.

The temptation, at this point in the analysis, is to blame journalism's trouble on everybody else but journalists. After all, the illogic flows, if every other institution is having similar trouble, it must be due to factors that we either can't much alter or about which we shouldn't be overly worried. True, the messenger whose duty includes the bringing of bad news may be blamed, and is thereby at an inherent disadvantage with a public at which he or she may frequently be at loggerheads. The problem with that point is that journalists can use it to ignore needed changes in their own behavior. They can use it to eschew dialogue with the public. Messengers can learn how to tell their messages better. The recipients can learn more about how and why those messages are gathered and relayed, and about the strengths and weaknesses of the system for bringing tidings. Both messenger and audience can learn to think more carefully about the ethics of journalistic communication. Progress can be made in all these respects. This book is for the frail humans who consume as well as those who gather the news.

The new salience of the news media in American society dates back at least to the 1960s. Since that time, a large scholarly and popular literature on the news media has accumulated. Journalism, communication, social psychology, political science, and sociology have all, as academic disciplines, contributed to this outpouring. Findings have made their way from the academic journals into university courses on mass media and society, the history of journalism, and—increasingly—the ethics of journalism.

Valuable new insights have come from a body of scholarship that identifies the organizational influences on journalists and examines the epistemology of journalism for factors that might help explain the limits on its role as a chronicler of useful truth and of reality itself. A supposedly strictly "objective" journalism has been shown to be, not necessarily deliberately opinioned or biased, but heavily influenced by occupational and societal values.

In the field of history, higher critical standards and a new group of historians have made less acceptable the kind of almost idolatrous treatment of major figures in journalism heretofore prevailing. Social and economic analyses, set in a historical context, are much more common than flattering narrative. A warts-and-all approach or a sophisticated historical interpretation is as likely to spring from the pens of scholars these days as an uncritical portrayal of the press.

Journalism and higher education are richer for this scholarship. However, the field is only recently beginning to develop a literature on normative ethics—that is, systematic reflections on what is right and wrong, good and bad in journalism. And the reasons for this tardiness are not hard to find. Those most likely to produce such a literature have been either preoccupied or otherwise restrained. Philosophers, with some important exceptions, have largely avoided the field. Journalists themselves are, by occupational nature, uncomfortable with the unavoidable abstractions of ethics, a disposition shared as well by some teachers of journalism. The journalism fraternity, too, is notoriously shy about writing on the field that might be interpreted as "preachy or self-righteous"—a reflection, perhaps, not only of humility but of just how problematic the ethics of the field can sometimes be.

Despite these built-in obstacles, substantial progress has been made. Walter Lippmann's books, of course, remain classics, beacons in the field. A generation has been enlightened by the now dated *Four Theories of the Press,* the University of Illinois Press volume by Fred S. Siebert, Theodore Peterson, and Wilbur Schramm first published in 1956. The scholarship of Schramm, and William L. Rivers of Stanford University, kept alive the social responsibility themes first struck authoritatively in the late 1940s by the Commission on Freedom of the Press, headed by the late Robert M. Hutchins. Professors John L. Hulteng, of the University of Oregon and Stanford, and J. Edward Gerald of the University of Minnesota contributed importantly in books and in their teaching. And John C. Merrill, now at Louisiana State University, continues to provoke important thought and discussion. More recently, significant surveys of the status of ethical practice in the field were written by Bruce Swain of the University of Georgia, in 1978, and by H. Eugene Goodwin of Pennsylvania State University, in 1983. Professor Clifford Christians at the University of Illinois, first chair of the Ad Hoc Committee on Ethics of the Association for Education in Journalism and Mass Communication, has helped stimulate interest in research and the teaching of ethics. Professor Everette C. Dennis, formerly dean at the University of Oregon School and now director of the Gannett Foundation's Center for Media Studies at Columbia University, has advanced the field not only by scholarship but by his organizational leadership. I have benefited from reading the works of these scholars and I would like to acknowledge the encouragement which their scholarship represents.

Three organizations deserve special mention. Indiana University's School of Journalism gave me the opportunity to teach ethics within a free-standing course, the Media as Social Institutions. Kenneth R. R. Gros Louis, vice-president in charge of IU's Bloomington campus, included me on a university-wide committee on ethics which, meeting at IU's Poynter Center, provided valuable encouragement and criticism. All of higher education owes a debt to the Institute of Society, Ethics, and the Life Sciences in Hastings-on-Hudson, New York—better known as the Hastings Center. Headed by Daniel Callahan, the center has encouraged the teaching of applied ethics in a variety of fields, including journalism. Finally, the Gannett Foundation, a stalwart in the support of journalism education, gave the School of Journalism at the University of Kentucky a generous grant with which to finance workshops in 1984, 1985, and 1986 on the teaching of ethics in schools and departments of journalism and mass communication. The task of organizing that workshop has been valuable and stimulating.

This book attempts to identify a framework of principles of ethical journalism from the articulated ideals, codes, and, most importantly, accepted best practice in the field. It presents and examines this framework not as a mechanistic panacea for moral dilemmas but as a useful approach for thinking through ethical problems, considering differences of judgment, and evaluating the performance of the news media. Far from being an individual contrivance, the framework consists of a set of principles deducible from the history, philosophy, and practice of journalism. Because it sets forth a normative approach, the book is polemical in nature but with sustained ethical dialogue rather than infallible judgment as its objective.

Chapter 1 argues that problems within journalism and in its relationship to the public require philosophic reflection that is more practical and adaptable to individual journalists than that which emerged from the 1947 study by the Hutchins Commission. Chapter 2 portrays and critiques the classical ethical theories as a journalist might apply them in a situation which, though hypothetical, is based on real world conditions and concerns.

Chapter 3 sets forth an eclectic system of journalism ethics, a framework of principles rooted in the historical and philosophic past of the press. Chapter 4 illustrates how those principles can be applied in a series of actual situations that required moral reasoning and ethical judgment. Chapter 5 summarizes the narratives of editors as they describe how they reached ethical judgments in a variety of specific encounters that required "close calls." These examples are used to make distinctions among values, virtues, and principles in journalistic contexts.

Chapter 6 reviews the substantial literature about organizational pressures on journalists and argues that the deterministic flavor of some of these studies obscures the potential for moral imagination and significant autonomy that journalists can and have exercised.

While *not* contending that journalism is a profession in the sense that medicine, law, and the clergy are, I view it as a craft with professional responsibilities. Chapter 7 construes media criticism, in its many forms, as one way journalists can seek to achieve under the First Amendment a degree of restraint and responsibility that the classical professions attempt to achieve through a method inimical to journalism—licensing.

Chapter 8 reviews some of the major collisions between the news media and the government within recent years and seeks to show how neither journalism nor the public is well served by the misleading vocabulary of "adversarialism." Chapter 9, reiterating the importance of investigative journalism, outlines possible criteria for making difficult decisions on what methods to use and how far to take them. It discusses the news media's credibility problem and suggests how investigative journalists might respond to it without compromising their work. Chapter 10 shows how the framework of principles might have been applied in several cases that have posed both important legal and ethical problems for the news media.

Chapter 11 sets forth a normative model of ethics in journalism and summarizes the findings of several of the key empirical studies of journalism ethics. It emphasizes the implications of those studies for individual intellectual and ethical development and commitment. Chapter 12 analyzes key events in the evolution of free expression and republican institutions. It shows how individual ethical commitment can be a companion concept to the social philosophy which underlies republican institutions. It outlines how the spirit and some of the forms of classical liberal philosophy persist as relevant guides to the modern journalist, even as changing times have withered some of its earlier features.

Portions of this manuscript were read and critiqued by Steve Weinberg, my successor as director of the Washington Reporting Program of the University of Missouri School of Journalism in Washington, D.C., now teaching at the Columbia, Missouri campus; Gerald Lanson, an assistant professor of journalism and science writing at New York University; Bill Kunerth, professor of journalism at Iowa State University; Walter Harrington, an assistant editor of the *Washington Post* magazine; David Weaver, director of the media research bureau at Indiana University's School of Journalism; and Ronald Farrar and Michael Kirkhorn of the University of Kentucky School of Journalism. In the book's earlier stages, members of the Ad Hoc Ethics Committee at IU, headed by David Smith, professor of religious studies, gave specific criticisms and encouragement, as did the late Dean Richard G. Gray, Walter Jaehnig, and Olatunji Dare, a former graduate student now teaching at the University of Lagos, Nigeria. Kathleen Ristow Harriman, Inez Woodley, Louise Davis and Manda Biddle typed the original version of the manuscript. My daughter, Mary Elaine Lambeth, patiently entered the final manuscript into a computer, and provided valuable editorial assistance. Naturally, whatever errors or shortcomings the manuscript contains are mine alone.

My family—the Lambeths of Kentucky, Alabama, and Florida, the Richardsons of Alabama, the Clarkes and Threshes of New York, and the Petersons and Andrewses of Michigan—provided moral support. This book is dedicated to my wife, Fran, whose encouragement and patient reading of every page reflect her friendship and characteristic commitment.

COMMITTED
JOURNALISM

CHAPTER ONE

Beyond a Socially Responsible Press

If a storm alarm is not sounding within the halls of American journalism, one should be.

Accumulated distrust of the news media, skepticism of journalists' ethics, and a resentment of media power are very nearly permanent features of the contemporary American scene. While the media themselves are not alone responsible for this state of affairs, it is past time for journalists and owners of newspapers and radio and television stations to articulate principles of performance that are publicly visible, ethically defensible, and rooted clearly in a philosophic tradition that continues to justify a free press. Not the least of the obstacles to such an articulation is a prevailing cynicism that any such idealistic undertaking will result in either piffle, repetitious generalities, or mischievous intrusion by outsiders no less and probably more guilty than the press in matters of ethics. While the nature and scope of the news media's power are matters not easily or quickly sketched, their salience in contemporary life can be. At grocery counters, the covers of *TV Guide* regularly entreat millions of readers to ponder the deeds and life styles of media celebrities. At their morning mirrors or during breakfast, countless Americans feed their minds with news pellets and feature dips served by network television news notables. Driving to and from work, a similar diet is dispensed by radio on the half hour. More highbrow fare reaches consumers on public radio. Less sensationally, perhaps, than in earlier times, the stars of the Gutenberg galaxy deliver printed news in daily, weekly, and monthly packages noted increasingly for their demographic sophistication and specialization of news and advertising content.

Yet salience means more than the mere widespread availability of news. News, at least to the literate on the planet earth in the final quarter of the twentieth century, often brings pain, disappointment, and a frustrating feeling of individual impotence. A colleague, Michael Kirkhorn, captured this feeling succinctly when he wrote:

1

Regularly, punctually, monotonously, our newspapers and radio and television stations relay listings of hazards, disasters, misdoings and undoings. Helplessly drawn to any dramatic situation, unanalytical accomplices in the zones of thought, journalists accumulate all kinds of bad ideas. They propagate notions which they poorly understand and discard those they assume others may misunderstand or refuse to tolerate. Preoccupied with the performance of individuals occupying official positions, journalists ignore the background. They see the spider, not the web. Relentlessly practical, they distrust dreamers, visionaries and utopians. They point us toward no detours but diligently cover our collisions.[1]

The public malaise has been registered rather graphically in a variety of ways. Most directly, it shows in polls. The National Opinion Research Center reported a steady decline in the proportion of Americans who had a great deal of confidence in the press. It dropped from 28 percent in 1976 to a low of 13.4 percent in 1983, climbing to only 16.7 percent in 1984.[2] The lowered confidence expresses itself in more tangible ways too. A study of 108 libel verdicts by juries of the late 1970s and early 1980s showed that 85 percent went against the media and almost two dozen carried with them damage awards exceeding $1 million.[3] It is true that a significant number of these judgments were reversed on appeal. However, the U.S. Supreme Court has paved the way for more libel cases to go to trial rather than throw them out on grounds of First Amendment violations. The high court has tightened the definition of public official, the major category of news sources who in libel cases must prove not only that what the press printed was false but also that the press knew it was false.[4]

Numbers alone, however, fail to convey the sense of erosion of trust in the news media. Historically, that can be traced, in substantial part, to the reporting of several major events which had a profound influence on the social, political, and economic life of the country. After a brief period during which it enjoyed righting the imbalance of postponed consumption necessitated by World War II, the United States was forced to confront a different kind of moral cancer, and at home: racial injustice. The civil rights movement, with its dramatic content and provocative style, cast the news media more actively than ever before in the role of carriers of the messages of dissident groups. This role, which fit so comfortably the professional conventions and ideology of the press, deepened as, successively, the news media covered the rise of consumerism, the environmental protection movement, the period of student dissidence in the 1960s, the Vietnam War, and the energy problems of the 1970s. A study of how 120 elite policymakers in Washington perceived the influence of the news media in these major episodes showed that impact was greatest in the case of such vivid and volatile events as the Vietnam War and the civil rights movements and less pronounced on the more intractable and diffuse problems such as energy and consumer protection.[5] Throughout the 1960s and 1970s, the news media left the public at large and many of the country's attentive elite groups with the feeling that such major events had been reported unfairly, especially by a new wave of muckraking and investigative journalists.

A swift and brief qualifying riposte is in order. Research now seems to establish what many suspected all along—that what news consumers view as "bias" or "unfairness" may well reflect instead their encounter with "information which is inconsistent with the picture of the situation they already hold in their heads."[6] As for society's policymaking elite, so often the source of news, they appear to have biases of their own as they look at the way the news media treat competing elite groups. Thus, for example, most interest groups and political blocs active during the height of the energy crisis perceived their competitors as having more access to the media than they themselves did.[7]

Clearly, where one stands with respect to the news media depends to some substantial degree on where one sits in the arena of public and private life. Bias and partial perspective are not the possessions of journalists alone.[8] Even so, journalists cannot cavalierly discount the evidence not only of widespread public disaffection but also of blatant unprofessionalism.

In the 1980s, a series of incidents raised the question of whether the news media might be not only unfair, but downright unethical. In the Janet Cooke affair, a young *Washington Post* reporter had her Pulitzer Prize revoked after confessing she had made up the existence of an eight-year-old heroin addict.[9] Shortly afterward, a columnist for the *New York Daily News,* Michael Daly, admitted that he had invented the name of a British soldier who had shot a youngster in Belfast, Northern Ireland.[10] Not many more months had passed before the round of exposés included the high temple of daily journalism itself—the *New York Times,* one of whose freelancers, Christopher Jones, acknowledged that a bylined story from Cambodia had actually been written from his home in Spain. Moreover, part of the story was lifted from André Malraux's novel *Voie Royale.*[11] In the spring of 1984, scandal hit the *Wall Street Journal,* regarded by many inside and outside journalism as a pillar of rectitude whose position as the largest circulating newspaper of general interest in the United States was well earned. Reporter R. Foster Winans, author of the popular "Heard on the Street" column, was fired after admitting that he had repeatedly disclosed in advance, to brokers and others, market-sensitive information that was to appear in the column.[12] To its credit, the *Wall Street Journal* broke the story itself, exposing many of the details of the government investigation and the fact that the probe included Winans's homosexual lover, a former clerk at the *Journal*.[13] Although the *Journal*'s thorough washing of its own dirty linen in public was widely praised, the episode was yet another breach of ethics damaging to the credibility of the news media. The damage is done despite the consensus that, as financial writer Harvey D. Shapiro puts it, "when it comes to trading on inside knowledge or selling it, there are very few rotten apples."[14]

There are ethical misjudgments of another kind which appear in the press with a regularity that understandably disturbs citizens in what many still like to think of as a humane, value-directed culture. For example, a major national magazine featured a career column in which a woman corporate executive advised women that they can sleep their way up the corporate ladder as long as certain prudential measures are observed. Said she: "It's wonderful to talk business in bed, share breakfast with a man who really understands your concerns without needing explanations." But she cautioned that one should "be careful, be canny, be daring. Make your corporate affair work for you."[15] Whether one reads this as an implication that women are incapable of succeeding in the corporate world on ability alone or as a pitch for hedonistic opportunism, such journalism raises ethical issues to which many in the public are sensitive.

Critical attention paid the news media goes far beyond periodic polls of public confidence, surveys of major news sources, and prominent reporting of individual lapses of ethical judgment. Less noticed, but accumulating rapidly over the past twenty-five years, is a body of scholarship that has penetrated the mystique the craft had acquired in the previous two hundred years. Although difficult to summarize quickly or to characterize briefly, this scholarly literature is substantial enough that it cannot easily be ignored or derided by journalists scornful of academe. While it is always difficult to generalize or specify the exact contours of scholarly consensus, the following points, I hazard to guess, enjoy a fairly wide backing among social scientists and other scholars who have studied the news media.

　i.　News is not an objectively defined product but the outcome of a fluid human process guided chiefly by "conventions" that serve the commercial as much as the public service goals of the media. If a situation embodies human conflict, engenders widespread human interest, affects many rather than a few persons, is recent, and contains elements of novelty or newness, then it may well emerge as "news"—provided it passes muster with "gatekeepers" whose judgment is often ad hoc and intuitive.[16]

2. Rather than being driven primarily by ideals of public service, news media establish work objectives and procedures that serve first and foremost the logistic and economic needs of the news organization.[17] News from a poor urban ghetto, a town remote from network news offices, or a third world nation stands less chance of being reported—other things being equal—than news from more convenient and affluent locales.

3. Objective reporting, in a strict sense, is impossible given the subjectivity involved in assembling facts and the frequent necessity for choosing to emphasize one set of facts rather than another.[18]

4. Any notion that the news media are comprehensive watchdogs of government is folklore. That governmental misdeeds are sometimes uncovered by the more aggressive news media, and subsequently corrected, are exceptions that prove the rule—namely, that media rarely take the initiative and are usually passive chroniclers of the status quo, often manipulated by those in power.[19]

5. Media independence, in the strict sense meant by many journalists, is a myth. The social and political system in the United States—as in any country—limits what news media can and cannot do. There are degrees of independence but the range of freedom of action open to reporters and editors is limited by owners or publishers, peer pressure, and social values, as well as statutory law and legal custom and procedures. The ideology of near-absolute media independence cloaks the fact that media are often trapped by their own need for a steady supply of news.[20]

6. Whether the news media actually equip the masses of citizens with the information needed for self-government is in doubt. Most use the media for individual, personal needs. Even among the attentive citizens who most diligently use the news media, the guidance supplied is less than expected under most definitions of the media's role in a democracy or republican form of government. "The reality," John Seigenthaler, publisher of the *Nashville Tennessean,* once wrote, "is that we do not have the manpower—and womanpower—or the space to provide our readers with all they need to know. But we will not admit that—to ourselves or the public."[21]

If these interpretive conclusions have the effect of diminishing the hubris of those few journalists whose arrogance rightly offends public sensitivity, so much the better. If they have the effect of forcing journalists to think more carefully about or improve the probity of their methods, the craft and the public will be well served. If the consumers of news come, through these scholarly findings, to see the news media in a more realistic context, the citizenry will be so much the wiser. And the result may well be more, rather than less, respect for the press. All these beneficial possibilities are made less than likely, however, because the books and articles in which these findings are contained are in scholarly renderings not easily available to the press or the public. However, many scholars and journalists and most members of the attentive public agree on at least one scholarly finding: the news media, despite and perhaps partially because of their flaws, are very influential, even powerful. The literature measuring the scope and nature of the media's power is legion,[22] and the volume of research shows signs that it is increasing rather than waning.[23]

What the literature on the press lacks is a positive statement on the ethics of journalism that is both conceptually rich *and* demonstrably useful. In short, the literature lacks a statement on ethics that is sensitive to the problems, limitations, potential, and power of the media which scholars and thoughtful journalists themselves have so carefully identified. "What is needed," concluded Professor Eugene Goodwin after an excellent and exhaustive survey of the status of journalism ethics, "is a set of principles based on a journalism that serves the public by aggressively seeking and reporting the closest possible truth about events and conditions of concern to people, a journalism that collects and deals with information honestly and fairly, and treats the people involved with compassion, a journalism that conscientiously interprets and explains the news so that it makes sense to people."[24]

The current need may be seen more clearly against the background of the results the last time an attempt was made to deal philosophically with the purposes and practices of journalism. Without much doubt, the document most widely known for such an attempt was the 1947 report of the Commission on Freedom of the Press, headed by Robert M. Hutchins. The report, "A Free and Responsible Press,"[25] is the chief source of the idea that has dominated discussion of journalism ethics for the past thirty-five years—the concept of the social responsibility of the press.

In contrast to the laissez-faire posture of a libertarian press, a socially responsible press is defined as having a positive duty to exercise freedom of expression. More specifically, the commission developed five standards of performance which, it asserted, are required of a free and responsible press. These are to:

1. Provide a "truthful, comprehensive account of the day's events in a context which gives them meaning."
2. Serve as a "forum for the exchange of comment and criticism."
3. Offer a "representative picture of the constituent groups of society."
4. Present and clarify the "goals and values of society."
5. Provide "full access to the day's intelligence."[26]

Rather than merely keep hands off the press, as libertarian doctrine demands, social responsibility theorists urged the press, government, and the public to actively promote not only freedom of expression but also the requirements the Hutchins Commission defined for a free and responsible press. Although the commission set limits on what government could or should do to promote responsibility, it did set for government the role—as William Hocking somewhat murkily put it—of "residuary legatee of responsibility for adequate press performance."[27]

Not surprisingly, criticism of the social responsibility theory has been frequent and fervid. Editors and publishers, none of whose names graced the membership list of the commission, reacted negatively at the time. The focus of their opposition was the likelihood of government intervention which was likely to fall on the press if it "behaved irresponsibly." Indeed, editors maintained that the country could not have a press that was truly free and fail to expect instances, and even periods, of press irresponsibility. In the ensuing decades, such scholars as John Merrill in the 1970s and J. Herbert Altschull in the 1980s have attacked the social responsibility theory on the grounds that it is either meaningless[28] or dangerous.[29] The latter worry stemmed from fear that the doctrine would lead to restrictions on the press that would curb its freedom. The former concern was based on the belief that "social responsibility" left totally unspecified the source or direction of the journalist's obligations.

Despite these strong and persistent criticisms, the legacy of the Hutchins Commission persists. Countless journalism classrooms consider and some even memorize its injunctions. Many media leaders, who long ago have forgotten (if they ever paid attention to) its philosophic substance, find the nomenclature of "social responsibility" irresistible. Even those who shear the word "social" away from the catchphrase use the generic word "responsibility" freely, perhaps unavoidably. Thus even while rejecting the use of government to foster improved media performance, the collective effect has been to keep alive the Hutchins tradition.

None of the foregoing is to suggest that the phrase "social responsibility" be cast into a semantic Gehenna, forever condemned. It may be unfair to assert that the term "social responsibility" is meaningless. It may be so only to those who believe themselves to be beyond the need or reach of exhortations to think about others. For to urge "social responsibility" upon a reporter, editor, publisher, or manager is to ask for an "other-directedness" in attitude and a willingness to consider the effects of individual actions and institutional practices upon others, upon the public. Although one would never think so from reading critics of the social responsibility theory of the press, there is something to be said for such a simple exhortation. Taken seriously, it can be a useful antidote to unbridled individualism, hedonism, or even the garden variety of journalistic carelessness.

But something more is needed of an ethical perspective. In short, the practical weakness of the Hutchins literature is that it contains little that would assist individual journalists in daily ethical judgments they have to make. There is no general framework that can be applied to specific decisions. In this, it is deficient in precisely the same way as the libertarian theory from which it sprang. Social responsibility theory can, as justly as libertarian doctrine, be judged as having failed, in Fred Siebert's phrase, to provide "rigorous standards for the day-to-day operations of the mass media—in short, a stable formula to distinguish between liberty and the abuse of liberty."[30]

Specifically, social responsibility theory, as currently developed, has little truly useful to say in answer to such questions as:

- What are the enduring principles which a journalist should consult, without fail, in making ethical judgments?
- Other things being equal, which of these principles is most important and which can be subordinated when they are in conflict? If none can always hold prime sway, what then?
- To whom or what does a journalist owe fundamental loyalty—to himself, the public, an employer, or colleagues?
- How best can a journalist approach such classic questions as means versus ends, especially when he or she is exhorted to serve as a watchdog over government?

One could argue that grappling with such questions was not the purpose of the Hutchins Commission, whose agenda was the proper role of the press as an institution in American society and of the government and law as guarantors of the liberty exercised by the press and the public. Certainly the commission's final report and associated volumes[31] are copious with commentary on institutional practices and responsibilities. It also could be noted that the ethics of journalism from the perspective of an individual journalist or organization cannot be treated in isolation from the role of the press in the larger society. Yet, still, the commission offered little to the individual journalist or media organization that could focus a dialogue on ethics.

Perhaps the lack of practical guidance can be traced in some substantial part to the weaknesses of utilitarianism, the philosophy that seemed to underlie much of the commission's report. In the most faithful utilitarian fashion, the commission's report was redolent with majoritarian values. In prescribing correctives for the laissez-faire, libertarian creed of the American press, the commission and its most vocal members repeatedly advocated measures that would protect the public more securely than existing libel laws;[32] require the media to function much like a common carrier; and require the government to intervene to supply news itself when the press performs inadquately.[33]

The utilitarian strain is strikingly evident in a passage from the pen of Hocking, who argued that the government should and could regulate the *conditions* under which the press conducts its activities without regulating the activities themselves. He wrote:

> To make rules and conditions for a fairer game interferes with no honest freedom of the players; it improves the game for them and for the onlookers. To consider the total output of free press activity with analogous questions in mind might offer similar advantages both to the press and the public. The ends in view would be the lessening of waste and disorder, the realizing of a genuine process of public thought, and the bringing of the best press service to the greatest number of people. The best service to the most people![34]

The Hutchins Commission report, the most important statement on the media in the twentieth century, philosophically brought utilitarianism under the media tent whether the ringmasters of the press noticed or not. But the practice of utilitarianism as, arguably, the news media's dominant mode of moral reasoning can be traced not only to the Hutchins report but to other factors as well. Chief among these are the structure of the industry, an occupational ideology linked to the media's role in the political and economic system, and a pervasive pragmatism in American culture that reinforces the journalistic sine qua non, "getting the story."

Media of mass communication seek to maximize their reach. While costs and the law of diminishing returns place limits on expansion, the normal orientation of media is to increase circulation or audience, or, in the face of competition, to hold fast to one's share of the market. This provides a built-in pressure on journalists to reach for the attention-getting story, the sensational. Pictures that offend good taste, stories that intrude upon privacy, and questionable methods used to "get the story" often are byproducts of the media's intrinsic need to capture and hold attention. The movement toward professionalism in the craft has markedly reduced flagrant lapses of judgment. But the pressures remain.

The commercial concern with numbers of readers or viewers has its ideological counterpart in the media's traditional role as a watchdog of government, as a representative of the people, preserving their "right to know." Indeed, the news media, as servants of the public interest, have an honored and indisputably ethical task to perform in doing what they can to monitor the performance of elected officials and the bureaucracies created to deliver public services. The question, of course, is how far can and should journalists go, ethically, to perform the watchdog role? When does the rubbery yardstick of the "greatest good for the greatest number" become a figleaf, a shibboleth, to justify use of flagrant deception or massive invasion of privacy in order to "get the story" for the majority (*and* for the press)?

Some journalists try to resist or cope with these utilitarian temptations. Some do, always have, and likely always will. However, the point is that, given the precarious position of the news media in public esteem and the need for greater press credibility, "some" may be too few. We live on a planet soon to be "bioengineered" if it is not first "biodegraded," in a world that could be incinerated and/or enervated by nuclear war, and in a society whose economy and culture are increasingly linked to those of other nations the American citizenry barely understand. In these circumstances, credibility, believability might serve as a better sine qua non than merely "getting the story." Or one might say, "get the story, but do it ethically, credibly." In these times, journalists need not only scruples. They need muscular scruples connected in a understandable way to the constitutional sinews that, despite stresses, have usually protected the press against body blows from diverse quarters. The utilitarianism implicit in most journalist pronouncement on ethics has thus far proved inadequate and unsatisfying, to the public, and, increasingly, to members of the press. Who counts the "greatest number" and who measures the "greatest good" are questions that ring painfully in the ears of the citizenry as well as sensitive observers of the press.

The intent here is not to attempt a repeal of the "public interest"[35] as a focus of journalistic labor. Nor is the purpose to argue for only one approach to the ethics of journalism. Rather, the objective is to show how a framework of principles can help individuals and organizations reach decisions in a way that fosters ethical behavior even while it disclaims ethical infallibility. The purpose, too, is to show that such a framework can be built from the same philosophic timber that gave rise to the free press in the first place.

But before attempting to construct a framework for an ethics of journalism, attention needs to be paid to the classical ethical theories. They need to be defined and applied, clearly, in a journalistic setting. Doing so will show not only their strengths and weaknesses, but will identify elements that can help the journalist develop a means for confronting his or her own decisions in matters of ethics.

CHAPTER TWO

The Journalist and Classical Ethical Theory

Five years of conscientious apprenticeship have won for hypothetical reporter Robert Earnest an assignment from the *Daily Argus,* a large eastern newspaper, to cover a presidential campaign. Knowledgeable about the politics of his own state, Earnest has inevitably been forced to learn the intricacies of politics in other states as well. In addition to extensive background reading, Earnest has made a point of befriending colleagues from other regions, especially Reginald Davis, veteran Washington correspondent for the *Morning Call,* one of the South's leading newspapers. Davis has shared unstintingly with Earnest from a reservoir of political knowledge accumulated not only in covering southern politics but five presidential elections as well.

While traveling with the presidential party in a week-long swing through the West, the members of the press find themselves with an unexpected block of time on their hands. The president, never a strong contender in the West, has decided to spend a morning and an afternoon taping political commercials set in unmistakably western locations. The tapings are closed to the press. Earnest, anxious to develop authentic sources of his own in California, spends the morning on the telephone and the afternoon visiting with local politicians of both parties. Davis, joining a group of seasoned writers who have been friends for years, takes the day off, heading first for a horse race, then a leisurely evening meal followed by a tour of night spots.

Earnest's scouting among California politicians uncovers what he thinks might not be widely known: the president has arranged an unannounced meeting early that evening with ten or twelve California political leaders, including some who heretofore have been un-enthusiastic about the president and pessimistic about his chances of winning the state. Earnest, with some reason, believes his day well spent; he has gotten the number of the hotel suite where the meeting is to be held.

That other reporters had learned of the meeting is obvious to Earnest when he enters the hotel lobby, which has been invaded by some three dozen journalists. They have been kept away from the upstairs suite, and told that the president would speak to them in the lobby following his meeting. The game plan is that the California politicians who met with the president would not accompany the chief executive to the lobby, and would let him do the speaking.

Candidly, the candidate admits that he has been told that three separate polls in the state report he is trailing his challenger by three to five percent. No, the president concedes, the key holdouts among the state's party leadership did not tell him at the meeting that they would endorse him. Yet, the president says, they had not foreclosed the possibility, and, indeed, they encouraged him with specific advice—none of which, however, he could share with reporters. Earnest's follow-up phone calls identify the politicians present at the session and uncover the interesting report that the president wants a Californian in his new cabinet, if reelected. Not a sensational story, Earnest thinks, but not a bad one either.

Earnest is surprised not to see Reginald Davis in the lobby. It is unlike him not to have been tipped on one of his customary periodic calls to the campaign, even if he was taking the day off. It is even more surprising to Earnest that Davis fails to show up for next morning's breakfast date during which the two reporters planned to discuss likely news developments of the day ahead. Davis doesn't answer a call to his room. The clerk says he has not checked out.

Finding no sign of Davis in the press room, Earnest decides to stop by Davis's room. He knocks, but there is no answer. The door, however, is not locked. Opening it, Earnest finds Davis sprawled across his bed, face up, still wearing yesterday's suit, snoring deeply. An empty bourbon bottle stands on the night stand. Next to it, the telephone's message light is flashing.

It is 9:00 A.M. If Davis hadn't filed an overnight story—and Earnest knew he hadn't—Davis should be filing right now. Davis merely grunts and rolls over on his face when Earnest tries to rouse him. Earnest can guess the message behind the flashing light. A call to the front desk confirms it: his office dictationist had called, as she promised, at 5:00 A.M. to take Davis's story. Davis's newspaper, unlike many others, wanted his own story each day, even if it duplicated the wires.

Earnest's eyes scan the room for signs of a story to dictate. Finding none, unable to rouse Davis, the younger reporter confronts his dilemma. What are his choices, and how does he, Earnest, plan to approach them?

TELEOLOGICAL ETHICS

Earnest might consult classical ethical theory, which takes two different postures toward the ethical obligation. One, the teleological stance, emphasizes the consequences of an act or decision. The other, deontological, focuses on the nature of an act or decision.

Teleology, in turn, has two basic forms, ethical egoism and utilitarianism.

EGOISM

If Earnest were to act as an ethical egoist, his decision would be based on what result would be best for him—and not for Davis, the *Morning Call,* or the readers of that southern newspaper. Earnest's friendship with Davis has taught him much about the organization and operation of political campaigns; Davis already has introduced him to a variety of contacts, and there are another three months before election day. Earnest still has much to learn from Davis. Clearly, it is in Earnest's interest to help Davis keep his own assignment to cover the campaign. Failing to file a campaign story might well hurt Davis with *Morning Call* editors, and might result in his being fired.

However, to help Davis will raise problems. First, whose story would be dictated? If he dictated his own story, the story already filed with the *Daily Argus,* Earnest might run the risk of incurring the wrath of his own editors if he is discovered. To avoid this, Earnest will have to alter his original story enough so that it would not be recognized. Second, if Davis cannot be awakened to dictate the story, who will? To Earnest, this is important because the press bus must leave soon, and there is not enough time to dictate the story himself. Thus, he must act quickly to hire or persuade someone at the hotel to do so while he attempts to get Davis in sober enough condition to board the press bus that will take them to the airport and on to another stop on the president's western campaign swing.

Earnest hires a hotel clerk to dictate the story and, after considerable effort, wakes Davis enough to guide him to the press bus. Earnest's devotion to his self-interest is basically in a tradition that stretches back to Epicurus (342?–271? B.C.), who believed persons should always seek what they believe will lead to their own satisfaction and avoid what they believe will inflict pain.[1] Contemporary egoists include such individualistic thinkers as Ayn Rand, whose books attempt to meld reason and self-interest into a coherent philosophy.[2]

It should be emphasized at the outset that Earnest's *behavior* is consistent with other ethical theories. Ethical theory focuses on moral reasoning, on the internal mental processes whereby ethical decisions are made. Thus, if Earnest had different motives, his actions described above could express that other major teleological philosophy, utilitarianism.

UTILITARIANISM

Utilitarianism seeks to promote what is best for the greatest number, or for all concerned. Reasoning as a utilitarian rather than as an egoist, Earnest would calculate that the greatest good for all concerned would be served by filing a story on Davis's behalf. Earnest's editors would receive the daily story they expect. Readers of the *Morning Call* would get a story not too dissimilar from the one they would have gotten from Davis—perhaps better because Davis would not have had time to do the research that led Earnest to the names of all those present at the session with the president. Because utilitarianism is concerned solely with maximizing the good and is neither a self-regarding nor a self-neglecting philosophy, Earnest considers his colleagues in the press corps in calculating the greatest good. The retention of Davis would help them all; here is another benefit to be gained by filing a story on Davis' behalf.

The founder of utilitarianism, Jeremy Bentham (1748–1832), described it as a philosophy that aimed at the "greatest happiness for the greatest number." Depicting humankind as governed by the competing forces of pleasure and pain, Bentham developed an elaborate "hedonistic calculus" that supposedly would guide individuals to the appropriate decisions. Although the calculus is viewed today as outmoded, the broader outlines of Bentham's utilitarian philosophy are very much alive. Reflecting Bentham's quantitative approach, some economists argue that happiness is maximized by free competition in the economy.[3] Others, with John Stuart Mill, argue for a utilitarianism that emphasizes the quality rather than the quantity of happiness.[4] Pluralists who want to maximize a variety of "goods" adopt a "nonhedonistic utilitarianism," rejecting the notion that only pleasure is worthy of pursuit.[5] Commonly these more modern versions of utilitarianism are classified in two ways—one focusing on acts, the other on rules as a means to fulfill ethical obligations.

ACT UTILITARIANISM

To the act utilitarian, rules and maxims—"never tell a lie," "thou shalt not kill," "never break a contract"—can provide only rough directions or summaries of moral experience. They are to moralists as radar is to the storm-tossed airline pilot, furnishing general indicators but not a detailed and specific description of the forces impinging on his aircraft. The act utilitarian, before acting, wants the assurance that the specific thing he *does* will maximize the good for all concerned.

As an act utilitarian, Earnest would have had to convince himself that filing a story on Davis's behalf would create the greatest good for the greatest number. In theory, the act utilitarian weighs alternatives scrupulously. Each is held against the other to determine which would maximize the good. Thus, before filing a story as though Davis had written it, Earnest might have considered the possibility of putting his own name on it, so as not to deceive. Yet that certainly would have astonished Davis's editors. Earnest might also have tried to delay the *Morning Call* editors, buying more time while trying to awaken Davis, allowing him to miss the press bus but giving him the chance to file his own story based on Earnest's notes. But that was rejected on grounds that it would have aroused his editors' suspicions. Moreover, Davis's deep drunkenness cast doubt on his ability to file an acceptable story. The course of action he finally followed appeared the best one to maximize the good—filing a story as though it were Davis's own.

RULE UTILITARIANISM

In contrast to the act utilitarian, the rule utilitarian puts great stock in precepts. He asks not what action will result in the greatest good, but what rule, when followed, will maximize the good. Discrete actions are examined not in relationship to other actions but in light of whether they conform to a rule that has been deemed to be morally useful in creating the greatest good for the greatest number. In our example, if Earnest were a rule utilitarian, he may well have concluded that, to a journalist, truth telling should be a cardinal rule. To mislead Davis's editors by filing a story written by someone else would represent falsification. But the rule utilitarian is not focusing on falsification per se so much as he is the wisdom of truth telling as a rule for journalists to follow. The reason it should be followed is that experience has shown that, for a journalist, it is most likely to maximize the good for society as a whole. One can imagine the negative consequences were truth telling not held in such a high regard by journalists. Indeed, one can easily see that it is through truth telling that journalism has its most beneficent result—in exposing scandal, educating the ignorant, informing the curious. As a rule utilitarian, he wants a rule that will maximize the good for all concerned, not just in the short run but in the long run, too. He does not file a story for Davis.

The "short run versus long run" question raises a subtle point. Utilitarians of whatever stripe must consider and try to maximize long range beneficent consequences. In making such judgments, not only the purity of their morals, but also the prescience and power of their minds play a significant part.

DEONTOLOGICAL ETHICS

Are there acts which by their very nature are moral or immoral? Those who belong to the other major school of ethics tend to answer this fundamental question in the affirmative. They disagree that results or consequences should be the *only* measure of whether the acts are ethical or unethical. "Tend to answer" is needed as a qualifier because deontology can encompass a wide variety of views and what unites these views is a disinclination to look *only* at results as a guide to ethical behavior.

There are deontologists who look primarily at the "nature of the act" in determining the rightness of an action, but who also look at the consequences. These persons are called "mixed deontologists" and they are defined on the basis of whether, while weighing results, the primary emphasis is placed on the act or the rule. They are thus called "mixed act deontologists" and "mixed rule deontologists." But before considering these more complex versions of deontology, we should look at the two simpler species of moralist—the "pure act deontologist" and the "pure rule deontologist."

This latter category can well be considered the progenitor of them all. Its patron saint, Immanuel Kant (1724–1804), is considered one of the seminal thinkers in the history of philosophy and ethics. After growing up in a lower middle class, religious family, Kant prepared for the ministry at the local Pietistic College. His brilliance led him to the University of Konigsberg in East Prussia, where he rose to a full professorship at the age of forty-six in 1770. Those who have read his highly rational, organized, and precisely defined works will not be surprised at an observation about him by one of his contemporaries: "Rising, coffee-drinking, writing, lecturing, dining, walking, each had its set time. And when Immanuel Kant, in his gray coat, cane in hand, appeared at the door of his house, and strolled towards the small avenue of linden trees which is still called 'The Philosopher's Walk,' the neighbors knew it was exactly half-past-three by the clock."[6]

It is significant that Kant's chief work on science and the nature of human knowledge, *Critique of Pure Reason,* appeared seven years before his principal book on ethics, *The Critique of Practical Reason* (1788). In the earlier work, Kant argued against a radical empiricism which the philosopher David Hume had developed more than twenty years earlier. Hume said that truthful statements could not be made about matters not actually experienced. By contrast, Kant described the mind not as separate from the things it observes, but as deeply *immersed* in all it observes. In short, the mind construes what it sees into coherent designs and concepts. Reason, in short, is the indispensable precondition for making sense of experience. Experience cannot be *the* guide to finding truth because it is the mind that orchestrates our knowledge of cause and effect. The structure of reality exists before and quite apart from experience and reason allows us to apprehend reality without experiencing it.

This supreme faith in a universal rationality, which Kant used in his writings on science, carries over into Kant's understanding of ethics. The mind, which has the capacity to discover physical reality, could likewise navigate its way to moral truth. Kant identified a principle which he thought all persons could apply, with reason, to determine the morality of particular actions. He would have us ask: "Can the maxim that underlies this action be made a maxim for all persons, everywhere, for all time?" In short, can it be universalized, without contradiction or inconsistency? As an example, Kant posed as a maxim the notion that when in difficulty each person could promise what he or she pleases without any intention of keeping such a promise. In this circumstance, Kant said, "the promise itself would become impossible, as well as the end that one might have in view in it, since no one would consider that anything was promised to him, but would ridicule all such statements as vain pretenses."[7]

Kant placed high value on the attribute of "a good will," defined as an implacable determination to do what ought to be done rather than merely seek one's own ends. Said Kant: "Intelligence, wit, judgment, and the other talents of the mind, however they may be named, or courage, resolution, perseverance, as qualities of temperament, are undoubtedly good and desirable in many respects; but these gifts of nature may also become extremely bad and mischievous if the will which is to make use of them, and which, therefore, constitutes what I call character, is not good."[8]

A good will is to be valued, Kant thought, not for what it does, but for what it is; it is good in itself. Humankind is endowed with reason not as the means of achieving happiness, but of perfecting a good will. And a good will meets the test of goodness when it acts from a sense of duty. When one acts from a sense of duty, one's acts are morally worthy. Morally praiseworthy actions are those done from an obligation to duty and are based on maxims that can be acted upon consistently by all humans.

PURE RULE DEONTOLOGY

If Earnest were acting as a pure rule deontologist, he would search for his duty in the circumstance. For a journalist one cardinal principle is that of truth telling. To file a story of his own as though Davis had written it would not be truthful. At the bottom of such an untruthful act would be the maxim, "If truth telling poses a problem for someone from whom you expect to benefit in the future and if you can alleviate that problem by an act of falsification, you may do so." Universalizing this maxim would multiply the deceit in the world, already in plenteous supply, and create havoc with the social system. Inevitably those who practice the deceit would themselves eventually be deceived. This scarcely comports with certain fundamental ethical universals, such as the Golden Rule: "Do unto others as you would have them do unto you." By contrast, truth telling, though it certainly does not promise a trouble-free existence, can be universalized. It is consistent with what is expected of a person of character in a society of character. To the journalist it is a cardinal virtue. As a Kantian pure rule deontologist, Earnest could forego filing on Davis's behalf, not being guided by any consequences that would ensue for himself, for Davis, or his editors or the public. Falsification would be a breach of deontological ethics.

Although the pure rule utilitarian and the pure rule deontologist above emerged with an identical decision, their moral reasoning was different. The utilitarian wanted to maximize the good consequences. The deontologist followed a rationally derived duty to tell the truth, quite apart from consequences.

PURE ACT DEONTOLOGY

At the other end of the spectrum we find the pure act deontologist. Such a person has been characterized as highly intuitive, spontaneous, and even "creative" in the way he reasons in morally demanding situations. To an act deontologist, no two circumstances are alike. Each is unique, so unique that the invocation of firm rules or codes is not possible. Not only is it not possible, it may actively prevent the doing of the right thing under the circumstances. The "right thing under the circumstances" must be what a diligent human, after searching consideration, *feels* to be the right thing to do. Thus, the act deontologist views reason as an unreliable means to determine moral conduct. One must consult one's innate ethical sense, one's inborn, inertial guidance system.

Were Earnest an act deontologist, he might well be influenced by the urgency of the moment. Here before him lies a human on the doorstep of trouble. Jean-Paul Sartre, existentialist and himself considered an act deontologist, would urge Earnest to "invent" his own response. No rules exist that are in any real sense applicable to this *particular* situation. With no thought of consequences, with a sense of empathy, Earnest might well file a story on Davis's behalf.

MIXED ACT DEONTOLOGY

Unlike a pure act deontologist, a mixed act deontologist holds that one should give some weight to the consequence of the act—that is, in addition to weighing which act best fits the moral demands of a particular situation. In this latter process, the mixed act deontologist also looks at various features of an act in deciding whether it is moral.

In Earnest's situation, failing to respond to help his colleague would represent, in a sense, a betrayal of friendship. Davis had helped him in his need—by introducing him to sources, by backgrounding him on political situations of which Earnest was ignorant, and, since they were not direct competitors, by swapping information. Not responding would be callous. Because Earnest is a new friend of Davis, he has no way of knowing how often Davis drinks so heavily that he misses story assignments. Earnest believes it would be unfair of him in these circumstances to conclude that Davis does *not* "deserve a break." As far as misrepresentation is concerned, Earnest will not file a story under Davis's byline. He will simply arrange for the dictation of a story without a byline. This is a deception. Earnest will not deny that to himself or others. But it is deception meant to help a good colleague and, having weighed both the consequences and certain features of this act, Earnest feels justified. Eschewing rules, he believes he has acted with due regard for the particular circumstances.

MIXED RULE DEONTOLOGY

Like the mixed act deontologist, the mixed rule deontologist is willing to consider consequences of his behavior in judging its morality. But he is different in that rules are important to him; they provide a stability and predictability in the moral order, he believes. He would like to view episodes from the kind of steady framework he thinks that rules can provide.

As a mixed rule deontologist, Earnest might well take into account the consequences of allowing his new colleague and friend, Davis, to run the risk of probable trouble with his editors. But, like the others whose positions allowed them to consider consequences, Earnest's imagination might have led him another step or two. It could well be that the best thing he can do for his friend is to allow him to face the consequences; a bracing shower may be, figuratively as well as literally, best for Davis. He may well *need* to face the consequences. If this is only a rare instance of inebriation on the job, his editors are likely to forgive him and give him the warning he needs. If it is a persistent pattern of behavior, how responsible is it to be a party to its probable continuation? The public is best served by sober reporters. Earnest does neither Davis, nor the *Morning Call* editors, nor the public a service by shielding Davis from responsibility for his own actions. Underlying Earnest's reasoning in not filing a story is his belief in truth telling and another rule that says professionals should suffer the consequences of their misdeeds. It is not as though the public truly suffers from the *Morning Call* missing Davis's own story. Two wire services and any number of special supplementary services' stories are available. Moreover, the probable immediate results of no story—an embarrassment to Davis and an inconvenience for his editors—are not worth what Earnest would have to pay to avoid them—violation of rules of professional responsibility and truth telling.

WEAKNESSES IN CLASSICAL ETHICAL THEORIES

A little reflection will uncover significant criticisms of the basic theories sketched above.

Universal ethical egoism, the belief that all persons should act in their own self-interest, offers bleak prospects in a newsroom—indeed in a society—that must find ways of solving disputes among its members. That's because, as philosophers have shown, it contains a fatal, internal contradiction. Take a situation in which two equally capable reporters, Erica and Ed, come across the same civic scandal. Each is ambitious. Each perceives it is in his own self-interest to publish the story *exclusively*. Each has modeled himself after the respected reporter turned editor Seymour Calumny. Indeed, Calumny is a universal ethical egoist, too. But how can he advise them? Shared bylines, legwork, and writing would be one obvious approach. But neither reporter believes that to be in his/her self-interest. And, if Calumny is a true egoist, he wants all persons to act in their own self-interest. He wants *all* to because he is a *universal* ethical egoist.[9] But he cannot give consistent ethical advice, as an egoist, when self-interests conflict. Erica and Ed cannot both have their own way.

As an operating ethic, universal egoism might be more realistic in societies in which individuals and groups are largely autonomous and self-sustaining. In modern societies, and in organizations which require intimate interaction and interdependence, it raises serious questions. It does so because in the modern world interests often conflict and the ethical egoist can do little to help resolve these disputes and still remain faithful to his beliefs.

There are other forms of egoism, but they are hardly less troublesome. One, which Jacques Thiroux calls "individual egoism," holds that everyone should act in that individual's self-interest. This is scarcely a formula for fraternity and fellowship or even civility among humans. Another form, "personal egoism," prescribes that each person should act in his own self-interest regardless of what anyone else might choose to do. This latter, which makes no reference to consequences to others, seems a fit credo for what Christopher Lasch has called "the culture of narcissism."[10] It is difficult to see how journalism, which is supposed to serve the public, can embrace such an ethic.

Finally, there is "scientific egoism," or the belief that, regardless of what individuals *say* they believe, individuals do in fact always or nearly always act in their own self-interest. Strictly speaking, this is not an ethical theory at all, but a psychological description of what *is,* or, rather what is thought to be. It is not *prescriptive,* which by definition all moral philosophies are. Adherents of this form of egoism face the difficulty of never being able to prove conclusively the arguments they advance. They cannot enter the head of an apparent altruist to disprove his charitable motives. They cannot, for example, prove that such reporters as the late Don Bolles, the investigative reporter murdered in pursuit of the Arizona crime syndicate, really acted in their own self-interest when practicing their risky craft.

Utilitarianism, that other major form of teleological theory, is not without weaknesses either. How is one to know that a particular decision will result in the greatest good for all involved? Take, for example, the decision faced by Erwin Knoll, the editor of *The Progressive* magazine, in deciding whether to pursue a story suggested by freelance writer Howard Morland explaining how to build an H-bomb.[11] The story, which the U.S. government attempted unsuccessfully to suppress, caused a furor. Morland, morally opposed to nuclear weapons, wanted to expose the government's nuclear secrecy practices as a fraud by publishing information he acquired legally. Had editor Knoll attempted to make a decision as a utilitarian on whether to publish the story, he could have found himself in a very thorny thicket. Would the published data actually help expand membership in the nuclear club, a result diametrically opposite to the magazine's intention? The argument actually made by the magazine, in part, was that the data it published could have been obtained by any nation wishing to do so. Getting the data was not the problem, but rather having the technical skills and money to actually design and build such a weapon. Over that, the magazine could and would have no control.

But how could one *know for certain* that proliferation would not result? How could one know that some *other act*—for example, announcing the magazine's possession of the data but not publishing it—would not have achieved the better result with less risk? These and other questions could be asked to show that predicting consequences, the skill most needed by the utilitarian, can be difficult if not impossible.

In the foregoing example, there are actually at least two difficulties. The first is in knowing the result; the second is in finding the act that will achieve the greatest good for all concerned. Act utilitarians assume that no one rule can be found that will wisely or adequately guide all moral decisions. One must scrupulously search to find the one act that, more than any other—now or in the future—will maximize the good. For humans acting under deadline pressure, as journalists must, the posture of the act utilitarian can be quite vexing.

Rule utilitarians might argue that they have just the solution for journalists. Act under guidance of a rule that maximizes the good, and one is more likely to cope adequately with time pressures of the journalist. But can a rule or rules be found that in all cases will maximize the good? Take the maxim that journalists should always tell the whole truth. If accepted literally, as presumably the "whole truth" is meant to be taken, reporters should decline when asked by police not to include in their stories of a murder the fact that police have fingerprints. Yet *not* to omit the fact that fingerprints have been discovered might encourage the flight of the criminal and prevent his apprehension. Society would suffer, in this case, by a strict, literal insistence on "the whole truth." As an alternative, one might construct a conditional rule. A journalist should always report the "whole truth," except when doing so would endanger life. But what about the *Progressive* case, in which the risk to American national security, American lives, was the key argument by the government? Some accepted the argument; some didn't. Yet clearly, the conditional rule—"tell the whole truth, except when doing so would endanger life"—poses serious problems for the working journalist. Predicting what would endanger life—whether act alone or act guided by rule—is tricky, and risky for the journalist who wants to be faithful to truth telling and robust debate. The same would be true, it can be argued, for other rules. The flux and sometimes vexing variety of human experience make rules difficult to apply in all cases without compromise, without failing, in short, to maximize the good.

Before leaving utilitarianism, a word needs to be said about the problems posed for a journalist who literally assumes the burden of attempting to maximize the good for all involved. To assume such a responsibility implies an almost obsessive concern over the exact effects of his reporting and editing. Obviously, an ethical journalist must weigh the consequences of his acts, to avoid libel or an authentic invasion of privacy. But the spirit of utilitarianism seems to call for a weighing and prediction of effects with a precision of which most journalists are incapable. Moreover, journalists may hobble themselves in pursuit of the truth if they allow themselves to become preoccupied with the effects and beneficial results of their work. To concentrate on effects can interfere with the gathering of facts. It can also put the reporter in a position of siding with a majority over a minority, a value judgment that may run counter to fair, unbiased reporting.

If egoism and utilitarianism have weaknesses, so likewise does deon-tology. What is an ethical system for if it is not concerned, in some way, with consequences? One can argue that, in fact, there is no such thing as a moral system that does not at least indirectly consider con-sequences. The Ten Commandments and other such beacons of ethics were not disembodied rules, unrelated to the lives within the com-munity from which they sprang. The prohibition against adultery was an admonition against deceit as well as an injunction meant to foster amity among households. Consider another weakness of rule deontology: what happens when moral principles appear to conflict? What should the journalist committed to truth telling do when he/she is asked to break a promise of confidentiality? Which moral rule should prevail? How grave must be the consequences of following one rule for the other rule to hold sway? (The careful reader will note that in the preceding sentence a consideration of consequences crept into a discussion of how deontologists might resolve one of their biggest dilemmas.)

CONCLUSION

The objective of this chapter has been to introduce the basic ethical theories, to explain these theories clearly by applying them to a single, hypothetical episode, and to critique these theories by identifying some of their key weaknesses.

The student is entitled to ask, "What good are they if they have weaknesses? If they all have weaknesses, then anything goes." The Committee for Education in Business Ethics responded to this reaction when, after its analysis of the teaching of ethics in higher education, it observed: "By criticizing the basic ethical theories, students often get the impression that each theory is equally faulty and that as a result ethical theory is not helpful. The standard critical approach can leave students with a kind of moral nihilism—a result not intended by philosophical criticism."[12]

Ethical theories are not like "black boxes," gimmicks that can be called upon to accept ethical questions and spit forth answers with mechanical regularity and precision. Rather, such theories are like windows onto the world of moral reasoning. They are meant to provide vantage points from which important ethical decisions can be considered. To anticipate certainty in every ethical decision is to look for what has seldom, if ever, been or ever will be. Moral reasoning is an art and not a science. It can be cultivated by careful and persistent reflection and diligent application. American journalism may lose its credibility unless its practitioners develop a greater capacity for moral reasoning. To those who say that "everything is relative," one must acknowledge that principles do compete with one another, but one must likewise emphasize the principles that *do* endure. To those who say one person's ethical decisions are as good as another's, one can accurately reply, "no, not necessarily." There is craftsmanship in ethical reasoning as well as in gathering the news.

Mixed rule deontology, the ethical approach favored in this book, values the steadiness provided by principles and the concrete rules that can often be derived from principles. Yet, it also values the guidance that can be gained by scrutinizing the likely consequences of alternative courses of behavior. It values such scrutiny not out of any expectation of maximizing the good but for assistance in making decisions when principles conflict or compete with one another.

To consult consequences and then choose among one, two, or more principles, or to find a way that respects each principle to some significant extent, is to exercise the moral imagination. It is an act of both judging and valuing, of making a value judgment. This book seeks to show how value judgments permeate the practice of journalism. It also argues that journalism and the public gain when such judgments are carefully and consciously made. Moreover, when the public interest is significantly at issue, both journalism and the public gain when ethical judgments are discussed openly.

The next chapter, drawing upon classical as well as more modern ethical theories, will attempt to develop a framework of principles through which journalists can confront ethical decisions. The objective is not to fashion a universal credo but to illustrate that a framework of principles is a sturdier guide in difficult times than unthinking intuitionism or knee-jerk, unrealistic utilitarianism.

CHAPTER THREE

Toward an Eclectic System of Journalism Ethics

In this chapter, an attempt will be made to develop a framework of principles for journalism ethics. It could be considered a "system" in the limited sense that its principles will be intimately related. It can be thought of as a system, also, in its attempt at comprehensiveness—that is, in its effort to be useful in weighing matters of right and wrong, in providing some standards for media criticism, and in helping decide what is worth journalistic attention in the first place. Lest the reader swoon at such an ambitious undertaking, recall the qualifying words "attempt," "effort," and "useful."[1]

The time is past when practitioners and teachers of journalism in western society can ignore the need to articulate at least the beginning of a system, and preferably one that blends journalism ethics with social philosophy.[2] What minimum expectations should such a system satisfy?

First, it should embody the values of Judeo-Christian civilization. Journalism is not a disembodied occupation. Conceived in the Renaissance, born in the Enlightenment, and nurtured to robust life in the modern west, journalism inherits the legacy of the larger society: the principles of truth, justice, freedom, humaneness, and individual responsibility. These principles pervade the numerous codes of ethics drafted by the various associations of journalism professionals and by individual news organizations.[3] However, a system of ethics should make clear, as codes cannot, how principles can be applied. A system should reflect working principles rather than mere platitudes or ossified collections of "do's and don'ts." Some means must be provided for resolving at least the most serious problems raised by cases in which principles conflict.

Ideally a system of ethics should, in its application, yield similar decisions when applied by different individuals in similar circumstances. Realistically, however, it cannot be a "black box" into which moral quandaries are confidently inserted with the expectations of certain answers. Slight differences in circumstance may suggest somewhat different courses of action. Different perspectives may prompt alternative emphases. A system of ethics must be flexible, but not so flexible as to be a mere rationalization for the personal preferences of those who invoke it. In short, a system must have bite and give direction. Its precepts should offer continuity and stability, though not necessarily invariant outcomes.

A system of ethics cannot ignore the classical approaches of deontology and teleology, or the variants of them, considered in the previous chapter. It should respond to the patent weaknesses of those approaches. It should do so by stipulating that both consequences and the nature of an act must be considered as anchors of moral reasoning. But it should attempt to provide a means to harmonize these different considerations in particular instances.

Finally, journalists, though sometimes they may seem not to be, are members of the species homo sapiens. No system should suggest that they inhabit a special moral universe which requires a special ethical stance.[4] Yet an ethical system for journalists should be one which journalists themselves find fair and useful in evaluating not only the morality of their individual behavior but also the worth of their collective labors. It should provide a basis for criticism and corrective reflection. This chapter will outline and illustrate the principles of an ethical system for journalists. The next chapter will show, in more detail, how they may be applied.

The framework developed here comes closest to mixed rule deontology. While journalists are expected to consider the consequences of their actions, they are viewed as best guided by rules derived from principles—telling the truth, behaving justly, respecting and protecting independence and freedom, acting humanely, and being a good steward of the resources, especially the First Amendment, that protect journalism and a free society. These broad principles are interpreted below as a journalist's guide, his voluntarily assumed obligation as a practitioner of journalism in a constitutional democracy. In the Lockean, contractarian tradition, the governmental trustee has been limited and enjoined to respect press freedom, among other freedoms. It has instituted rules of law to govern disputes over how such freedom should be defined. One of the oldest codes of ethics of journalism, the Statement of Principles of the American Society of Newspaper Editors (ASNE), begins: "The First Amendment, protecting freedom of expression from abridgement by law, guarantees to the people through their press a constitutional right, and thereby places on newspaper people a particular responsibility." The system of ethics here described is offered as one journalist's definition of that "particular responsibility."

THE PRINCIPLE OF TRUTH TELLING

The word *truth* has many dimensions, each of which a journalist must recognize and respect. There is truth in the sense of factual accuracy, reflected in the ASNE code's admonition that "every effort"—not just "some" effort, but "every effort"—"must be made to assure that the news content is accurate, free from bias and in context, and that all sides are presented fairly." Most fundamentally, the need is for a habit of accuracy, of checking and rechecking to establish the accuracy of questionable information. The habit includes acquisition of the skill to anticipate likelihood of error.

Such basic learning does not appear magically, like a Platonic spark generated by rubbing two press cards together. Long hours of apprenticeship, dialogue, and attention to detail are essential. It was the apparent absence of such learning, both cognitive and ethical, that led to the tragic professional death of Janet Cooke, the *Washington Post* reporter whose Pulitzer Prize was revoked after it became known that her winning story, about an eight-year-old drug addict, was a hoax.[5] Deliberate falsification, of course, is the most egregious breach of the ethic of truth telling. Fidelity to fact assumes that a journalist will not only not falsify but will diligently establish the authenticity of stories written or broadcast. That human frailty, deadlines, and large volumes of words in the daily news will guarantee some error should in no way induce laxity in a journalist.

Journalist could not do their work in a satisfactory way, however, if satisfied only by a standard of factual accuracy. In recent decades it has become almost a cliché that a journalist should seek not only the facts but also the larger truths behind the facts. In one of the earliest formulations of such an objective, the late Paul Y. Anderson, winner of the 1928 Pulitzer Prize for his reporting of the Teapot Dome scandal, told an audience of journalism students:

> I have said it is the duty of the reporter to do something more than merely observe and record what comes his way. Genuine devotion to the truth demands far more than that. The truth is not always to be found on the surface; it cannot be picked off like peaches from a tree. There are concealed truths, the existence of which is but faintly indicated on the surface. It is the reporter's business to get at them, nevertheless.[6]

Concealed facts or truth can be uncovered by a variety of means—document searches,[7] in-depth interviewing,[8] and participant observation,[9] to name a few. Also, in a complex, modern society, professionals and experts communicate with one another in specialized ways. The journalist who is not knowledgeable enough and ambitious enough to become fluent in the vocabularies of specialists may well forfeit the opportunity to report more than the surface of the news. Thus, journalists need to gain some understanding of statistics, econometrics, and computer programming. For these are among the specialized languages used by important sources in the large, formal organizations that constitute journalism's traditional beats: government, business, law enforcement, and science, among others.

Reflection will show that there is an intimate relationship between competence and a journalist's capacity as a moral agent. "The primary purpose of gathering and distributing news and opinion," according to the ASNE code, "is to serve the general welfare by informing the people and enabling them to make judgments on the issues of the time." How well a journalist reports the effects of school integration on the academic achievement of blacks may depend heavily on his ability to understand the logic and limitations of multiple regression analysis, a statistical technique used by social scientists to measure the relative influence of different variables. How effectively a reporter compares alternative economic forecasts for a key industry of the community he or she covers may depend on the ability to comprehend the uses, strengths, and weaknesses of econometrics. How accurately a writer covers a dispute over the privacy risks raised by a new computerized system of police record keeping may depend on how well he or she understands computers and computer programming.

It is not that a reporter is unethical if he fails to understand statistics, econometrics, or computer programming. The point is that without one or more of these skills he or she may come far less close to the truth in his work, may fail to realize his potential as a moral agent, as a truth teller. The point is as effectively made if the specialist is a sports writer. To effectively cover sports, or any other beat for that matter, one must perfect talents of observation, memory, and detachment.

As a caution to the foregoing implicit expression of faith in the efficacy of the news story as an instrument of civic enlightenment, one must turn, as all students of the media eventually do, to Walter Lippmann. As long ago as 1922, he warned that "as social truth is organized today, the press is not constituted to furnish from one edition to the next the amount of knowledge which the democratic theory of public opinion demands."[10] Although there have been strides made in stimulating the dialogue between the media and the social sciences,[11] and in teaching social science techniques to journalists,[12] one still may be forced to conclude that the "social truth" the public needs to govern itself will not appear in sufficient quantities in the news media day by day. Rather, it may be expected to emerge, as Lippmann himself hoped, with a vital but by no means exclusive contribution from the news media.

Thus, journalists in their work must be aware of and heed the demands of factual, contextual, and social truth, plus the truth of the physical and natural sciences. But there is also a fifth level of meaning, and that is truthfulness in the news gathering process. To what extent, if at all, should journalists employ deception in gathering the news? Can a morally acceptable distinction be made between "active" and "passive" deception? These are crucial questions. The position taken here, elaborated in future chapters, is basically that of a mixed rule deontologist. Only truthful means should be used, and in those rare and carefully justified instances where deception is permissible the means so employed must be fully described and explained in the news story, along with the justification.[13]

Because timely, reliable information is the currency of power in a democracy, it is especially important that the currency not be debased. The ethical value of truth telling doubles as a news value. Deception, prevarication, or lying—whether in government, business, science, or law enforcement—is usually news.

THE PRINCIPLE OF JUSTICE

At the day-to-day operating level, the principle of justice is reflected in the journalist's concern for fairness. Typical is the standard of the *Washington Post,* whose code of ethics derives rules from the principle of justice:

> While arguments about objectivity are endless, the concept of fairness is something that editors and reporters can easily understand and pursue. Fairness results from a few simple practices:
>
> 1. No story is fair if it omits facts of major importance or significance. So fairness includes completeness.
> 2. No story is fair if it includes essentially irrelevant information at the expense of significant facts. So fairness includes relevance.
> 3. No story is fair if it consciously or unconsciously misleads or even deceives the reader. So fairness includes honesty—leveling with the reader.

4. No story is fair if reporters hide their biases or emotions behind such subtly pejorative words as "refused," "despite," "admit," and "massive." So fairness requires straightforwardness ahead of flashiness.

Reporters and editors should routinely ask themselves at the end of every story: "Have I been as fair as I can be?"[14]

After a *Washington Post* reporter once highlighted a middle-aged political candidate's visits, back in his college years, to a massage parlor, the *Post* recanted, confessing in a major editorial that it had invaded the candidate's privacy: "One is forced to conclude that the paper knew not just more than it could print, but more than it should have known and more than anyone other than [the candidate himself] needs to know about his past personal life."[15] When the falsity of Janet Cooke's story became known, and when the injustice it had perpetrated on police and the black community became clear, the *Post* ran a special section explaining how its transgression occurred and highlighted on the front page the conclusions of its ombudsman's investigation.[16] Among these conclusions were that the editors had ignored signs that the story of the boy heroin addict may have been untrue; that the emphasis on prizewinning at the *Post* "clouded good judgment"; that "a young talent was pushed too fast"; and that "absolute trust in a reporter was betrayed." These findings seem to indicate that to achieve fairness requires more than individual reporters observing a few simple rules, and that the ethos of the newsroom and sensitive management of reporters by editors play major roles in creating a climate conducive to high ethical standards. Bill Green, the ombudsman, concluded that the *Post*'s transgression in the "Jimmy case" was the exception rather than the rule.

To emphasize the climate of the newsroom as a key ingredient in fairness is not to downplay the importance of guidelines for sensitive news coverage. Important efforts have been made to devise such guidelines to achieve fairness in covering criminal trials,[17] terrorist episodes,[18] investigative stories,[19] and others that run a risk of libel.[20] The journalist who aspires to behave justly will consult and weigh them. Beyond this concern with fairness in his deportment toward news sources, employers, colleagues, and the public, there is another and equally fundamental sense in which a journalist must be concerned with justice. This relates to his voluntarily assumed responsibility, as a practitioner under the First Amendment to the U.S. Constitution, to monitor the status of the larger contract of which the First Amendment is a part. That is, the journalist in a free society seeks to know whether and to what extent it is a free society, whether the preamble's promise to establish justice and promote the general welfare has, in fact, been fulfilled.

Stated in such general and hortatory terms, the assumption of such a "watchdog" responsibility might seem arrogant and perhaps even foolish if one expected the news media alone to conduct such monitoring. In fact, however, attention to injustice is a staple, occupational orientation of American and most western journalism. It furnishes the basis for the most coveted of the Pulitzer Prizes,[21] and is reflected in the ASNE's code in the injunction: "The American press was made free not just to inform or just to serve as a forum for debate but also to bring an independent scrutiny to bear on the forces of power in society, including the conduct of official power at all levels of government."

John Rawls, a philosopher in the contract tradition of Thomas Hobbes and John Locke, has written an intricate, highly abstract, but nonetheless useful theoretical analysis of the just society.[22] He assumes a hypothetical original condition in which founders of society, standing behind a "veil of ignorance," choose the principles that will govern society. These are the principles selected without knowledge of how chance, natural ability, and unequal access to wealth would affect the individual founders. First, each individual in society has an equal right to the maximum liberty compatible with the same degree of liberty for all others. Second, the only inequalities permissible are those that work to the advantage of all and arise under circumstances of equality of opportunity. In a carefully developed treatise that contrasts with what he sees as the dominant utilitarianism of modern times, Rawls asserts: "Each person possesses an inviolability founded on justice that even the welfare of society cannot override. For this reason justice denies that the loss of freedom for some is made right by a greater good shared by others. It does not allow that the sacrifices imposed on a few are outweighed by the larger sum of advantages enjoyed by the many."[23]

In a treatise that is faithful to the complexity of his topic, Rawls formulates what can be taken as an even firmer theoretical basis for the watchdog ethic than the one currently asserted by the ASNE code. In short, a just journalist should pay attention to the "way in which the major social institutions distribute fundamental rights and duties and determine the division of advantages from social cooperation."[24] In covering major social, political, and economic institutions, a reporter should ask: Are agreed-upon rules and procedures followed consistently and uniformly? Are some groups or classes of persons enjoying more than their fair share of goods or bearing more than their fair share of the burdens? Do some groups have more access than others to the policymaking process? Do citizens have the minimum requisites of life? On occasion the journalist may thereby stimulate the delivery of justice or the righting of an injustice; regularly he can report debate over competing claims in a society that asserts justice as a value.

THE PRINCIPLE OF FREEDOM

Liberty has just been considered as an indispensable element in the idea of justice. In western society, a denial of liberty to individuals or groups is one of the gravest of injustices. That concern for liberty is elaborated now under the more general concept of freedom.

In the most literal sense, the journalist must guard that particular freedom under which he enjoys protection, the First Amendment. He does so because, in the words of the ASNE code, "freedom of the press belongs to the people. It must be defended against encroachment or assault from any quarter, public and private." The *New York Times,* the *Washington Post,* and other newspapers did this in the Pentagon Papers case, successfully overturning a federal court injunction that prevented publication of a massive series of articles based on secret official records describing the origin and conduct of the Vietnam War.[25] Formation by journalists of the First Amendment Congress and, earlier, the Reporters Committee for Freedom of the Press[26] are examples of two specific approaches to defending what are perceived to be incursions on the First Amendment. Likewise, in a spirit of open debate, the journalist should consider and even solicit viewpoints critical of his own.

But there is another meaning to the word *freedom,* freedom in the sense of autonomy or independence. It is clear that autonomy is an important journalistic value. The ASNE code speaks of "independent scrutiny" of the power blocs in society. It also asserts: "Journalists must avoid impropriety and the appearance of impropriety as well as any conflict of interest or the appearance of conflict. They should neither accept anything nor pursue any activity that might compromise or seem to compromise their integrity." Other codes explicitly prohibit acceptance of gifts, free or reduced travel, outside employment, certain financial investments, political activity, participation in civic activity, or outside speaking engagements.

More vexing than these overt, tangible threats to a journalist's independence are the subtle, insidious risks the journalist confronts day by day. In a classic article, Warren Breed showed how reporters may lose their potential as moral agents by a socialization process in which the reporter is taught to accept newsroom policies inimical to wider public needs.[27] A constant concern of journalists is the risk of becoming so close to and dependent upon sources that they lose the critical perspective, becoming co-opted by sources.[28]

Not all the decisions journalists must make to preserve their independence are clear cut. One collegiate journalist, for example, was asked by a Pulitzer Prize–winning computer scientist for permission to inspect, before publication, a completed story that the reporter had written based on an interview with the scientist.[29] The scientist said he would check for accuracy only, not for purposes of editing or changing style or news emphasis. Some news organizations prohibit such a practice out of hand, as did the college newspaper for which this reporter worked. The assertion of autonomy which led the reporter to reject the scientist's request led to a major factual error, embarrassing to the editor and the reporter of the newspaper as well as to the scientist. As a subsequent analysis of this and other specific cases will show (see Chapter 4), principles sometimes conflict, and the weighing of competing considerations (autonomy versus running a risk of error, for example) poses difficult problems.

THE PRINCIPLE OF HUMANENESS

In their capacity as fellow human beings, journalists should obey what John Rawls has called "the natural duties."[30] Other things being equal, these require that a journalist give assistance to another in need. Likewise, journalists should do no direct, intentional harm to others, and should prevent suffering where possible.

These duties seem innocent enough on the surface. A journalist familiar with cardiopulmonary resuscitation should give it to a news source stricken during the course of an interview, if that seems the best or only means of helping. Covering a football game on the sidelines, a journalist will warn unsuspecting fellow bystanders of a ball carrier lurching on a collision course toward them. The departure dates and times of troop ships in time of war are not divulged by the correspondents who happen to know them.

But the decisions are not always easy. Shortly before the Central Intelligence Agency's invasion of the Bay of Pigs in Cuba, an operation aimed at the overthrow of dictator Fidel Castro, the *New York Times* was ready to print a story about preparations for the invasion. President Kennedy, learning of the impending news story, called the *New York Times* and persuaded its editors, on national security grounds, not to

publish it. The *Times* acquiesced. Later, however, reflecting on the loss
of lives and the damage done to American interests, President Kennedy
said that, in retrospect, he wished the *Times* had printed the story, thus
preventing the harm that resulted from the defeat of the Bay of Pigs
operations.[31]

Often the issue of whether a story has a potential for direct harm to
life arises in local police news. For example, in Miami a lawyer was
abducted at gunpoint and his captors demanded ransom. Rumors of the
incident reached reporters, who were asked to withhold news of the
kidnapping. The reasoning was that captors typically warn those from
whom the ransom is sought not to contact police. If the abductors read
news accounts of the kidnapping, then, obviously, police have been
alerted. This is thought usually to induce a panic in the kidnappers
which increases danger to the person kidnapped. In the Miami case, the
news media withheld the news for eighteen hours, and the attorney was
subsequently freed.[32] Such withholding of news would seem to be an
innocent and constructive enough way to heed the ethical injunction to
do no harm. However, when news of the kidnapping of newspaper
heiress Patricia Hearst was delayed, one Associated press editor
charged the wire service with suppressing the news. "None of us, of
course, would ever want to do something which would jeopardize the
life of anyone. But the police and others are always asking us not to
print something—and they always have an urgent reason. Since when
do we make those censorship judgments?" This editor specifically cited
what he termed the *New York Times*'s "unfortunate decision" to suppress the initial story on the Bay of Pigs invasion.[33] His concern, which
many will find misplaced, nonetheless reflects a residual conflict between the journalist's desire for freedom and autonomy and the instinct
to obey the natural duty to do no harm.

For purposes of this ethical system, the principle of humaneness (do
no direct harm, prevent harm, render needed assistance) implies natural duties, the very minimum that one human owes another. As such,
these duties are not part of a positive injunction to do good or to
maximize the good. Such an injunction is purposely excluded here to
avoid the trap of utilitarianism, the weaknesses of which were alluded
to in Chapters 1 and 2. There is, of course, a sense in which every
ethical system has a concept of the good and the values of truth, justice,
freedom, humaneness, and stewardship are part of the "good" a journalist seeks to advance. But a journalist takes risks by assuming that he
knows how to maximize the good, or that doing so for "the greatest
number" is possible, or part of his duty.

THE PRINCIPLE OF STEWARDSHIP

In most discussions of journalism ethics, the topic of this section is addressed under the name "responsibility" in mass communication. That concept is central to the idea of "stewardship" developed here. However, by using the word stewardship, an attempt is being made to identify and to establish more graphically and more sturdily the notion of a commitment to trusteeship which a journalist is free to assume in a constitutional democracy. *Webster's New Collegiate Dictionary* gives a definition of stewardship as "the individual's responsibility to manage his life and property with proper regard to the rights of others." That is the basic sense in which it is used here. A journalist—reporter, editor, publisher, or media owner—is in a unique position to *help* keep the wells of public discourse unpoisoned, if not wholly clean. From the vantage points which his occupation gives him, he is in a better position than many citizens to monitor the condition of justice within or between institutions. As a special beneficiary of the First Amendment, the journalist has a material motive to *protect a protection* meant for all. It is his responsibility to do all of this, for he is a steward of free expression. Although citizenship in a constitutional democracy makes each citizen a steward, the journalist's occupation gives him unique resources for this role. He manages his resources of communication with due regard for the rights of others, the rights of the public, and the moral health of his own occupation.

The idea of "social responsibility" was developed in its most influential form in the work of the Commission for a Free and Responsible Press, the so-called Hutchins Commission, in 1947. The requirements the commission identified for a free and responsible press are worth repeating. They are:

1. A truthful, comprehensive, and intelligent account of the day's events in a context which gives them meaning.
2. A forum for the exchange of comment and criticism.
3. Coverage of the opinions, attitudes and conditions of the constituent groups of society.
4. Vigorous editorial leadership, by presenting and clarifying the goals and values of society.
5. Full access to the day's intelligence.[34]

Leaving aside for the moment the question of which, if any, of the five points are achievable, in whole or in part, it is clear that a journalist who heeds them has assumed a prodigious responsibility. To behave responsibly, he will, of course, avoid libeling others, invading their privacy, harming their persons, and he cannot ignore their legitimate, newsworthy petitions or claims in the larger society.

Beyond that, as indicated in the section on truth telling, he must develop and be an effective steward of his own talents. He has a responsibility to do so. W. D. Ross, a philosopher generally regarded as a mixed rule deontologist, has termed this the obligation of "self-improvement," the duty to improve oneself "in respect of virtue or of intelligence."[35] In journalism, this requires that reporters and editors be alert to the relationship between the intellectual demands of the bodies of knowledge behind the news and their responsibilities under the codes to which they pay heed. Modern journalism abounds with opportunities for self-improvement.[36] These range from the oldest such program, the Nieman Fellowships in Journalism at Harvard University, to more recent efforts, such as the Walter Bagehot Fellowships in Economics and Business Journalism at Columbia University, aimed at specialists.

CONCLUSION

To describe the ethical journalist as a humane truth teller who seeks justice and protects freedom as a faithful steward of his craft may well invite incredulity. To modern, late twentieth century eyes such an occupational portrait may seem to exude hubris and vibrate with impracticality. No living, breathing journalist and none of the departed greats—not Ida Tarbell, O. K. Bovard, Walter Lippmann, or even Lou Grant—could have squared all his or her decisions with the principles articulated above. But the reason, of course, lies not in the principles themselves but in the fact of our humanity. Making this elementary observation may help us distinguish between journalism's clear need for ethical principles and the less than ideal distribution of human virtues—wisdom, courage, temperance, fairness—required for carrying out those principles.

This qualification need not blind us to reasons for encouragement. A team of researchers examining the moral development and belief systems of journalists in the late 1970s concluded their study with a value judgment:

> The largest proportion of our journalists appear to have given serious thought to their professional commitments. The longer they have been on the job, the more likely they are to be open-minded and thoughtfully responsible. The majority are anything but the narrow-minded cynical curmudgeons popular rhetoric tells us we can expect to find prevalent in America's newsrooms."[37]

In addition, researchers such as William G. Perry, Jr., as explained in a later chapter, have found an empirical basis for a scheme of intellectual and ethical development that appears to be both realistic and hopeful[38]—though certainly not a panacea—in countering the moral malaise of the late twentieth century. That malaise was well described for the journalist by Edna St. Vincent Millay:

Upon this gifted age, in its dark hour,
Rains from the sky a meteoric shower
Of facts . . . they lie unquestioned, uncombined.
Wisdom enough to leech us of our ill
Is daily spun; but there exists no loom
To weave it into fabric . . .[39]

In the belief that each person must build his or her own loom, the next chapter will seek to apply one loom to several episodes that posed ethical problems for contemporary journalists.

CHAPTER FOUR

Applying Principles to Cases

The new decade of the 1980s had scarcely begun when Chicago readers, as used to sensational journalism as any in the nation, confronted a front page *Chicago Tribune* story by nationally syndicated columnist Bob Greene:

> LOS ANGELES—This is for the man who calls himself "Moulded to Murder."
>
> I am in Los Angeles, waiting for you to call. My telephone number is being printed in the Daily Signal, the evening newspaper in southeastern Los Angeles County in which I am told you read my column.
>
> You have said that all your life you have been isolated to the point of pain. We want you to know that you are not alone anymore. We want only one thing: for you to get in touch, so that we can talk about the torment that has driven you to your threats of murder.[1]

To his sick communicant (call him MTM, for "Moulded to Murder"), Greene said later in the same column:

> A few things to set your mind at ease: This is not a police phone number. I am sitting in a hotel room, waiting for your call. The phone is a direct line that has been installed for this purpose. It is not tapped. No one is going to try to trace the call.

Two days later, sitting in a Los Angeles hotel room with a twenty four-hour bodyguard, Greene advised the readers of his column that "things are happening," but declined to elaborate:

> Every reporter's instinct inside me screams to write about what is happening; my entire life as a newspaperman has been devoted to dis-seminating information, not holding it back. But the homicide detectives say that if our purpose here really is to help the troubled man and prevent the killings, then the writing of a newspaper story has to come second to performing a public service. Under the circumstances, I think I agree, but it is not an agreement that has come easily. So this will be the last column I

write until the case is resolved one way or the other. There is a story here, in many ways the most amazing story in which I have ever been involved. I will tell it as soon as I can.[2]

Three days after Greene's first column appeared, police traced a call from MTM and arrested him in one of several pay telephone booths from which he had been calling Greene to make arrangements for a personal meeting. Greene had kept in sympathetic contact with MTM, in part by printing in his column a letter to MTM from a young suicide-prone woman whose own published letter to Greene had itself originally prompted MTM to reach out to Greene. At Greene's request and to fulfill a promise Greene made to MTM, police shielded MTM from personal publicity. The sick man underwent psychiatric counseling and at last public report appeared on his way to coping with his deep personal problems.[3]

This case involves all five of the principles of the ethical framework described in the previous chapter. Direct harm could have come to both MTM and his potential victims had Greene conducted himself irresponsibly, had he exploited the "exclusive" that was his as the only columnist contacted by MTM. The nature and extent of his obligation to tell the truth was directly involved in Greene's promise to MTM that "no one is going to trace the call." Certainly, an injustice would have resulted if innocent people were murdered. Greene's freedom and independence as a journalist came under direct pressure and Greene was forced to define how much he valued autonomy, compared to the values enhanced by cooperation with police. Finally, Greene had, by all his actions, to define "responsibility," to decide, under those circumstances, what it meant to be an effective steward in his position as a nationally syndicated columnist.

However, the pivotal principles in this case appear to be humaneness—the "natural duty" to do no harm and prevent harm—and truth telling. On the latter point, Greene, after an interview with MTM following his capture, wrote:

> I told him that I was sorry we had to put tracers on the telephone in my hotel room. In one of my first columns, I had told him that there were no taps on the phone, and that the calls were not being traced. That was true. But after he made his first contact with me Thursday night and indicated that the murders might be about to begin, police decided they had no alternative other than to put the tracers on the phone.[4]

One can argue (and I do) that Greene did not actually lie in phone call No. 1—not only because the phone was not tapped but because he apparently did not then know or contemplate there would be taps in the future. It also could be argued that to have lied in phone call No. 2 Green would have had to tell MTM, *again*, that the telephone was not tapped while knowing the opposite to be true. These technical considerations tend to obscure the larger reality: Greene let stand MTM's impression that the conversation was not tapped. In later publicity revealing this deception, Greene ran the risk that the credibility of his newspaper might suffer were it read by someone who later might find himself or herself in a position in which trust in the word of a journalist was deemed critical. That MTM later expressed himself as unconcerned about the matter—indeed, he said he was "glad" to be caught—does not diminish the fact of the tradeoff Greene made. Better to avoid the inhumane, palpable harm likely to ensue in the MTM situation—death of innocent persons—than pay heed to the abstract and perhaps undefinable possibility that his newspaper's and journalism's credibility would suffer. Indeed, not to have cooperated with police under the circumstances would have irresponsibly damaged the standing of the press.

Greene's reasoning in the MTM case illustrates how persons give "weight" to competing principles; indeed, some philosophers argue that all ethical decisions involve such weighting, whether explicitly recognized by the decision maker or not. One way to give more rigor to an ethical system or framework is to give preference, or special weight, to the principles therein. Toward that end, the framework being here applied gives the following initial—though not absolute—priority:

1. The principle of truth telling.
2. The principle of humaneness, specifically doing no direct harm to persons, preventing direct harm wherever proper and appropriate, and assisting another human in compelling cases of need.
3. The principle of justice.
4. The principle of freedom
5. The principle of stewardship.

The sequential listing does not fully indicate the nature of their position in the framework of ethics, hence an explanation is necessary.

The first two principles are "prima facie" obligations.[5]

The obligation to "tell the truth" goes to the very heart of the journalistic function. One would be hard put *not* to classify it as obligatory on its face. Indeed, one can argue that truth telling is inextricably linked to the other four principles. To be just, whether one means in the sense of fairness in written work or fidelity in monitoring justness of institutions, it is difficult to see how one could dispense with truth telling. Nor could one ignore truth telling and expect freedom to long remain intact, or expect to receive the respect due a responsible steward of free expression.

The injunction to do no direct harm, prevent direct harm, and render assistance to fellow humans—in short, humaneness—is on its face an obligation humans should assume. Its inclusion here is not ritualistic but deliberate, emphasizing that journalists should live with this primary obligation and actively consider what it means in their work. Perhaps the failure of *Washington Post* editors to make it their business to find and help "Jimmy"—when they *first* believed him to exist—is a classic illustration of how concern for getting and publishing or broadcasting the news can blind journalists to elementary obligations.

How absolute are these principles? Can one truly say that never under any circumstances should a journalist tell an untruth in published or broadcast work? What if MTM, or some other such sick person, had demanded a second assurance, in writing, that no tap would be placed on the telephone line? What if that assurance were made the condition of any other conversation with the journalist, and yet the police and psychiatrists were unanimous in their judgment that an end to the conversations would prompt a killing spree? Many, probably most, would have deceived a sick man rather than risk innocent lives. Absolutes in ethics, in the narrow sense depicted in the MTM example, can be unrealistic if not, on rare occasion, irresponsible.

What can be asserted with confidence is that there can be an absolute commitment to principled reasoning in matters of right and wrong and to enduring principles that are near-absolutes. They can be no more than "near-absolutes" because life, it seems, is seldom so uncomplicated as to confront us with important moral decisions which do not involve weighing and weighting competing principles. When we are very lucky, our decisions can be unambiguous and we can merely invoke the appropriate principle; in short, we respond in these circumstances with our moral reflexes, perhaps made sharp by early family, school, church, and other influences. However, most of the time we must decide how we weight competing principles. At such times we must inevitably inspect the context in which we find ourselves. According to the approach suggested here, truth telling and humaneness— construed strictly to mean avoiding palpable physical or irreparable psychological harm to a particular person or persons—come first. These "prima facie" principles should be respected unless the journalist is confronted with a situation in which to do so would be to ignore a *vital public interest.* "Vital" in this sense means of "utmost importance," something that is, as Webster's puts it, "essential to continued worth and well being." Greene's benign deception in the MTM case clearly served a vital interest, saving the lives of persons who otherwise may well have been murdered.

Some important qualifications need to be made specifying the limits on an injunction to the journalist to do no harm. Already indicated is the restriction of the principle to palpable physical harm or irreparable psychological harm. These are the types of harm for which we can justify imposing the almost absolute prohibition. Were other types of harm included, mere emotional suffering for example, one can see the professional paralysis a journalist would risk. A minister's son is arrested on charges of robbery soon after his father's installation in a new pastorate. The minister, concerned for his son and for his own reputation, asks that the story be withheld, pleading emotional suffering to both. To honor such a request when the policy of a newspaper is to publish all such arrests would be unjust to others who suffered embarrassment from the publicity given such a crime, and to the public, which wants and needs to know of such episodes as part of the media's report on community crime. But more relevant to this discussion, it is not the journalist's job to censor the news based on anticipations of how he or she anticipates people might possibly react to it. Little would be printed or broadcast were the journalist expected to avoid harm of whatever kind.

A second restriction is that of intentionality. Journalists cannot be considered culpable for the unavoidable consequences of the behavior of others. Discussing such situations, Charles Fried, who has helped significantly in defining limits to categorical norms, has written of unintended cases of harm: "If that result occurs inadvertently or as a mere concomitant of one's conduct or because one failed to seize an opportunity to prevent the result, then whatever else may be said of the conduct—it may be careless or callous, and may be condemned for that reason—it does not violate the categorical prohibition to do no harm."[6]

But in many instances, if not most, a news story can be handled in such a way as to meet both journalistic standards of accuracy and substantive truth and still avoid the most egregious, unacceptable levels of harm. Doing so requires sensitivity, imagination, craftsmanship, and resoluteness in the face of possible criticism from peers or the community.

In Michigan City, Indiana, a black assistant principal of a high school—call her Joy Calder—was arrested and charged with shoplifting. She had put a $15 ham in a handbag and failed to pay the cashier for it.[7] The initial decision by Ray Moscowitz, then editor of the *Michigan City News Dispatch,* was to print a separate story rather than list it routinely among the police news items. Rationale: a role model, one who, in fact, was responsible for discipline matters in the school, had been charged with violating the law. The community needs to know about such events.

A sensitive black reporter who knew Calder well wanted to verify with Calder herself whether the theft had occurred. If it had, he wanted to explain why the newspaper had to publish the story. During the reporter's visit, Calder said her shame was so great that she would commit suicide were the incident published. After a brief conversation, she grabbed her coat and left the reporter, who was struck by the depth of her depression. Moscowitz felt what many humans feel when faced with such moral dilemmas: a need for more information. Friends of Calder told Moscowitz that they had heard the suicide "rumor" too, which was enough to convince Moscowitz that Calder would indeed commit suicide.

When the *News Dispatch* asked school authorities about the episode, they had not yet heard of the arrest of their assistant principal. They suspended her. Moscowitz recalled: "We could not, of course, ignore the story forever, but decided we would not print until we were sure Calder was emotionally well. A week went by, and calls to the paper began as word of the arrest spread around our town of 37,000. We were called, among other epithets, nigger-lovers."

Twenty days after her arrest, Calder, having recovered emotionally, resigned at a school board meeting. The *News Dispatch* reported the shoplifting incident in the body of the school board story. She was sentenced to twenty to thirty days of community service. "A sidebar on her resignation, I felt, was not necessary and could cause her additional emotional harm," Moscowitz wrote.

Moscowitz's reading of the facts led him to believe that an immediate story would have caused Calder irreparable emotional harm, an emotional harm so intense that Calder would have tried to kill herself. Truth telling was not avoided but postponed. In the weighing and weighting, the immediate avoidance of grievous harm took precedence over the immediate telling of the news. Moscowitz defied both those whites who charged he was covering up and those blacks who wanted him to print nothing.

The point should be made that, often, when people disagree over ethical decision making they disagree not so much over matters of principles as over whether sufficient information is at hand on which to base a decision. Differences also arise over how to interpret the significance of the information available. In the above episode, some editors in the same situation might have wanted more evidence of Calder's suicidal intent before deciding to delay publication. Other editors, confronted with mounting rumors within the black community, might have assessed the calls to the paper as a signal to print the story immediately so as perhaps to prevent a serious racial disturbance in the school or in the community stemming from distortions and rumors. The important thing is that editors and reporters use principled reasoning, that they engage in ethical dialogue, both before and after the resolution of ethical decisions. Such dialogue can sharpen their moral judgment and sensibilities. Shared within their larger professional communities and with the public, this moral concern can help make ethics a more vital part of the civic culture. Such dialogue is increasing within many newsrooms and in the profession at large. However, this is not a development with which the public is familiar. Hollywood, as it has done with other occupations, muddies public understanding of journalistic norms and prevailing standards of best practice. In the movie *Absence of Malice,* a reporter seeking to test the authenticity of a murder suspect's alibi discusses the case with the suspect's friend, a woman who was with the suspect on the night of the crime in a city far removed from the scene of the murder. But she was with him because she was undergoing an abortion, during which she needed his help. The reporter, apparently to make her story more believable, uses not only the true alibi but the woman's name. The woman is an employee at a Catholic school, and her parents had been spared any knowledge of the abortion. When the story is published, the suspect's friend kills herself. Even neophyte journalists cringed at that needless name-telling. The story in the movie could have been told and the alibi verified with the exercise of reportorial craftsmanship and moral imagination. Presumably hotel records would verify the presence of the wrongly accused man and the woman as guests of the hotel on the day of the crime. The public could have been told and assured of the existence of such authenticating documents but with one name deleted. The reason for the deletion could be explained; namely, the need to protect the woman's right to privacy. The newspaper could have treated the matter in this fashion with reasonable confidence that the public would understand the use, in this particular instance, of an unidentified source.

Although instances in which journalistic decisions are linked to palpable physical harm are infrequent, they are not rare.[8] Much more common than episodes involving the natural duties are those which require careful interpretation of the principles of truth telling, justice, freedom, and stewardship. A classic case was the *Chicago Sun-Times*'s undercover investigation of corruption among city inspectors, law enforcement officials, and a covey of accountants who specialized in the small businesses regulated by the city.[9] A twenty-five-part series by *Sun-Times* reporters documented shakedowns, payoffs, and failure to perform official duties. It prompted official investigations and prosecutions as a result of which more than a dozen city and state employees, including building, health, fire, and electrical inspectors, were fired or suspended. Many were indicted and convicted of soliciting bribes. The series won a number of prizes, including one from the Society of Professional Journalists/Sigma Delta Chi, but was rejected for a Pulitzer, apparently because of the elaborate form of deception used by the newspaper to expose municipal misdeeds.

To locate and identify wrongdoing by city health, fire, and building inspectors, the *Sun-Times* leased a run-down bar, complete with flagrant violations of the city codes, which its reporters dubbed the Mirage. The management of the newspaper provided funds to open the bar and operate it long enough to serve as bait for the corrupt inspectors. The bar was deliberately overstaffed by reporters in order to corroborate the soliciting of payoffs by inspectors. Tape recording conversations without the consent of the parties involved would have violated Illinois law, so several reporters had to take notes immediately after every instance in which a payoff was solicited by the inspectors and paid by the tavern staff. Also, to comply with the law, the *Sun-Times* made sure that each violation of the law was reported, by prearrangement, to the Illinois Department of Law Enforcement. Photographic evidence was obtained surreptitiously by *Sun-Times* photographers by means of a dimmer system that allowed enough light at just the right moments, with patrons none the wiser.

David Halvorsen, managing editor of the *San Francisco Examiner,* has summarized the issue: "Was it classical journalistic enterprise for *Sun-Times* reporters to be posing as saloon keepers with a hidden camera monitoring the scene? Or was it a form of entrapment that some editors do not countenance on the part of law enforcement, much less their own reporters?"[10] To debate the issue, Halvorsen arranged a forum in the Bulletin of the American Society of Newspaper Editors between Clayton Kirkpatrick, president and editor of the *Chicago Tribune,* the *Sun-Times*'s competitor, and Eugene Patterson, president and editor of the *St. Petersburg Times.*

Kirkpatrick defended his competitors, dismissing the argument of entrapment by stressing the care taken to avoid it. Indeed, Pam Zekman, one of the *Sun-Times*'s reporters, has asserted: "I can say unequivocally that there was no entrapment at the Mirage. We were very, very careful about it. We consulted with both the *Sun-Times*'s attorneys and, in the abstract, with the prosecutors. We found that there is no way a reporter can, in a legal sense, commit entrapment. Nonetheless, we set a much higher standard for ourselves than policemen are required to follow. Our rule was that we would never plant the suggestion that a payoff would be made. We would wait until an overture was made by an inspector."[11]

Said Kirkpatrick: "The scheme was a little more elaborate than such time-honored journalistic enterprises as sending a reporter out in the role of ordinary citizen to test the service practices and pricing policies of television or automobile repairmen, but the approach was basically the same." He gave three other reasons why he thought there should not be an ethical prohibition against role-playing: (1) An undercover approach sometimes is the only way to avoid physical harm to the reporter. "I find it difficult to accept that ethical considerations would require that a reporter announce his identity and purpose at a Klan cross-burning, or a violent picket-line confrontation, or a civil riot." (2) Direct, corroborative evidence, usually obtainable by undercover approaches, is often needed to "stimulate corrective action, to bring about lasting administrative or legal remedies." (3) Readers like to personalize their newspapers and to impart human characteristics to them as crusaders against evil." Calling this a "philosophical" argument, Kirkpatrick added: "The drama of an undercover expose is a powerful factor in persuading a newspaper reader that his newspaper will go to extraordinary lengths to defend his rights. It could be sacrificed by unnecessary and uncompromising adherence to a mistaken standard of ethical purity."[12]

Patterson, applying what he termed "the scale of distinctions," found nothing wrong with "plainclothes reporting." The *Times*'s restaurant reviewer "doesn't wear a press card on her lobster bib"; its consumer reporter doesn't volunteer her non-consumer status" when investigating a bait-and-switch advertiser, he said. But, going up the scale a notch, Patterson said that, although his newspaper had done it in the past, he would not go undercover to expose a nursing home's abuse of its patients or a real estate agent's racial discrimination in the sale of houses. "Both of those stories could have been reported by straight means if we'd been willing to work harder," he said, then added another reason why he, in those cases, would not have resorted to subterfuge: "We've inflicted pretty high ethical standards on public and private institutions with our editorials in recent years and I worry a lot about our hypocrisy quotient if we demand government in the sunshine and practice journalism unnecessarily in the shade." Significantly, however, Patterson said he reserves the right to let reporters infiltrate "if fakery is truly the last resort and the only way to serve a vital public interest."

But fakery, he said, puts "our pursuit of truth on a tainted tangent . . . and I don't think we ought to take it as a norm."

Clearly, the reporters and editors of the *Sun-Times* were concerned about the injustice of the web of corruption they knew to exist among city inspectors. They weighted justice more heavily than the principle of truthful, deception-free methods. The end of exposing the injustice of shakedowns and payoffs justified the undercover means, or so the reasoning ran. The difference between the philosophies of the *Sun-Times* and Patterson would seem, then, to reduce to two questions: Could the exposure of bribe-taking and systematic corruption have been accomplished by other, undeceptive means in Chicago? And, in doing the Mirage bar series was the *Sun-Times* serving a "vital public interest"?

The first question is one that cannot be answered without access to specific facts about the Chicago municipal inspection force and without tapping the experience of a variety of knowledgeable investigators. It is not an ethical question but a pragmatic one. What else, short of infiltration or subterfuge, would have worked? We need not answer that question to make the important point, again, that differences between journalists may hinge on matters of judgment and on interpretation of fact rather than on matters of principle. It is an important point, one often overlooked by critics quick to judge.

The second question is one that strikes at the heart of the fifth principle, that of stewardship. The *Sun-Times* no doubt saw itself as not only correcting an injustice but also as being responsible, as a good steward of the watchdog ethic, for exposing civic misdeeds. But was there a "vital public interest" involved, one sufficiently vital as to justify an elaborate ruse? In short, were untruthful means justified by the objective of bringing to light an injustice and prompting a prosecution to correct a wrong? One needs, of course, to define "vital public interest." If one were to invoke a utilitarian mode of reasoning, one could reason that the overwhelming majority of Chicagoans are affected by the city's codes. When the enforcement of these codes is corrupted by bribe-seeking, shakedowns, and payoffs, then the public clearly suffers. The definition of the public interest by majoritarian calculation is easy, too easy. Among other things, that method ignores the effects of deception and lying on the parties involved, as will be developed in a later chapter on ethics in investigative reporting. By utilitarianism's loose standards, too much that is shabby can be justified under the journalistic mantle of watchdog of the public interest. A more stringent standard is needed, one that, at a minimum, would provoke more rigorous weighing of fact and weighting of competing principles.

When a journalist or news organization seeks to establish a standard defining "vital public interest" in cases that seem to require the use of deceptive means, it might ask the following questions:

1. Is the wrongful condition, problem, or practice to be exposed systemic or likely to become systemic or is it only partially or selectively present in the institution under investigation?
2. If the condition is systemic or nearly so, are there compelling reasons for believing that it cannot or will not be corrected without the news media and without the news media's use of deceptive means?
3. Does the wrongful condition, problem, or practice strike at the heart of the "social contract?" That is, does it violate one of the principles of humaneness, truthfulness, justice, and freedom in such a way that a reasonable and faithful adherent of the contract would clearly adopt deceptive means to expose it?

The position taken here is that if all the answers to these questions are yes, and if the journalist is willing to justify his methods in the subsequent stories, deceptive means can be acceptable.

The careful reader will note a flavor of utilitarianism in the use of the word "systemic" in the first of the foregoing measures of a "vital public interest." However, the third measure, a deontological one, is pivotal. Consequences are considered but principles are meant to govern. It should be emphasized that responsible ethical dialogue can result in two or even three different, equally defensible positions. This need not signal the futility of ethical discourse but merely that different value judgments and/or assessments of facts or likely consequences have been made. While common judgment or one party's successful persuasion of the other might seem desirable, a case can be made that robust differences can just as well signal moral vitality as ethical disarray.

Up to this point, less has been said of freedom and how it competes with other principles than has been said of the tension that often arises among truth telling, justice, humaneness, and stewardship.

A young college reporter, who will be called Richard Woods to avoid any unnecessary damage to his reputation, once interviewed Douglas Hofstadter, a computer scientist who won the Pulitzer Prize in 1980 for his brilliant book *Godel, Escher, Bach: An Eternal Golden Braid*. The story was to appear in one of the finest college dailies in the country. "I felt uneasy with the fact that he had no tape recorder with him," Hofstadter recalled, "since it seemed to me that most of what I was saying was going unnoticed." At one point, Hofstadter asked that Woods go get a tape recorder. Woods left and returned with one, only to find that it did not work. Later, he sent Hofstadter a note assuring him that there would be no distortions.

"Unfortunately," Hofstadter said, "this was not the case, as I found out when the article appeared in the paper shortly thereafter. The problems began in the first line, in which my name was given as 'Richard Hofstadter.' Then, my title was given incorrectly. From there, the article went on, misquoting me, distorting many of my ideas (even to the point of directly contradicting my statements), garbling other ideas, and, in my opinion, making me sound incoherent and confused." What made Hofstadter doubly angry was that he had made a request to check the story for technical accuracy in advance, and confronted a policy that banned such an inspection.[13]

As a result of an ensuing imbroglio, the college newspaper adopted the following policy:

> Sources may read a story before it is printed only to check the accuracy of the story and only after the reporter has gotten the approval of the editor-in-chief. This, however, does not give the source a license to rewrite the story; it only gives the source an opportunity to review and clarify.
>
> As a general rule, sources embroiled in controversy or involved in a highly sensitive matter may not read the story before publication.
>
> Striving for professional standards should be the goal of all of us. By going to great pains to assure accuracy you will not only be helping yourself and the paper, you will be enhancing the much-needed credibility of the paper.[14]

This controversy and its denouement highlight an important ethical issue: to what extent should a reporter sacrifice his professional freedom or autonomy in an effort to assure factual accuracy? To his credit, Hofstadter said he understood how reporters would deny an inspection privilege to someone involved in a poltiical story. He argued: "To me, it is a mark of professionalism and personal pride to make sure that an article is accurate. To insist on some sort of independence in reporting technical ideas is to confuse political reporting with informational reporting, and to have upside-down priorities."[15]

It may be that in some instances the distinction between "informational/technical" stories and "political" ones is unambiguous. It may be in some or many instances scientists or other specialists will limit themselves to factual inaccuracies. It may be that the self-confidence of editors and the good judgment of reporters are sufficient to protect against abuse in the infrequent instances in which prepublication inspection of copy is permitted. But it also is true that (1) few other circumstances have a greater potential for mischief than source-inspected copy; (2) scientists and other specialists often are involved in a kind of politics affected by media coverage; (3) relying on source inspection can turn into a crutch for a person unwilling or unable to develop his or her own understanding of a specialty: and (4) alternatives are available that can often make unnecessary a risky practice. These latter include review of the story by an equally competent but uninvolved third party who is a specialist in the same field as the source, the reading back to the source of selected passages and quotations, and, most importantly, scrupulous preparation by reporters in advance of such difficult interviews. In short, only in the rarest of circumstances, and only when the foregoing alternatives are all inadequate for a story of compelling significance to the news medium involved, should a journalist consider allowing a source to inspect copy in advance of publication.

The journalist with moral imagination seeks aggressively to discover alternative courses of action that will allow him to observe the central principles of his craft/profession. Where tradeoffs and the weighting process are made necessary by circumstance, a search will be made for ways to minimize the extent of the tradeoff. The journalist lucky enough to work for an ethically sensitive organization will consult with editors and peers whenever their advice might clarify options available in ethically taxing circumstances.

An ethical bind can develop suddenly and unexpectedly, even for journalists of long experience, if they are momentarily careless in the fundamentals they think they have mastered. This seemed to have been the case for Wayne Thompson, associate editor and editorial writer for the *Portland Oregonian*. Some six months before Janet Cooke's case came to light, he confessed to making up quotes in an exclusive interview his newspaper had with Dixy Lee Ray, the Washington governor defeated in a Democratic primary.[16] Thompson told fellow reporters later he felt obligated to meet the next-day deadline which his newspaper expected. Doing so, however, resulted in fabrication, which the governor's press secretary quickly detected. After Ray informed the newspaper, the *Oregonian* suspended the forty-five-year-old Thompson, whose admission of error ran on the front page, supplemented by an inside-the-paper retraction that identified errors paragraph by paragraph. Almost all of the quotes in Thompson's two stories on the governor were invented, with the result that almost all the quotations were inaccurate. Specifically, instead of being "stunned and bitter" by her defeat, as Thompson wrote, she asserted she was not bitter. Ray was quoted as describing herself as "victimized by a deeply biased press that opposed me from the day I filed for office and never let up." But a tape recording made by the governor showed that it was Thompson who said that, not Ray. In addition, there were other discrepancies between the transcript and the published stories. Thompson's tape recorder had malfunctioned. When he made the decision to go ahead anyway, he was "tired and drained." In subsequent interviews, he made clear the problem may have stemmed from the fact that years earlier he had ghostwritten for the governor a series of articles on energy that had appeared in the Oregonian. Thus, a close association with a politician may well have compromised Thompson's independence, and, ultimately, the accuracy of his work. Thompson accepted an eight-week suspension without pay, then went back to his editorial writing job with a vow to live down a transgression for which he had offered to resign.

CONCLUSION

Although at one point he acknowledges the "possibility that there is no way to get beyond a plurality of principles,"[17] John Rawls labels as "intuitionists" those who believe in a group of principles and who simultaneously deny there is a foolproof system of priority for resolving conflicts between principles. The argument made here, and made elsewhere by persons concerned with standards of ethics in modern life, is that, even though not set in rigid priority, principles, when articulated and continually defined with respect to particular cases, provide a solidity that strict reliance on intuition never can.[18] Many if not most important ethical decisions by journalists wind up in print or are broadcast for public inspection and public retort. The others, less visible, can themselves be made public with improvements in methods of media criticism and ethical dialogue within news organizations. Therefore, serious violations of principle can be the subject of censure and widespread debate in a way that can help prevent or minimize lapses. "Close calls" of one principle taking precedence over the other can be made the subject of rigorous discussion and professional accounting.

Such discussion and accounting have developed and do take place within journalism, though not nearly as frequently or as vigorously as needed. Principles illustrated by application here are implicit, if not explicit, in most codes of ethics of media organizations and professional societies. With their more explicit identification and use in studying cases and the quality of news coverage, perhaps journalism can less accurately be called an underdeveloped profession.

CHAPTER FIVE

Values, Virtues, and Principles

A set of principles, carefully calibrated and weighted, can serve as a compass to point to the polarities of clearly right and clearly wrong, as well as to the ethical directions that lie between. Yet a set of principles cannot furnish all the wind for the sails or, usually, the whole reason for the journey. These are provided with the help of values and virtues. Values, both moral and non-moral, define what is good and bad, as principles define right and wrong. Virtues are those traits of character or personhood that help one live up to or live out the principles of an ethical system. The extent and range of a person's virtues—and their opposite, vices—shape the ethical impact of his or her life. The purpose of this chapter is to show the interplay of principles, values, and virtues in a series of actual ethical decisions that editors themselves have identified as their toughest.[1] Drawing sharper distinctions among these concepts may allow journalists to see ethical problems in a clearer and richer context. It also may give a welcome human dimension to a subject too often treated as a mechanistic exercise. A later, concluding chapter will discuss ideals.

Obviously, there can be overlaps in the use of the above terms. Such principles as humaneness, truth telling, justice, freedom, and stewardship are moral values, even as they are also guideposts for discovering our moral obligations. But there are also non-moral values—as distinct from immoral ones—that play a major role in the conduct of journalism.

This appears clearly when we list some of the functions of modern journalism and identify the corresponding non-moral values implied by those functions. Thus, conscientious news media aspire to:

- Acquaint people with their environment, providing the informational wherewithal for daily life. (Knowledgeability)
- Equip people with the information they need for important decisions. (Usefulness)
- Provide the news, background, and interpretation with which peo-

ple can give meaning to a complex world. (Understanding and
Community)

- Monitor, within the limits of available resources, the community's
  key public and private institutions, especially those that affect the
  quality of justice in society. (Feedback and Community)
- Transmit and/or enrich the culture by mirroring and reflecting on
  humanity's own efforts to feed, clothe, house, secure, enrich, enter-
  tain, and inspire itself. (Education and Community)
- Help distribute the goods and services of society by crafting a
  communication product that will attract and effectively serve advertisers. (Entrepreneurship)

In the context within which these values are identified, they can be
viewed as good and worthy. But judgments of right and wrong do not
inhere in knowledgeability, usefulness, community, understanding,
feedback, education, or entrepreneurship. In fact, with only a little
imagination one can see how these values can be twisted for purposes
most persons would call bad. It is this malleability that prevents our
using the word "moral" to describe these values, even though most
people commonly supply a moral purpose or meaning when they refer
to them.

The distinction is important for journalists because, frequently, the
non-moral values of their calling are the very ones that create pressures
on moral principles. Take a journalistic value widely shared in American culture—competitiveness. It is embodied in the "scoop," the story
told first, exclusively. Although critics deplore journalism's so-called
scoop mentality, a strong argument can be made that it has served not
merely journalists but society well. But for the scoop, and the rewards
journalists attach to it, many a civic boil would have festered, and much
immorality affecting the public weal would have remained uncleansed
by the disinfectant of publicity.

Alex S. Jones felt the pressure of competitiveness in spades when, as
editor of the *Greenville* (Tenn.) *Sun,* he declined to publish a scoop: a
federal grand jury's investigation of a South American marijuana buy
that implicated a local bank loan officer and a former assistant attorney
general. Having learned the details of the investigation, the *Sun* refused
to publish them because officials would not confirm them. To have
published in this case, Jones said, "would destroy the man's reputation
without his ever being charged with a crime" (87). In a situation in
which the principles of truth telling and justice were in tension, Jones
chose to postpone truth telling in favor of the fairness rule on his
newspaper, which embodied the principle of justice: do not use infor-

mation from unnamed sources in such cases "unless there was reason to think that justice was not going to be done" But "the law enforcement apparatus was working well" and the names were not used (89).

Unfortunately, exactly the opposite position had been taken by a competitor forty miles distant, who named names repeatedly and trucked the rival product daily into Greenville. To make matters worse, the rival newspaper bought and aired radio spots suggesting that the *Sun* was covering up for prominent local citizens. Jones, now a correspondent for the *New York Times,* summarized the enormous pressure:

> Staff morale was on the floor, and character assassination was rampant. The town was whipped into hysteria, and the opposition's newspapers were selling like hot cakes. . . .
> The reputations we had set out to protect until and unless indictments were forthcoming had been shattered. The opposition's news stories had named them, and they were common currency.
> Was there any reason not to run with the ball and print all we knew, using unnamed sources like our rivals? (88)

But Jones stuck to his guns and, when the indictments finally came down, he postponed his press run four hours to be "first and complete—with the story" (89).

The tension between the principles of truth telling and justice was resolved by Jones and his *Sun* colleagues with the help of the virtues of fortitude and courage. The gift of discernment led them to the judgment that, painful as their predicament was, the facts did not justify buckling before the competition and making an exception to their rules restricting the use of unnamed sources.

Few values are as strong in the American newsroom as toughness. It is a legacy of an almost bygone era of hard-driving, hard-drinking, iron-fisted reporters and editors. The city editor as newsroom mogul embodied the value in the way he leashed and lashed errant reporters. A grammatical sin, a missed deadline, an inaccuracy—any of these was certain to evoke from him at best a devastating grunt or piercing reprimand, and at worst actual dismissal. The criterion of publication was anything newsworthy that the Good Lord permitted to happen. In the 1920s and earlier, not only would real city editors not eat quiche, they would not write nor abide by anything so sissy as a code of ethics. But the reflexive reaction to print everything regardless of the consequences is being rethought, if not eroded, in the recent new concern of editors—and the public itself—with journalism ethics.

William Burleigh, general editorial manager of Scripps-Howard, was one of thirty-one editors who told their experience with tough ethical decisions in a book entitled *Drawing the Line*. He said he had learned his trade on a "tough, we-print-everything, no-exceptions-to-the-rule newspaper" (51). Like Alex Jones, Burleigh once confronted the necessity to choose between the imperative of truth telling and justice, or fairness, and humaneness. The question was whether to print two court records which would have, in effect, publicly identified two young girls as incest victims. He wrote of the experience:

> This once it was time for the young city editor to start asking himself some ethical questions. Did he really want to be the agent for branding these girls for life? If there was even a remote chance of causing such harm, no rule, however venerated, seemed worth that. Even if it did make him less of a macho city editor. (52)

Burleigh wrote that he "felt guilty" at the time for cutting out the records without telling his managing editor. In recent years, however, such newsroom reticence has given way to spirited office debates, Burleigh wrote, "and the exceptions to the old rule grew"(52). In his case, the virtue of compassion softened the application of the value of toughness.

Novelty, often an ingredient of "what's new," is a pervasive and well nigh permanent non-moral value in journalism. Arnold Rosenfeld, editor of the *Dayton* (Ohio) *Daily News and Journal Herald,* certainly encountered that value when the lifestyle department of the *News* developed a sensitively written, edited, and photographed feature on a special education class for youngsters with severe deformities. Not long before the story was to be published, Rosenfeld received a call from the parents of a young woman, "Mary," whom his reporters had found to be a leader in the class. She was a dwarf, and her parents, irate at what they considered to be a thoughtless invasion of their privacy, were threatening to sue. When Rosenfeld informed them the paper had obtained permission from those involved, including Mary, it made no difference. Rosenfeld called attention to the obvious good such a story would do, including demonstration of the splendid job the parents had done with Mary, who emerged as a study in courage and self-confidence. The parents would have nothing to do with such reasoning. Nor could they see the significance of reporting the special education class itself.

Struggling with the parents' request to kill the story, Rosenfeld struck a compromise. He would remove references to Mary in the story, and leave out the pictures of her. It considerably lessened the journalistic value of the story. Wrote Rosenfeld:

It was not a great day for journalism.

But I still feel good about the decision. People who are dwarfs, I decided, have greater claims concerning privacy than most. Their objections, particularly in the softer news area, must carry almost ultimate weight with us.

This story counts for almost nothing in its narrowest sense. It is important journalistically, only because it proves that the search for an all-purpose, one-size-fits-all ethical code will inevitably be frustrated. Everybody is searching for such rules, a statement for which this book [*Drawing the Line*] is best evidence. (29)

The virtue of prudence informed Rosenfeld's weighing and weighting of the claims of truth telling on the one hand, and justice or fairness on the other.

At the other pole in ethics of privacy, the sifting and valuing of competing considerations led to a decision to publish in the case of the *Milwaukee Sentinel* and Milwaukee County Supervisor Richard C. Nowakowski. Elevated to the chairmanship of the county board in a tough election battle, Nowakowski occupied a key position affecting the public interest. While investigating his personal and political life, the *Sentinel* discovered questionable activities, "including campaign law violations and his involvement in swinging parties," wrote *Sentinel* editor Robert H. Wills (22–23). The newspaper's stories led to eight felony indictments. Nowakowski was acquitted of accepting a bribe, and five counts of soliciting perjury were dismissed. But ultimately he was convicted of violating the state's Currupt Practices Act and fined $1,000 for accepting $800 in postage stamps as part of a campaign contribution. Nowakowski, as a convicted felon, was removed from office. He later moved to Florida, where he died of a heart attack in 1982.

The newspaper's executives concluded that their truth telling role as a watchdog over government overrode any caution that might otherwise have restrained their making public details of Nowakowski's private life. Wrote Wills:

Our reasoning? We believed that we had the responsibility to let the community know of the personal background, character and the activities of this elected official. We were certain that the judgment he used in his personal life would be the same kind of judgment he would use in his governmental decision-making, and we were equally certain that an enlightened citizenry would reach the same conclusion. (23)

The *Sentinel's* efforts in the Nowakowski case reflected, among several values, the non-moral value initiative, a value pervasive in American culture and one especially important to American journalism. The principles in tension were truth telling and justice or fairness. To stand up to the criticism for bringing details of Nowakowski's personal life to light, the newspaper had to exercise the virtue of fortitude. As often occurs in a case of major investigative journalism, the arbiter was the court system. Investigative reporting and other forms of entrepreneurial journalism are fostered and supported by an esprit de corps that permeates most effective newsrooms. It is a non-moral value that propels much of the best journalism.

Nothing is more destructive of such newsroom solidarity than a decision not to publish something that a news staff has uncovered, especially when it appears that not publishing will be pleasing to the most powerful in the community. Such was the dilemma that once faced William F. Thomas, editor and executive vice-president of the *Los Angeles Times,* after his staff conducted a wide-ranging interview with the politically ambitious son of a very successful California politician. In the midst of some "fanciful musings" on medical experiments on humans, the son had made an "ambiguous reference" to Hitler (33). When the father got wind of its inclusion in the story, he telephoned Thomas and insisted that his son's political career would be aborted if the newspaper printed the son's foolish remark. To make matters worse, the father also telephoned the reporter involved and threatened him in a way that led both the reporter and his immediate supervisor to infer that the politician had and would exercise his supposed influence with Thomas and the newspaper's publisher.

Thomas, hoping the story would be so strong that he could avoid having to side against his staff, read it and came to the "melancholy conclusions that: (1) the reference to Hitler was more puzzling than relevant; (2) it had no bearing whatever on the thrust of the story, which mainly portrayed the father's determination to shape a political future for his not-so-sharp son; and (3) the son, apprised of what he'd said, declared that, for God's sake, he didn't mean he agreed with that monster about anything" (34). It was a close call, because the staff argued persuasively that the remark showed the son's thinking processes, an acceptable reportorial objective, given the nature of the article. But Thomas concluded that using the remark, especially after the son's emphatic disclaimer, would be "overkill" (34).

In weighting the obligation to justice over a literal interpretation of truth telling, Thomas had to muster a number of virtues—wisdom (that word so seldom employed by moderns), courage, and not a little prudence. The distinctions he made—in recognizing the context of the young politician's remarks and their disavowal, not to mention their likely impact—showed an exercise of moral imagination.

Few non-moral values inhere more tenaciously in journalism than celebrity or prominence. The famous or widely known, whatever the reasons for their making news, generate wider and more attentive response in readers and viewers, a response which itself has an economic value given advertising's relationship to circulation. Celebrity provided the context for a 1976 decision by Robert H. Phelps, then managing editor of the *Boston Globe* and now vice-president of Affiliated Publications. The topic was the release of Bob Woodward and Carl Bernstein's book *The Final Days,* which chronicled the demise of Richard Nixon's presidency. At issue was a *Globe* Washington bureau story that included a reference to Nixon's relationship with his wife, Pat. The version of the story which Phelps allowed to be published was a New York columnist's summary of a passage asserting not only that Mrs. Nixon once threatened divorce, but also that she and Nixon "had not had sexual relations for 14 years" (16). Actually, the Woodward and Bernstein book had merely reported that Nixon and his wife "had not really been close since the early 1960s" and that "her rejections of his advances . . . had seemed to shut something off inside Nixon" (16).

In letting the passage on Nixon run, including the columnist's summary of that portion of the book, Phelps was swayed by the uniqueness of a presidential resignation in the news and his need to provide whatever information he could to help explain it. Later, Phelps regretted his decision:

> I had let my feelings about the evils of the Nixon Presidency override professional ethical standards that should protect the privacy of every individual whether good or evil. The relationship between the Nixons was based on sheer rumor. In the case of the sexual relationship, the report had come not directly from the *Newsweek* excerpts but from what a gossip columnist had heard about the excerpts. There was no evidence to support the statement, no evidence that even if true, the absence of a sexual relationship had an effect on Nixon as a key Watergate figure or as President. I'm sorry I let that passage stand. (17)

A lack of craftsmanship in secondary reporting and editing, influenced by a felt need to "get and print the story," had compromised truth telling. The pressure of covering a celebrity whose news making was truly unique contributed to an injustice. The virtues of honesty and candor brought the tale to light as an object lesson for fellow journalists.

Journalists are not uniformly serious-minded in their tale telling, and somber affairs of state are not the only grist for ethical recollections in tranquility. That much was clear from Seymour Topping's account of a 1958 French Indochina experience when, as an Associated Press reporter, he covered an exchange of letters between Harry Truman and Norodom Sihanouk, then king of Cambodia. To express his gratitude for American aid, the king had decided to present the White House with an elephant. Truman, as best he could, tried to deflect the king's generosity. But Sihanouk would not relent, and the beast was placed aboard ship to cross the Pacific. To everyone's surprise and "to the vast relief of the White House, the elephant succumbed," Topping recalled, before the ship reached his adoptive country.

The cables between Truman and Sihanouk were turned over to Topping by a senior official in the American legation in Indochina and became the basis for an entertaining AP feature by Topping that was widely reprinted in American newspapers. The use of diplomatic language to discuss the gift of an elephant provided the spice of the story. But there was a hitch. King Sihanouk, offended by the story, objected to President Truman and his protest had repercussions not only at the State Department but in the legation in Indochina. Topping's source was reprimanded and his personnel record thereby received a hurtful blemish.

The source was as surprised by the publication in Topping's story of the full text of the lowly classified cables as Topping was about the subsequent impact of the tale. Topping, managing editor of the *New York Times,* later reflected:

> Mea culpa to my source's immediate boss did little good, but a subsequent conversation with an assistant secretary of state in Washington mitigated the reprimand in his personnel file.
>
> As for my lesson, never again would I write a sensitive story without carefully weighing whether I had been fair to my sources. Certainly, the first journalistic obligation is to the reader, particularly if the public interest is involved. But sources should not only be quoted accurately and in perspective, but also protected, if circumstances require. Frankness, rather than manipulation, should be the rule in obtaining information from the innocent and naive. (82)

Justice, as reflected in journalistic rules to achieve fairness, is a moral value. It also takes the form of a virtue when expressed by a journalist who actually tries to make amends, as did Topping, for a wrong done to a source. The tale also shows that such non-moral values as humor and entertainment—welcome tonics for the human condition—can nonetheless sometimes encourage an unwitting carelessness in journalists.

Curiosity, that quintessential non-moral value of the journalist, has a special talent for jumping ethical bounds. That seemed to be one message in a story written by a former tennis prodigy turned reporter about a tennis mother's excessive devotion to her son's development in the game, and published in the lifestyle section of the *Detroit Free Press*. Collected after hours and hours of interviews and phone conversations, it depicted in pervasive detail the imposingly vicarious life the mother pursued through her son's tennis (18–20). The story was a masterfully written parental object lesson in how—and by inference how not—to relate to a child's interest in sport. No question pertaining to the mother's most private fears and aspirations went unasked or unanswered.

Scott McGehee, managing editor of the *Detroit Free Press,* knew the story would be criticized, but that it would also be "read and talked about." Although libel-proof, the story nonetheless caused pain. The mother told McGehee that the story was "mean" and "unfair," and that it had "ruined her marriage, her relationship with her son, her life."

McGehee, reflecting a contrition common to many of the thirty-one editors who contributed to *Drawing the Line,* said that "the woman's voice still haunts me," adding:

> So do the questions I didn't ask: Did the reporter have some unresolved problems from her own tennis-playing youth that colored the story unfairly? Would the story have worked just as well without the mean tone? Did the reporter get too close, allowing the mother to assume she was a friend, not merely a reporter? Did the story unfairly take advantage of a woman who had no previous experience dealing with the press? (19)

McGehee's questions, asked retrospectively, reflect the curiosity of the moral imagination. Her post-mortem scrutiny of the case shows the non-moral value of curiosity in the service of the virtue of conscientiousness. It also shows that curiosity, a non-moral value, is in itself neither bad nor good. Much depends on context—in short, on the facts. Thus, there is a legitimate "relativity" not only in the application of principles but in the expression of values that are not relative, but endure.

If, to the journalistic ear, there is an uncomfortably pompous or pious ring to the vocabulary of moral discourse, it may well be that the hard value of self-detachment has crept up on the craft/profession's blind side. Instead, the vocabulary and occupational ideology of journalism—specifically, a misunderstanding of objectivity as an ideal—may be interfering with the cultivation of moral discourse as a habit. How, journalists may be implicitly asking themselves, can we be objective while discussing such squishy-soft matters as values, virtues, and principles?

The answer may lie in cultivating within journalists not only the ideal of objectivity but the wisdom to see how the hardy empiricism of their craft is inescapably influenced and enriched by non-empirical considerations—in short, by values and virtues. It may just be that the explicit recognition of this fact will emerge from the increasing emphasis on ethics in journalism and the importance of ethics to the credibility, and hence the economic well being, of the news media. If that link is forged convincingly enough by the leaders of American journalism, then the pursuit of the ethical way may become not the pursuit of puddin' heads, but a characteristic of the toughest minds and the truest spirits in the field.

CHAPTER SIX

The Journalism Business

Handling the Organizational
Pressures on Media Ethics

Thus far, several major theories of ethics have been sketched and some of their strengths and weaknesses identified. In the light of these strengths and weaknesses a framework of principles has been constructed, using classical values, the experience of journalists, and the existing codes of journalism ethics. Examples have been used to show how such a framework can be usefully applied to daily problems facing reporters and editors. Values and virtues that enrich or detract from ethical journalism have been identified and distinguished from one another. To leave it at that might leave an erroneous impression that the journalist is entirely a free agent, that all he need do is internalize major principles and then act on them. If there are such ethical automatons, their existence has been well hidden.

Journalists live their lives, for the most part, within organizations; even the freelancer, working in one of the remaining outposts of individualism, must contend with the conventions, pressures, and objectives of organizations that purchase the product of his or her pen. The purpose of this chapter is to identify the subtle as well as more palpable ways in which news organizations affect the nature, range, and impact of the ethical decisions journalists make. An attempt will likewise be made to identify, in general, some ways journalists can and do respond to organizational influences on their professional lives.

Earlier chapters described utilitarianism—making ethical judgments on the basis of the greatest good for the greatest number, in short, maximizing the good—as a potential trap for the journalist. Identifying what is best for a majority and picking the best means for maximizing the good are formidable, perhaps impossible, undertakings. While these are difficulties that will dissuade many from embracing utilitarianism, there is yet another more insidious feature of the doctrine. It is ever so easy and often tempting to choose as a "maximizer of good" the path that suits the individual journalist's and/or the media organization's interest rather than the course a journalist, as a moral agent, would decide. Reasons for this are not hard to find.

Within most media organizations there is an arithmetical imperative to maximize audiences. The larger the circulation or audience of a newspaper, magazine, or broadcast property, the more it can charge for advertising, the economic lifeblood of news media. Sensational news—news that invades privacy, exaggerates, or titillates—attracts attention and can expand the audience. What the Good Lord allows to happen, runs an old journalistic tradition, an alert editor will not hesitate to print or broadcast. After all, the public has a "right to know" what is happening in society, be it ever so gruesome or unseemly. True, a minority will find it repelling to turn on the six o'clock news and see live footage of policemen inspecting the latest victim of the local axe murderer. But—so goes the reasoning—perhaps the majority, reflecting on the gore it has witnessed, will install burglar alarms or lock home doors. Thus, showing such footage and banner-headlining the seamier side will work "the greatest good for the greatest number." Local TV stations' practice of playing up sensational news shortly before ratings time graphically illustrates both the pressure to expand audience and the invitation to rationalize journalistic behavior on utilitarian grounds.[1]

Making an analysis at deeper levels, scholars within the past decade or so have shown organizational influences in the very definition of news and how it is gathered and presented. Collectively these studies suggest that limitations on the freedom of action of the journalist are built into the organizations in which they work in the form of economic, social, and bureaucratic constraints. Warren Breed, one of the earliest researchers, interviewed 120 reporters and editors on middle-sized newspapers in the Northeast to study how "policy" or "slant" was bypassed or maintained.[2] Policy was defined as a more or less consistent orientation in news stories and editorials toward selected issues and events in a community. These may range from local elections to school controversies or urban renewal. He found that staffers can "often, if not always" be prevented from counteracting policy. The reasons are several. An editor can usually keep "touchy" assignments from potentially troublesome reporters, and fire those who attempt to transgress policy. But the fear of reprisals is sometimes enough. Often, however, reporters respect or admire an editor, and positive obligations can likewise deter. Heeding policy also may expedite career advancement. For that matter, the entire newsroom may frown on friction over policy, or, as Breed reported: "Instead of mobilizing their efforts to establish objectivity over policy as a criterion of performance, their energies are channeled into getting more news." Subsequent studies by Ruth C. Flegel and Steven R. Chaffee[3] and, more recently, by Mark Popovich[4] seem to credit reporters with more independence than found by Breed. But Breed's study no doubt identifies influences prevailing in many news-rooms. Noticed far less frequently but as important for our purposes are the means (Breed identifies several) that can be used to bypass policy,[5] which will be discussed later. Breed examined, and emphasized that he examined,[6] only "policy" stories, ignoring the vast majority of stories that have nothing to do with policy. News, however, has been the focus of a second generation of scholarship. Using organization theory, these later scholars have sought to define "what it takes" for an organization to stay in business. They then sought to show how those "organiza-tional maintenance needs" shaped the news and whether those influ-ences were stronger than the individual judgments that journalists themselves advanced as the primary determinants of news. Among the more significant of these studies was Edward J. Epstein's *News from Nowhere,* an analysis of network news. His research showed the impor-tance of (1) a predictable supply of stories—hence the heavy flow from news locales such as Washington, New York, Chicago, and Los An-geles; (2) film with compelling visual qualities; (3) novel events and graphic detail; (4) newscasters with whom audiences could identify; (5) short, economical stories, and (6) uncomplicated, readily digestible rhetorical style. These organizational preferences do not eliminate the role of the individual journalist, Epstein said, but he emphasized: "As long as the requisites remain essentially the same, network news can be expected to define American society by the problems of a few urban areas rather than by the entire nation, by action rather than ideas, by dramatic protests rather than substantive contradictions, by rhetorical dialogue rather than the resolution of issues, by elite news makers rather than economic or social structures, by atypical rather than typical news, and by synthetic national themes rather than disparate local events."[7]

Using a similar analytical schema to study the *New York Times* and the *Washington Post,* Leon V. Sigal sought to explain the behavior of these powerful national print media in covering government.[8] Central to his approach was the idea of the newspaper as a bureaucracy whose members are forced by the logic of their positions to bargain. The stakes in bargaining are the use of available staff and space (the dimen-sions of which are both influenced predominantly by economics) and time, which is always limited by deadlines. The object of journalistic labor, whether consciously defined or not, is a product that will appeal to and not offend—at least drastically or consistently—large numbers of advertisers and readers. While encumbered by these constraints, the journalist must at the same time furnish some evidence that the special protection given the press by the Constitution is deserved and not merely a shield for commercial greed. Day by day, from the "glut of occurrences," there must be selected those stories, and only those stories, capable of sustaining these often contradictory imperatives of the Fourth Estate. But how? Enter Sigal's version of "the journalist's creed."[9]

Uncertainly among journalists over what constitutes news is overcome not by verifiable standards but by what Lippmann called conventions, or customs that pass for standards. One is "objectivity," meaning news devoid of personal opinion and overly subjective judgments. Where strict factuality might prompt offense, it must be accompanied by a balancing fact or attributed perception or viewpoint. Objectivity, in short, must not be achieved at the expense of fairness. The more authoritative the source, usually meaning the more official he or she is, the better. Subjectivity and reportorial value judgments are more likely to be minimized if news is "pegged" to a discrete, recent event of significance to many people. If one can obtain news before anyone else does, fine. Scoops attract readers and increase prestige. Above all, after getting news, give it to the reader in language that simplifies the complex and converts the difficult into a currency which all may use at the civic marketplace.

Sigal argues that while many different groups of Americans have learned to gain access to the press for their ideas and opinions, there is still unequal competition. High administration officials, knowledgeable in the ways of the media, enjoy quicker and fuller access than anyone else. He sees problems with the status quo: "So long as news organizations concentrate large staffs in their Washington bureaus, so long as newsmen adhere to the existing routines and conventions of news gathering, so long as editors hesitate to counteract absorption on the beat, in short, so long as the organization and politics of newsmaking remain as they are, the press will primarily offer news from official sources passed through official channels."[10]

Essentially agreeing with the findings of Breed, Epstein, Sigal, and others who have used organization theory to study the news media, sociologist Herbert Gans's research nonetheless is richer for having been conducted over a longer period of time and, I would argue, with a more empathetic concern for not only the sensibilities but also the possibilities of journalism. Gans spent the better part of ten years interviewing and content analyzing "CBS Evening News," *Newsweek,* and *Time*. News, he concluded, can best be explained by the terms "power" and "efficiency."[11] Reporters and editors, all of whom face deadlines, work with an epistemology and a definition of news that allow them to efficiently allocate their scarce resources of print or air space and production time. Powerful elites in society are the most important sources of news not only because their activities satisfy the conventions of news gathering but also because they are the most efficient sources of news.

Former Vice President Spiro Agnew, the watchdog group Accuracy in Media, and the business community, among others, have argued that the national journalists Gans studied are primarily liberal, which exerts an unsettling influence on contemporary American culture. While Gans acknowledges the effects of media coverage of the Vietnam War protests, the civil rights movement, and the student movement of the 1960s and 1970s, he believes that a deeper and longer look shows that the content of the media reflects "enduring values,"[12] enumerated and illustrated as follows:

1. Ethnocentrism. While the news media's relentless coverage of Watergate might seem to denigrate the United States, the denigration actually was of a small group of politicians whose attempted subversion of American justice was thwarted by an invincible constitutional structure, "our system."

2. Altruistic democracy. The frequent focus by the news media on injustice, corruption, non-feasance, and stupidity in government reflects a belief that politics should *always* uphold the public interest.

3. Responsible capitalism. "The underlying posture of the news toward the economy," Gans writes, "resembles that taken toward the polity: an optimistic faith that in the good society, businessmen and women will compete with each other in order to create increased prosperity for all, but that they will refrain from unreasonable profits and gross exploitation of workers and customers."[13]

4. Small-town pastoralism. Combining an affection for "nature and smallness per se," this enduring value can be seen in stories emphasizing the troubles of big cities, the vapid life of suburbs, and the threat to individuals from Big Technology and bigness in all walks of American life.

5. Individualism. Typified by the many staunch individualists who once appeared on CBS newsman Charles Kuralt's "On the Road" series, this value also appears in news that highlights threats to the

individual from computers, "group think," or conformity induced or coerced by corporations, cults, or political parties.

6. Moderatism. Anything, including individualism, can be taken too far, and extremists are unwelcome. "The news is scornful of the overly academic scholar and the oversimplifying popularizer: it is kind neither to highbrows nor to lowbrows, to users of jargon or users of slang," in Gans's view.[14]

7. Order. Fully aware that media critics argue that "liberal journalists" report disorder to foster political change, Gans cites "pro-order" stories in the wake of urban riots of the 1960s and in the aftermath of the Nixon resignation. He said they indicate a decided preference instead for the restoration and preservation of domestic peace. In many respects, critics are ignorant of how a journalist's obligation to news values requires the airing or printing of news of violence. Therefore, they are unable to see that journalists in fact value an orderly society.

8. Leadership. Because so much of the news features leaders, their hopes, successes, near-misses, and failures, it is not surprising that Gans would identify this as an enduring value reflected in the news. From presidents to county commissioners, from FBI directors to police chiefs, from national corporate executives to local chamber of commerce leaders, the predominance of these "authoritative sources" in the news makes evident the value journalism places on leadership.

Thus far, this reconnaissance of the scholarship on journalism has outlined the more or less indirect influences that may limit the degree of latitude allowed reporters and editors in decision making. By osmosis, a newsroom can absorb and assimilate newcomers into the ways of "policy," constricting choice. By using a subtle definition of news more geared to organizational maintenance than individual autonomy in news judgment, the range of permitted behavior is narrowed. And by traditions which reflect the values of the larger society, the options open to a journalist may be limited.

Indirect influences and a host of direct ones as well emerged vividly in *Behind the Front Page,* a remarkable analysis by a social scientist, Chris Argyris, of a major metropolitan newspaper. Identified in the book as "The Daily Planet," the now open secret is that the object of his study was none other than the *New York Times.* For three years during the early seventies, with the permission of top management, Argyris sought, in addition to academic objectives, to "discover what must be done to create newspapers that are self-examining and self-regulating."[15] His work there took place at a time when the relationship of the national newspapers to the government had become corroded by coverage of major social upheavals—the civil rights movement, the student revolt, the Vietnam war, the Watergate scandal, not to mention major apparent changes in moral values and the structure of the American family. It was a time of internal debate not only at the *Times* but also at other key institutions, media and non-media, as well.[16] His attempts to apply organization theory and other tools of social science to the perceived problems of an honored journalism organization were both novel and strategically timed.

Argyris subtitled his book *Organizational Self Renewal in a Metropolitan Newspaper.* The "living system" he described[17] was characterized by intense competition and low level of trust among reporters and editors in the newsroom. Emphasis was placed on winning rather than cooperating to achieve goals. A judgmental atmosphere prevailed in which innovation was discouraged and the lessons of newsroom experience had a less cumulative effect than might have been possible in an open, accepting environment. Differences among groups and departments were often suppressed rather than discussed. Secrecy about personnel and other matters was common. Decision-making was centralized. Among management, Argyris found, these conditions fostered leadership that either domineered or withdrew. In both cases, they reinforced negative attitudes in the "living system," he said.

Argyris acknowledged at the end of his study that it had "not shown an unambiguous and clear cut causal relationship between the distortion of the news or the tone of editorials on the one hand, and the living system and type of reporters on the other."[18] But he said there is a distinct possibility that the living system "may act as a magnet for reporters who will be predisposed to create credibility problems by reporting subjectively, distorting inferences, and selecting news to fit their unresolved, and in many cases only partially recognized, needs."[19] These and other problems, Argyris reported, were recognized by his study and the editors.[20] But Argyris reported he had little if any success in his intervention to make the *Times* a more open, self-renewing organization.[21] He concludes his study with a doleful lament that an institution protected from outside intervention by the U.S. constitution should so consistently carp and criticize the secretiveness of other institutions in society, yet resist the very process of self-renewal it needs to perform its job effectively.[22]

Argyris wrote that the "credibility gap," then as now much on the minds of editors, may be caused as much by problems in the internal dynamics of news organizations as by the commercial motives of the media so widely noted. But while there is considerable support for this view,[23] there is nonetheless continuing concern about the direct and indirect role of economics on news gathering performance.

The rise of media conglomerates and groups (the term "chain" having almost disappeared from common usage) has been dramatic. In newspapers, by the late 1970s, the number of group-owned newspapers had grown to about 60 percent of the total,[24] and by the 1980s, the percentage had climbed to 72 percent.[25] Attributed to poor local management, family disputes that forced sale of newspapers, and tax laws that induced sales to groups, this decline of competition and rise in one-ownership towns has been widely deplored. Critics argue that chain or group ownership discourages diversity of news and opinion and makes for less quality in performance. However, scholarly studies of both news and opinion content fail to support this verdict.[26] In addition, a comprehensive assessment by the Rand Corporation of newspaper chain ownership and broadcast-print cross-ownership concluded: "The results of assessing the current knowledge about concentration of media ownership can be expressed in a well-known Scotch [sic] verdict: 'Not proved.' Evidence relating media ownership to economic or content performance is generally weak and unconvincing."[27]

There may be differences between group and independently owned newspapers in their impact on reporters and editors. William T. Benham, John Finnegan, Jr., and Patrick Parson of the University of Minnesota have shown, for example, that independent editors were more likely to stay at their current jobs than those at group newspapers.[28] An American Society of Newspaper Editors' survey showed that 22 percent of group editors and 28 percent of independent editors viewed *high* turnover of editors as interfering with the effectiveness and credibility of newspapers. Only 7 percent of group editors and 3 percent of independent editors saw any corresponding benefit in high turnover. Whatever future scholarship may document on the group vs. independent debate, evidence is beginning to accumulate that newspaper management styles and newsroom expectations have an important impact on the performance of journalists. Thus, an in-depth analysis of 489 reporters and editors at ten different newspapers in eight locations concluded:

> The image described was one of an increasingly competitive, politically charged communication environment where at least some energies were diverted from news-gathering and editing toward solidifying one's standing with higher-ups in the status hierarchy.
>
> The question for managers is whether undue emphasis is being placed on career advancement to the detriment of cooperative, amicable working

relations among peers and at the expense of professional dedication to the organization's overriding concern, producing an accurate, timely enterprising, and thorough newspaper.[29]

The study by Judee K. Burgoon, Michael Burgoon, and Charles K. Atkin of Michigan State University also found many journalists isolated from their communities[30] and not consistently in tune with their readers' interests or background.[31] "Overwhelming majorities" found their jobs satisfying, but 59 percent perceived them as "not healthful,"[32] with deadlines named as the biggest source of stress.

A fledgling journalist, a thoughtful mid-careerist, or even a mellowing veteran might be forgiven for being at least momentarily daunted by the seeming juggernaut of scholarly and anecdotal evidence of organizational influence on the moral and professional autonomy of media practitioners. I am not here rebutting the evidence, but do wish to emphasize that in this world the potential for the exercising of individual initiative and values still exists and that there are those whose professional competence and principled acts have made a difference in the behavior of organizations.

At the outset, it should be noted that the pressures of organizational life are not visited solely upon journalism. In the twentieth century, indeed, the bittersweet fruits of bureaucracy are shared by many private and public institutions. Lawyers in impersonal corporate firms, doctors in mammoth hospitals, clergy in the clutches of ecclesiasticism, and scientists with corporately influenced research agendas—all must deal with ambiguities about the nature of their work, the direction of their obligations, and the effectiveness or impact of their labors. To admit as much is not to confess moral leprosy but to acknowledge complications common to the moral and professional lives of many if not most persons.

Such an acknowledgement does not make a journalist's problems evaporate but it should make him or her foreswear wearing the scarlet letter of sinfulness or near-impotence that scholarship seems so willing to proffer. Read aright, however, scholarship should help a journalist face straightaway the problems of the craft/profession. None of these is more central than his or her capacity as a truth teller.

The obligation of objectivity arose as a fading political press gave way to a commercial one serving readers of diverse backgrounds and persuasions. To write "objectively," without expressing opinion, thus was to serve not only the pristine value of truth but a motley audience attracted by common interest in a factual version of news acceptable to most if not all. This ideal of objectivity, often substituted as a synonym for "truth," also helped journalists of the 1920s and 1930s gain respectability and remove the stigma of unprofessionalism bequeathed by their predecessors. Serviceable as the concept was, it was inevitable that the limitations of absolute objectivity as a lodestone for professionalism would be exposed and fought.

Those who led the battle, which continues to this day, are a testament to the potential of individuals to influence the organizations in which journalists work. Among reporters, Paul Y. Anderson of the *St. Louis Post-Dispatch,* who won a Pulitzer Prize for helping reopen the Teapot Dome scandal, repeatedly spoke of printing not only the facts, but the truth behind the facts.[33] Curtis MacDougall, a Northwestern University journalism professor, pioneered by introducing "interpretive reporting" to several generations of college and university journalism students through a textbook that has sold about 400,000 copies.[34] In the profession, the belief that a journalist should interpret the news was aggressively fostered by such well-placed editors as Lester Markel of the *New York Times.*[35] Almost as influential were the failures of "objective journalism," demonstrated by the press's parroting of charges by the late Senator Joseph McCarthy of widespread Communist infiltration of government. These charges, often printed without background, interpretation, or verification, were later proved to be largely unsubstantiated. The knowledge that the press had been duped by "objective" journalism led many, some hitherto hesitant to do so, to embrace interpretative reporting and practice it.

Lest he or she be boggled by semantics, slogans, or solipsism, a serious journalist needs to work through the viewpoints of the "objectivity" versus "interpretation" debate. The seeming hoariness of the argument is itself a danger to the field. The topic actually is as fresh, as palpable, as the next recession to be explained or the next war to be reported or the next budget to be interpreted. The view proposed here, which agrees essentially with that of Donald McDonald, is that no news account can be totally free of subjectivity. Values, in the form of judgments of importance, influence the selection of what to write about, the facts gathered, and the emphasis placed on those facts. "But objectivity as meaning a substantially truthful account of contemporary public affairs is well within the possibility of the mass communications media, despite many practical difficulties," McDonald concluded.[36] As Elmer Davis, reporter and commentator, wrote:

> The good newspaper, the good news broadcaster, must walk a tightrope between two great gulfs—on one side the false objectivity that takes everything at face value and lets the public be imposed on by the charlatan

with the most brazen front; on the other, the "interpretive" reporting which fails to draw the line between objective and subjective, between a reasonably established fact and what the reporter and editor wishes were the fact. To say that is easy; to do it is hard.[37]

Authentic interpretation retains the fidelity to fact central to the "old objectivity" while furnishing perspective and fullness of meaning. It supplies background information unavailable from or omitted by news sources; it translates complex data or terminology so that it can be understood; it provides enough context to allow readers to judge the news for themselves and not be misled; it tells candidly what information is unavoidably missing from a story; and, when necessary, it is explicit enough about methods used to gather the story to let the reader assess its probity and fairness. Authentic interpretation—"objective interpretation," if you will—explicitly rejects the facile assertion that because news judgment unavoidably contains subjective elements there is no such thing as a substantially objective story. Authentic interpretation also rejects the insidious notion that the journalistic obligation of justice and fairness requires that favorable information, even though it is not strictly relevant, must be included in a story to, literally, provide balance. "Balance," to a just journalist, means essential fairness, not a counting house allocation of favorable and unfavorable paragraphs contrived merely for effect. In short, authentic interpretation is scientific in spirit, and the truth it portrays is subject to addition and revision. "Truth" writ large is never encapsuled completely in one, two, or even several stories. Yet, as Walter Lippmann has suggested, the democratic faith is that the media, with the help of other republican institutions, can contribute to its eventual discovery.

Despite organizational constraints, and not infrequently with direct support from the organizations for which they work, journalists have striven successfully to expand the domain of "reportable truth." Philip Meyer, now teaching but formerly a reporter and executive with Knight-Ridder newspapers, helped introduce the use of the techniques of survey research in newsrooms.[38] Donald Barlett and James Steele of the *Philadelphia Inquirer* have perfected the use of government documents as sources,[39] and their prize-winning techniques, including computer-assisted analysis of documents, have been imitated. Steve Weinberg, executive director of Investigative Reporters and Editors, wrote a widely respected book showing how Washington's myriad government sources can be used to give perspective to not only national news but government news in communities of all sizes across the country.[40] The television documentary, developed most effectively by the late Edward R. Murrow of CBS and his colleagues, has its contemporary counterpart in such public affairs programs as "60 Minutes," the format for which has been imitated by the better local stations. Investigative Reporters and Editors in Columbia, Mo., has been formed to perfect techniques of enterprise journalism in both print and broadcast media. For years, special mid-career fellowships and seminars have been established to help reporters of public affairs and other specialists to improve the state of the art of their craft profession.

These examples and numerous others that could be cited provide a counterargument to the pessimism of some scholars[41] who have focused on constraints (and helpfully so) but have largely underestimated the influence of individuals and professional organizations on the ethical capacity and performance of journalists. Truth telling need not be a captive to the conventions of daily news gathering. The emphasis in recent years on background stories, news analysis, and interpretive features, and the availability of sophisticated new reporting tools are strong evidence of a capacity, when necessary, to transcend conventions. Moreover, especially on medium-sized and metropolitan dailies, news magazines, and larger TV stations, a new generation of journalists is prepared to be freed of artificial constraints. As indicated by anecdotes and surveys showing deadlines and ratings as sources of unhealthy stress, conventions such as "timeliness" and "human interest" do exist. These take their toll. However, the *capacity* to report and interpret news objectively and in depth is or can be within reach of most media in the United States. The newsroom is not nirvana. Journalists are by no means supermen and superwomen. Their flaws and limitations are real and, indeed, are made public daily. But the organizations for which journalists work need not make them intellectual or ethical eunuchs, at least not without individual consent. That much is clear.

If significant strides have been made in expanding the definition of news to include enterprise journalism, at least a beginning has been made in raising the formal standards of ethics. Although there are differences[42] over the extent to which codes can or should limit employee prerogatives, such as private group memberships and family activities, there is a widespread acceptance of at least the basic provisions of the many codes of ethics promulgated by professional groups and individual media organizations.[43] The reservations about codes are several—that they are too general; that their adoption was largely for public relations purposes; that they are hypocritical if they do not at the same time cover publishers and station owners; that they do not provide—or that they might some day contain—enforcement mechanisms; that they foster a false sense of purity; and that they potentially promote an aloofness from sources and the community that tends to dangerously isolate sources.[44] The very restiveness with codes may reflect an awareness, at least by some journalists, that the essence of ethics can never be codified and must ever be the habit of examining alternative courses of action in light of principles that sometimes conflict.

Indeed, a strong case can be made that a combination of moral imagination, professional ingenuity, and interpersonal communication skills is more effective in establishing and maintaining ethical standards in the newsroom than codes of ethics. Once in upstate New York a young reporter was assigned to report on a petition from the company that owned his newspaper to the Federal Communications Commission, asking for permission to build signal boosters so that its decidedly inferior UHF-TV station could compete more effectively for advertising dollars with the local VHF station, which was clearly the leader in viewership and advertising revenue. Part of the story dealt with documenting the disparity between the stations. The reporter handed in a five-page story, the length and detail of which angered the editor-in-chief, who also was general manager of the station. Returned to the savvy city editor, the story became the subject of a conversation between him and the reporter. Upset, anticipating he would be forced to compromise, the reporter told the city editor he would resign if asked to alter his story. "That would be dramatic," the city editor said, indicating, first, that the original article was truly overwritten and, second, that resignation was a sure if melodramatic way of losing control of the story. Then he helped pare the piece, omitting none of the essential facts.[45] He thereby indentified and put to rest a phony ethical issue and avoided a situation in which a shoddy story could have emerged had he and the reporter made a spurious issue of the editor's reaction.

Journalists have other options when confronted with authentic cases in which they are asked to write a story they think might compromise their ethical standards. In the early 1980s, the *Miami Herald* was confronted with a single-spaced, ninety-nine-page critique of its coverage of the black community by a veteran former *Herald* reporter and editor, Robert Hardin. Basically, Hardin accused the powerful Knight-Ridder flagship newspaper of pandering to the black community in its coverage of police brutality and events leading to the city's riots of May 1980, allegedly with the objective of building circulation there. After agonizing over the memorandum, which Hardin had made public and discussed on local broadcast media, the *Herald* decided to treat it as a news story. *Herald* reporter Carl Hiaasen was asked to write the story. However, he told his editors it would not be ethical, and explained to the *Columbia Journalism Review:* "I am good friends with the writers involved. They bent over backwards to be fair to the police."[46] As for writing about Hardin, Hiaasen said, "it would elevate him to an immediate authority," and would be "harmful to our morale." As Hiaasen's decision indicates, reporters can use their brains and tongues, and ask not to cover stories they believe would compromise their ethics. In the Miami case, it was a matter of who *should* write the story. The *Herald* then asked its Washington correspondent, Tom Fielder, to write it. Fielder did so, but only after asking for and receiving a guarantee that *Herald* editor John McMullan, who had publicly disputed the issue with Hardin, would not inspect the article before it was published. The example of Hiaasen and Fielder in this case can be a source of instruction and encouragement to reporters who mistakenly believe that all managements are inflexible and insensitive to ethical standards.

In other circumstances, the reporter may have no alternative but to resign. "The newspaper or station that does not carry out its obligations to the staff—a decent salary, adequate staffing of reportorial and editing positions, full support of penetrating journalism, intelligent and independent leadership—cannot demand the loyalty of the staff," writes Melvin Mencher, professor at the Columbia University Graduate School of Journalism.[47] In preparation for such an eventuality, Columbia's Dean Edward W. Barrett advised students to accumulate from their salaries a "go to hell fund" to make it easier to leave irresponsible organizations.[48]

Breed suggests that journalists in timid or policy-laden organizations can use their initiative to originate stories, especially on beats where editors and publishers have comparatively little knowledge and in areas where policy is unclear.[49] He even suggests that a reporter whose story has been rejected or who believes it is certain to be rejected can "plant" the news with another rival news organization. Thereafter, Breed says, the reporter can plead "the story is now too big to ignore."[50] This latter approach is tantamount to a deceit that would invite a habit of lying in the newsroom, creating perhaps as much or more distrust than before. Breed's basic point, however, is that the emphasis in most newsrooms on "getting the news"—what he calls an "instrumental orientation"—reduces the moral potential of journalists.[51] But that potential often can be reclaimed or defended by acts of moral imagination, by dialogue with management, by originating one's own stories, or by quitting, to name a few options.

In addition to these stratagems, there may be traditions within the newsroom that can protect journalists from the more egregious forms of pressure to compromise on ethics. As an example, Alan Parachini, while an investigative reporter for the *Chicago Sun-Times,* uncovered evidence that commercial blood pressure measurement machines in the Windy City were inaccurate. The manufacturer of the machines noted that the devices were located in stores of one of the newspaper's biggest advertisers, and that publishing criticism of the machines might result in loss of advertising. Parachini dismissed the threat, confident that his employer, then Field Enterprises, would respect the autonomy of the newsroom and reject any advertiser's overture.[52] When the *Wall Street Journal* was faced with a threat by General Motors to pull its advertising if the newspaper printed news of the company's new line of automobiles before the release date, the *Journal* published the information anyway.[53] But not all such stories have a happy ending. William A. Emerson, editor of the *Saturday Evening Post,* said he believed that advertisers' opposition to a *Post* editorial led to the loss of $13 million in advertising, hastening the magazine's demise as a staple of the American magazine scene.[54] The Coca-Cola Company once withdrew substantial advertising from NBC after an NBC documentary showed the company to be a beneficiary of the exploitation of migrant workers in the South.[55] Nor is the price of resistance always paid by corporate wealth. A 23-year-old reporter for the *Trenton Times,* then under control of a management that was retrenching financially, was fired after he rewrote an advertiser's press release which had been ordered to be printed verbatim.[56] He lost his job, despite the publisher's later admission the management had erred in agreeing to run the press release verbatim.

These traditions against advertiser interference with the news product—in short, this emphasis on the principle of freedom and independence—have a long history. The early muckrakers spoke out against it. Thus, *Collier's* in 1910 revealed that patent medicine companies' advertising contracts with newspapers allowed automatic cancellation if states in which the newspapers were published adopted bans on proprietary medicines.[57] In the 1930s, George Seldes, the media critic, exposed advertising's continuing influence. In the more enlightened days of the 1960s and 1970s, food pages—where many of the previous sins were committed—became the focal point of a brand of consumer journalism that often vigorously explored product quality on behalf of the consumer. Concerned that the more somber economic mood of the 1980s is eroding that beachhead, a practitioner of the specialty, Goody L. Solomon, documented her concerns and publicly criticized the drift away from enterprise consumer reporting in an article in the *Columbia Journalism Review.*[58] That this article, in the tradition of Seldes and others, is only one of many such pieces currently published does not weaken—in fact it strengthens—the point: the principle of stewardship must be practiced to be kept alive and well. Bruce Brugmann, who established his feisty *San Francisco Bay Guardian* on a shoe string and gut determination, put it well: "The defense of journalism as more than a business and more than a monopoly—though a business it is and a monopoly it has become—is properly the journalist's duty. It is they who must understand that many (but certainly not all) of the basic problems are attributable to the exigencies of business monopoly as applied to the gathering of information, which was once considered so important it was granted constitutional privilege and protection. The journalist has both a professional and public obligation to look after his inheritance.[59]

In summary, the scholarship on organizational constraints and influences on journalists has, as Anthony Smith noted, "demystified" the processes of reporting,[60] laying them open for public debate and professional response. Less than full mileage will be gained from this new understanding, however, if either the public or a segment of the profession is led to believe, as Edward J. Epstein would have it, that reportorial tools are so weak that journalists must declare themselves "agents for others."[61] Any given year's crop of investigative journalism will refute such an assertion. The point, in fact, is that journalists, as a group, have enough professional competence and enough moral freedom to fully face and accept the responsibilities implied by the constitutional protection granted them. The times are such that the twin demands of ethics and competence are no longer merely matters of special interest to journalists alone.

CHAPTER SEVEN

In Lieu of Licensing

A First Amendment Remedy for a First Amendment Business

At ninety, his steps were as swift as the eyes of the collegians whose smiles also followed the old man's dogged walk across the lawn toward Dartmouth's Baker Library. Two visitors in tow, he descended to the lower floor entrance and straight to the west wing of the hall, where he was to begin his guided tour. It would be, he made clear, not only his visitors' but his own high point of the day: viewing "An Epic of American Civilization," murals circa 1932–1934 by Jose Clemente Orozco.

From an Aztec ritual of human sacrifice to the arrival of a Mayan-Toltec hero-god named Quetzalcoatl ("The Plumed Serpent"), Orozco's art is a pageant of human struggle. Peace, plenty, and pyramids arise in Quetzalcoatl's reign, only to be followed by a regression to violence and evil which frightens away even the hero-god himself. Then comes the stout Christian conqueror, Hernando Cortez, then, in its time, the age of machines, human exploitation, and modern war; an unknown soldier suggests the earlier Aztec sacrifice. The masses of Latin America, rising up, throw off their chains in a bloody outburst. Finally, there stands a colorful Christlike leader and idol smasher, waving a fist and urging us to act to right the wrongs we have seen. Behind him, as in a junk yard, are broken religious, national, and political symbols. Even the leader's own cross has been snapped in two, as if to suggest that that symbol too had become perverted by demagogues and hypocrites.

The old man's tour of the murals ended, and he waved his right hand, palm upward: "Uplifting, the most inspiring painting in the world." The enthusiastic tour guide, then ninety years old, was none other than George Seldes, pioneer media critic and publisher of the muckraking newsletter *In Fact,* circa 1940 to 1950.[1] Sampling the titles of his eighteen published books, one sees that his tastes in art and journalism have galloped together toward idol smashing, debunking, exposé, and exhortation. With *You Can't Print That: The Truth Behind the News,* in 1929, Seldes began his career as a media critic, upbraiding the European press for its distortion of the news in the post–World War I era. *Sawdust Caesar* in 1935 exposed the evil machinations of fascist Benito Mussolini, the ambitious Italian journalist. *Freedom of the Press* in the same year showed in vivid detail those threats to the press arising from the influence of advertising and the business office. Kenneth E. Olson, then dean of Northwestern University's Medill School of Journalism, called it "the most stinging indictment of the American press since Silas Bent's 'Ballyhoo.'"[2] In it, Seldes also appealed for journalism graduates to enter the profession with "minds . . . opened by courses in journalistic ethics."[3] In *The Lords of the Press* in 1938 Seldes named names of newspapers and identified scores of specific examples of journalistic transgressions. A nostril-quivering polemic in the tradition to which the readers of his bestselling books had become accustomed, the volume and its immediate predecessor made Seldes famous. However, Seldes's more sweeping assertions and broad-brush inferences caught the attention of critics even in his finest hours during the 1930s and 1940s.[4] Despite faults of overstatement and inconsistent documentation, and despite a twenty-year fall from grace as a result of a brief period of Communist infiltration of his newsletter, Seldes's contributions have come to be recognized as having lasting significance. Professor Emeritus Curtis MacDougall described Seldes in 1980 as "the man who more than anyone else living made critical analysis of the press' performance popular and important."[5] The first journalism organization to officially honor his work was the Qualitative Studies Division of the Association for Education in Journalism, whose 1980 plaque rests on Seldes's mantel in his Vermont home overlooking the White Mountains of New Hampshire. Two years later, the George Polk Awards included a special citation honoring Seldes's efforts at media criticism.[6]

Although Seldes sustained his criticism for more than twenty years,[7] he was not without both predecessors and lineal descendants. Will Irwin, one of the original muckrakers, wrote the premier critique of the press in a series of fifteen articles in *Collier's* in 1911. Published under the title "The American Newspaper: A Study of Journalism in Its Relation to the Public," this work was noted for its extensive documentation, balance, completeness, and sense of journalism history. Nothing quite like it had ever been published before.[8] In their depiction of the influence of advertisers and commercial interests, denunciation of yellow journalism, and allegations of press failure to serve the public interest, Irwin's articles bore what modern scholarship has recognized as a "striking"[9] resemblance to the findings of the Commission on Freedom of the Press, chaired by Robert M. Hutchins, in 1947. In short, by the end of World War II, the stage had been set for such critics as A. J. Liebling[10] and, in the 1960s and 1970s, Ben Bagdikian.[11] Liebling's irreverent and penetrating articles in the *New Yorker* established the hope, still unfulfilled, that evaluation of the media might conceivably become an art form as fully developed, and certainly as important, as music, art, or theatre criticism. Bagdikian's articles and books established the fact that media criticism could become an accepted specialty within journalism.

The history of media criticism and the works of media critics are worthy of study in themselves. They are especially important, however, when viewed against the background of the debate over whether journalism is a profession—and, if not, what it must do to become one. Although this is a hoary topic on the conversational menu of journalists, it is considered here to establish a context for a discussion of the ethics of media criticism.

Wilbert E. Moore has identified at least six characteristics that can be used to help identify a profession.[12] First, it must be a full-time occupation, not a trade that can be practiced as the mood strikes or merely as an occasion requires. Second, it must not be an occupation taken lightly; that is, one must have a "calling" that involves deep commitment. Third, a profession must carry itself in society by means of a formal authoritative organization that can set terms for entry and continuance in the profession and maintain professional standards. Through organization, an occupation, as Moore contends, can "set itself apart from, and above, mere tasks set aside by the administrative wisdom of superiors."[13] Fourth, a professional is one who has been prepared for his calling by long, presumably arduous preparation by means of specialized knowledge obtainable only through schools organized by the profession or with its blessing. Fifth, a profession must serve society. And to guarantee such services there will be codes of ethics, as Moore says, "to protect the ignorant client and the legitimate practitioner against the charlatan or the improper practitioner."[14] Finally, an occupation buttressed by such concrete protections must certainly deserve and require autonomy to deliver its services. No outside interference or amateurish dabbling can be allowed within the bailiwick of the licensed, certified, professional practitioner.

Whether journalism is or is becoming a profession, and whether it should be, are important questions. Generally, this research has shown that, compared to other occupations, journalism is not yet a profession but in some respects is becoming professionalized.[15] The journalist's status as an employee the product of whose labor can be accepted or rejected prevents him from attaining as much autonomy or control over his work as do doctors or lawyers. Moreover, controls over entry into journalism, while they exist, are not centralized in a professional sense and are certainly not based on any uniformly accepted standards of preparation. That may result, in part, from the lack of an agreed-upon body of knowledge that news media are willing or able to impose upon entrants in the form of educational requirements.

However, the service function of journalism in a democratic society is so important and its ethical component so imperative that to expunge journalism from the ranks of the professions would be folly. Briefly put, the argument made here is that journalism is a craft with professional responsibilities. Licensing, which is common to medicine, law, and some developing professions, cannot be instituted for journalists. To do so would violate the First Amendment to the Constitution by involving government in abridging the rights of some persons to publish or to enter journalism and practice it. That much—and it is a great much—is clear. What, then, can be done to give the public—which shares the rights of the First Amendment—the assurance that journalists are behaving competently and responsibly? How can journalists provide an assurance comparable to that given, say, by medicine and law? And, perhaps, first of all, *should* journalism, *need* journalism, provide such an assurance?

Slowly, sometimes fitfully, but nonetheless perceptibly, the news media of the United States have, on the whole, come to accept some form of accountability. The vast majority have eschewed anything like a licensing system—certainly not a governmental one, and not even a private one.[16] The methods of accountability embraced vary widely.[17] But even those opposed to the most advanced forms—such as the National News Council that lasted from 1973 to 1984—recognize elementary obligations to correct errors and receive and respond to criticisms.[18] Wayne Godsey, in his term as president of the Radio Television News Directors Association, opposed the news council but recognized the self-interest in at least rudimentary forms of accountability. Wrote Godsey: "Our First Amendment rights (even the restricted rights of the broadcasters) come from the people. If we cease to serve them, or if they *believe* we cease to serve them, our rights will be imperiled."[19] In fact, as the 1970s and 1980s brought what seemed to be increasing reversals or qualifications by the courts of journalists' rights, media leaders responded by urging greater responsibility and responsiveness lest the media's standing be further eroded.[20]

But there is a perspective, an ethical perspective, that recognizes and attempts to transcend media self-interest. In its code of ethics the Society of Professional Journalists/Sigma Delta Chi declares that journalists "should be accountable to the public for their reports and the public should be encouraged to voice its grievances against the media," adding: "Open dialogue with our readers, viewers and listeners should be fostered." Although the code does not define accountability or prescribe particular mechanisms, it ends with a "pledge": "Journalists should actively censure and try to prevent violation of these standards and they should encourage their observance by all newspeople. Adherence to this code of ethics is intended to preserve the bond of mutual trust and respect between American journalists and the American people."[21] The SPJ/SDX code thus gives media criticism a central place in the ethical stance of the journalist. It appears to reflect the principle of stewardship by which a journalist voluntarily assumes the role as *an* overseer of the exercise of the First Amendment.

The article "an" is emphasized because it suggests that a journalist who chooses stewardship as a media critic does not have to presume omniscience. He or she does not have to become the journalistic Quetzalcoatl, rushing to the rescue of the American media. Certainly there need be no more hubris and no less humility in media criticism than in any of the other forms of criticism urged by the media codes of ethics. Thus, the Associated Press Managing Editors' code urges a newspaper to "report matters regarding itself or its personnel with the same vigor and candor as it would other institutions or individuals."[22] Undoubtedly influential in today's world, the media certainly can be interpreted as being one of the "forces of power in the society" which the newspaper editors' code says should be subject to "independent scrutiny." The goal of media criticism, of perfecting mechanims of accountability, is to furnish the functional equivalent of licensing without any resort whatsoever to the formal power of government or some supposedly equal, informal power of licensing by an organization of professionals. In short, the craft/profession's response could be to use the First Amendment's guarantee of free expression to collectively oversee and upgrade the performance of the business benefitting most from the First Amendment. This is the First Amendment approach to making journalism accountable.

A caveat must be entered immediately. To introduce media criticism as an expression of media ethics is not to put forth a panacea. It is merely to identify concretely an opportunity to act on the principle of stewardship. Because media criticism takes many forms, there are many opportunities, each with strengths and weaknesses.

NEWS COUNCILS

What was known for slightly more than a decade as the National News Council had its roots in the recommendations of the Hutchins Commission for an independent agency to evaluate press performance and make public reports on its findings.[23] Before establishment of the council in 1973, there developed a long, sometimes acrimonious debate within the American Society of Newspaper Editors and elsewhere[24] over whether such an organization would infringe on the rights of journalists. Finally, with financial support from the Twentieth Century Fund, and despite opposition from some media heavies such as the *New York Times,* the self-appointed council was founded. It served as a recipient and assessor of complaints against the media—but only in those cases in which the media themselves declined to respond. Grievances were heard by a council of eighteen distinguished citizens, with the help of a small professional staff. Only eight members were from the communications industry. Lawyers for both the media and the complainants were permitted at hearings. The only cases accepted were those in which the complaining party signed a waiver of rights to file a lawsuit in matters brought before the council. The council's findings, published with majority and dissenting opinions, if any, were intended, through the publicity given them, to stimulate an atmosphere of media responsibility.

Academic critics such as John Merrill objected, in principle, to such groups on the ground that "ultimately" they would lead to government intervention and control. "The only way a 'theory' of social responsibility could have any significance in any country is for the governmental power elite to be the definer and enforcer of this type of press."[25] Merrill wrote. *New York Times* publisher A. O. Sulzberger said he was concerned that the council "would encourage an atmosphere of regulation in which government intervention might gain public acceptance."[26] And *Boston Globe* editor Tom Winship declared, "they have no damn business meddling in our business."[27]

In addition to these objections on principle, there were complaints about the council's staff work, its composition, and the scope of its activity. For example, while investigating a complaint against *Life* magazine, the staff did not interview the reporter, Hillary Johnson, whose article was the subject of the investigation. The council found *Life* at fault for paying $8,000 to Bernard Welch, a professional thief and accused killer of the late Dr. Michael Halberstam, a prominent and widely admired Washington physician.[28] *Life* also was criticized for failing to tell readers about the payment. However, the council said it did not find enough evidence to rule on whether reporter Johnson had deceived Dr. Halberstam's widow in gaining an interview. Johnson had said she wanted to reply directly to the deception charges. When criticized for failing to interview Johnson, the council said it had relied on *Life* editors' "unequivocal defense" of Johnson's reporting and that, in doing so, it was following a policy "never to go to reporters or sub-editors for comments or complaints unless the course is suggested by the publication."[29]

Another complaint involved the council's handling of one of the three stories that won for Teresa Carpenter the Pulitzer Prize. Ironically, it was the very Pulitzer Prize that the *Washington Post* had returned in the wake of the Janet Cooke scandal.[30] Carpenter's story in New York's *Village Voice* recounted the murder of Allard Lowenstein, former congressman and prominent New York Democrat, and his relationship with Dennis Sweeney, a former student. First charged with the second-degree murder of Lowenstein, Sweeney was later committed as insane. Lowenstein's family and friends accused Carpenter of inaccurately suggesting that Lowenstein was homosexual. Despite her editors' backing of her story, the council concluded that there were "a number of valid challenges" to the authenticity of Carpenter's portrayal of Lowenstein. It found the article "marred by the overuse of unattributed sources, by a writing style so colored and imaginative as to blur precise meaning, and by such reckless and speculative construction as to result in profound unfairness to the victim of a demented killer." The *Voice* had refused to cooperate with the council's investigation. Yet it accused the council of failing to include evidence that would have upheld the reporter's allegations about Lowenstein. Norman Issacs, council chairman, said the testimony which the *Voice* wanted included was not definitive and would have diverted the investigation.[31]

A council member, Margo Huston, a Pulitzer Prize-winning writer for the *Milwaukee Journal*, argued in the Halberstam case that the council had "crossed a potentially hazardous boundary line," adding: "Instead of properly confining its decision . . . to fairness and accuracy, it marched blindly into the quicksand of values, news judgment and good taste by suggesting it was 'unfortunate' for *Life* to compare the life of a prominent doctor to that of an alleged murderer."[32] And others have suggested that the ten council members who were considered "public" as distinct from "media" representatives included some who, in fact, had close ties to the media.[33]

In response to criticism, the council at one point considered splitting itself into two parts—a board of trustees of chiefly non-media persons who would raise money and handle administrative matters, and a separate council of press representatives to weigh complaints. But those within the media opposed to the reform would have nothing of it. Shortly after, the National News Council voted to terminate itself.[34]

During its eleven years, the council reached decisions in 242 complaints brought to it. Of these, 82 were found warranted in whole or in part, and 120 were found unwarranted. The council dismissed 37 complaints, and 3 were withdrawn by the complainants. Some media organizations, such as CBS News and the *Louisville Courier-Journal and Times,* broadcast or published the results of council proceedings. But Elie Abel, a distinguished journalist and professor of journalism at Stanford University who served on the council for five years, put much of the blame for the demise of the council at the feet of other "great newspapers and broadcasting networks that smothered its proceedings in silence."[35] Without publicity, the council was denied the strength it needed to give influence to its findings. Abel called seemingly "forlorn" the idea that such careful investigating and reporting on allegations of bad journalism would contribute to higher professional standards and, ultimately, greater public confidence in the news media. But others were keeping the faith even at the council's burial. Said its 1984 president, Richard S. Salant, former CBS News president: "We remain convinced that the concept of a news council—national, and perhaps even more important, local and regional—is a sound one. It is capable of making an important contribution to improvement of press performance, to public confidence and understanding, to press freedom and, hence, to the whole of our society."[36]

Interestingly, the papers of the National News Council will be housed at the University of Minnesota, whose Walter Library and School of Journalism has been asked not only to keep the council idea alive intellectually, but also to foster new mechanisms of accountability. Minnesota is the only state with a news council. In existence since 1971, it has issued dozens of rulings on controversies surrounding accuracy, fairness, invasion of privacy, sensationalism, letters to the editor, and access to advertising space. It is accumulating what its leaders believe to be the equivalent of a body of common law with respect to media ethics.[37]

INTERNAL MECHANISMS OF CRITICISM

The first line of defense against unethical, inaccurate, or unfair journalism is within the newsroom itself. Reporters, editors, and news directors do in fact police their own ranks. Occasionally, dramatic evidence of this reaches public attention. Thus, in the late 1970s the

Lewiston (Idaho) *Morning Tribune* published a full-page exposé of its reporters, its editor, and its publisher, focusing on possible conflicts of interest.[38] The newspaper analyzed how news coverage had been affected by its publisher's presidency of the Idaho Board of Education. It showed conflicts of interest between the assignment of its business reporter and her husband's ties with a forest products firm. It exposed the executive editor's public relations work for a U.S. senate candidate, and numerous other staff links that raised ethical questions about how fair its staff could be on certain topics. Neither James Boylan, then editor of the *Columbia Journalism Review,* nor Jerome Walker, Jr., managing editor of *Editor & Publisher,* could recall anything like the "full scale undressing" by the *Tribune.*[39]

In the 1980s, in the wake of the Janet Cooke affair, producers of the CBS network's award-winning "60 Minutes" program turned the tables on themselves by staging a self-critique.[40] Panelists assembled to grill correspondent Mike Wallace and Producer Don Hewitt were Herb Schmertz, vice-president of the Mobil Oil Co. and a vociferous critic of news coverage of business; Ellen Goodman, syndicated columnist; Eugene Patterson, board chairman of the *St. Petersburg Times;* and Bob Greene, investigative reporter for *Newsday* and head of the project conducted by Investigative Reporters and Editors to probe the mob murder of reporter Don Bolles. Lively dialogue brought into sharp focus such questionable "60 Minutes" techniques as hidden cameras and microphones, the ambush interview, and deliberate law violations by reporters in search of a story. Among highlights of the program was Hewitt's vow to eschew the ambush interview—a sudden confrontation in which a source is caught by surprise by a reporter's questions. "It's like getting a man to testify against himself," Hewitt said, promising not to use the technique routinely, if at all, in the future. On the idea for the show, CBS producer Philip Scheffler said: "After all, we question everybody else's ethics, so why not our own?"[41]

Another form of internal criticism is the ombudsman, a person designated to monitor a news medium for accuracy and fairness, explain the news business to the public, and/or convey reader/viewer viewpoints to the management. Although retaining a strong vein of fidelity to the original Scandinavian institution, American media ombudsmen are wholly private and non-governmental. The specific mix of duties of an ombudsman varies, of course, with particular employers. Some write long memoranda to management evaluating the performance of reporters and editors. Others write critiques posted on bulletin boards within the newsroom. Still others write critical columns published in the newspaper either regularly or periodically. Almost all receive complaints from readers, investigate the complaints, and arrange for an appropriate response, usually a correction.

John Herchenroeder was appointed as the first ombudsman of the *Louisville Courier-Journal and Times* and, after many years on the job, reported his belief that readers had a better understanding of how the newspapers worked and a new willingness to express their views on news and public affairs.[42] A survey by Suraj Kapoor and Ralph Smith reporting the experience of 132 newspapers showed twenty-four had full or part-time in-house critics or ombudsmen. Among the accomplishments reported by these overseers are the following:

1. A regular place in the newspaper for corrections was created.
2. Advertising of pornographic movies was banned.
3. Extra space was allocated to headlines on important news to prevent distortion and foster accuracy.
4. Important local news in zoned editions received greater front page play.
5. Attention to local groups and local sports increased.
6. Addresses of witnesses of local crime were no longer included in news stories.
7. Systematic accuracy checks were begun by mailing published stories to sources and asking them to identify any errors.
8. Reader opinion polls were checked more closely to ensure proper wording of questions.
9. Coverage of racial controversies became fairer.
10. The approach used in telephone solicitation of subscribers was revised.[43]

These achievements no doubt reflect perceptions of accomplishments of ombudsmen for a great variety of newspapers, from very small dailies to those with metropolitan circulation. Whatever the merits of their work, ombudsmen with recognizable responsibilities as such have not appeared on more than a few dozen American daily newspapers. Perhaps this reflects a judgment by most editors and publishers that there are weaknesses in the concept. Robert J. Haiman, managing editor of the *St. Petersburg Times,* outlined these six arguments against ombudsmen in a presentation to his peers:

1. What journalists need is not necessarily more criticism from within the ranks but more systematic, independent, and sophisticated criticism from the outside. The ombudsman is an insider, despite precautions often taken to foster independence.
2. Rather than opening up the lines of communication between edi-

tors and their readers, the ombudsman stands between them. Says Haiman: "If we want to get close to readers, then why don't we answer our own phones and open our own mail?"

3. The public criticism of the ombudsman prompts reporters to ask, "Who the hell do I work for?" and readers to ask, "Who the hell is in charge down there?" Hence, the ombudsman approach is bad management because it fogs the lines of authority.

4. Although ostensibly the ombudsman is supposed to raise the level of reader understanding of the media, in reality the effort too often becomes "sort of a more accurate version of the Lou Grant show." Said Haiman, "This Hollywoodizing, this turning of the press into a studio of stars is a mistake. It can blind us to what we are supposed to be and make us forget which side of the footlights we are supposed to be on."

5. Ombudsmen are "not the best way to direct the attention of the staff to the need to avoid errors, to seek them out when they occur, and to correct them." That job best belongs to reporters themselves and their editors, Haiman said.

6. Ombudsmen most often do not get involved until after mistakes have been made. "And perhaps that," said Haiman, "is what's most wrong with ombudsmen."[44]

Haiman argues that the experience of the *Washington Post*'s ombudsman in the Janet Cooke case illustrates the sixth criticism. The ombudsman, Bill Green, wrote a widely read and admired explanation[45] of how the *Post* happened to print a fabricated story about a boy heroin addict named Jimmy, submitted it successfully for a Pulitzer Prize, and then returned the prize after *Post* executive editor Benjamin Bradlee and others discovered the story was false. Had Green not been working on the principle that he should intervene only *after the fact,* perhaps the *Post* reporters and the sub-editors would at least have spotted the error before it was compounded by award of the Pulitzer.

Whether they are internal ombudsmen without critical columns to write or whether they are columnists only, the work is difficult. David Shaw, the *Los Angeles Time*'s veteran critic, indicated as much when discussing the reaction he often gets when gathering his stories: "Newspaper reporters and editors are not one whit better than politicians, crooks, businessmen, athletes, doctors or lawyers when it comes to dealing with the press. They are guarded, suspicious, and quick to tell me 'no comment,' 'I was misquoted,' 'I was quoted out of context' or 'I didn't realize I was being interviewed.' "[46] In fact, the discomfort created by the work was recognized in 1970 when Richard Harwood of the *Washington Post* pioneered the critical appraisals of his own newspaper.[47] Harwood's immediate successor, Ben Bagdikian, resigned the spot after a dispute with management over whether the ombudsman should handle reader complaints as well as write media criticism. The two duties conflicted, in Bagdikian's opinion.[48]

Freelancer and press critic Cassandra Tate, in a study of ombudsmen's columns, reported instances in which they pulled their punches, looked down on readers, "explained" rather than criticized, and served as apologists for their newspapers rather than as authentic links to distraught or angry readers.[49] It is difficult, she noted, to assess the effect of ombudsmen's columns. "Furthermore," she concluded, "the major benefits are nebulous: the creation of a climate that makes it easier to admit mistakes, a heightened awareness of ethical issues, what Bradlee, *Washington Post* editor, calls 'influencing the attitudes of reporters and editors.' "[50]

It is worth recognizing the limits of analyses of ombudsmen's impact. Not all benefits are tangible enough to register on the calipers of media critics. And in a culture which often eschews the reality of the intangible, Bagdikian's summary judgment, quoted by Tate, is worth heeding:

> It's been a kind of self-indulgent, self-congratulatory gesture by a lot of publishers but I think it's also been a useful mechanism, and frequently very effective. It's a beginning step in the realization that most newspapers are increasingly detached from their communities, and it may be a way to get the leadership of the paper more closely acquainted with the real community, and not just the community they go out to lunch with every day. On the whole, it's been a healthy development. It's certainly been better than nothing.[51]

Perhaps the prominence and visibility of media critics such as Shaw, Bagdikian, Charles Seib, and Green have obscured the importance of more traditional means of delivering criticism, praise, and professional evaluations. Prof. William Blankenberg of the University of Wisconsin sent questionnaires to 340 newspapers asking what methods of internal criticism they used (Table 7.1) and how they felt internal criticism could be improved (Table 7.2); 243 responded.[52]

On the average, one of four daily newspaper editors wanted more frequent individual conferences devoted to criticism. One of five editors wanted more regular group conferences. Almost a third wanted to improve existing methods. Far more preferred these approaches over those likely to publicize criticism more broadly within or outside the newsroom. Although these results are somewhat dated and include only editors, they show a preference for face-to-face criticism over less

TABLE 7.1   **Methods of Internal Criticism Used at 243 Newspapers**
(percentages)

	Used	Used Regularly
Individual conference	92.7	43.3
Group conference	73.5	56.4
Memoranda	74.4	57.4
Bulletin board	53.8	42.9
Employee publication	19.7	

(Mean number of methods used: 3.1)

SOURCE: News Research Bulletin No. 9, June 3, 1970 (results of research of William B. Blankenburg, commissioned by the ANPA). Reprinted in Lee Brown, *The Reluctant Reformation* (New York: David McKay Co., 1974), p. 215.

personal methods. They do show, however, that internal criticism is important and techniques are worth improving.

JOURNALISM REVIEWS AND OTHER EXTERNAL MECHANISMS

Perhaps no mechanism better reflects a First Amendment approach to professionalizing journalism than the institution of the journalism review. And no journalism review better symbolizes that approach than the *Columbia Journalism Review*. Established in 1961–62 at Columbia University's Pulitzer School of Journalism, *CJR* carries on its contents page this excerpt from a founding editorial in the publication's Autumn 1961 issue: "To assess the performance of journalism in all its forms, to call attention to its shortcomings and strengths, and to help define—or redefine—standards of honest, responsible service . . . to help stimulate continuing improvement in the profession and to speak out for what is right, fair, and decent." That such an undertaking did not meet with immediate commercial success can be inferred from the fact that *CJR* operated at a loss for the first seventeen years.[53] Under the leadership of former Columbia Dean Edward W. Barrett, the *Review* attracted support from the Ford and Markle foundations and from such individuals as Louis G. Cowan, the late CBS executive; Laurance Rockefeller, business executive and conservationist; and the late James P. Warburg, financier and author. But in the late 1970s, *CJR* began reaching the black, and on its twentieth anniversary in 1982 Barrett could feel confident in writing that "it's doing well enough to have an assured future."[54] An examination of *CJR* shows that it has assumed many important roles, among which are to:

- Embarrass those whose errors and misjudgments *CJR* thinks it can document; typical is its "darts and laurels" section.
- Bring to light questionable practices hidden from view of the profession; Peter Dreier's and Steve Weinberg's 1979 study of interlocking media directorates was a classic.[55]
- Encourage the improvement of reporting methods; *CJR* has paid

TABLE 7.2 **Suggested Methods for Improving Internal Criticism from 243 Newspapers Surveyed, by Size of Paper (percentages)**

	All	*Small*	*Medium-Small*	*Medium*	*Medium Large*	*Large*
Refine present methods	28.7	12.5	40.0	24.1	38.7	29.0
Have more individual story conferences	24.8	25.0	23.3	37.9	12.9	25.8
Add regular group conferences	20.3	43.7	16.7	24.1	6.5	9.7
Add full-time critic or supervisor	9.8	6.3	3.3	0	19.4	19.4
Use Winners & Sinners publication	7.8	3.1	3.3	3.4	12.9	6.5
Use outside consultant	2.6	3.1	3.3	0	6.5	0
Seek more staff participation in criticism	2.6	3.1	3.3	3.4	0	3.2
Other	3.9	3.1	0	6.9	3.2	6.5

SOURCE: News Research Bulletin No. 9, June 3, 1970 (results of research of William B. Blankenburg, commissioned by the ANPA). Reprinted in Lee Brown, *The Reluctant Reformation* (New York: David McKay Co., 1974), p. 221.

consistent attention to polling and survey research as means of upgrading the coverage of politics and social problems.[56]
- Defend unpopular positions it regards as in the interest of journalism; it supported *The Progressive*'s right to publish H-bomb secrets in the face of the federal government's attempt to suppress the article.[57]
- Evaluate media performance on key stories and issues in the news; such critical evaluations are the staple of each issue.

Although it is difficult to assess the impact of *CJR*, its 34,000 circulation does provide some measure of its reach. In addition, it is widely read among students about to enter journalism.[58] Said Elie Abel, Barrett's successor as dean at Columbia: "We have reason to believe that certain crude political smears are less likely to recur in particular newspapers as a result of staff roarbacks ignited by *Review* articles. Some newspapers have been prompted by exposure in the *Review* to reconsider old, established forms of malpractice."[59]

During the 1960s and 1970s when social protest movements focused on the shortcomings of established institutions, a bevy of local journalism reviews appeared on the journalistic landscape. These small, critical, activist publications were often gestated by staff discontent with media performance. They were as frequently breech-born, over the opposition of local media management, and lived short lives. The *Chicago Journalism Review* died at age seven. So did *More,* the national media review that went through three publishers before succumbing to advertising, management, and reader support problems.[60]

Although the record might seem to indicate that there is a dim outlook for media criticism, that may represent only a superficial judgment. A new national magazine, the *Washington Journalism Review,* has established itself. The *Quill,* published by the Society of Professional Journalists/Sigma Delta Chi, reaches a national audience with its news about the media. Moreover, media criticism has become standard fare in such national magazines as *Atlantic, Harpers, National Review, New Republic,* and *Esquire,* not to mention *TV Guide.* In addition, some newspapers and television stations voluntarily monitor media performance. When CBS's "60 Minutes" celebrated the work of a Chicago tutor in "The Marva Collins Story," a CBS affiliate, WBBM-TV in Chicago, later did a follow-up account, raising questions about its coverage and about the effectiveness of Collins's attempt to remedy the defects of the public schools.[61] The *Wall Street Journal,* long before it was "in" to establish an ombudsman, carried on its front page critical evaluations of media ethics and it has continued such coverage over the years.[62] Moreover, the survival of the *St. Louis Journalism Review,* established in 1969, has kept alive the hope that a formula might still be found to make local journalism reviews economically viable.

The 1960s and 1970s witnessed the formation by interest groups of a wide range of organizations to monitor the media's performance. Accuracy in Media, a conservative watch group formed in 1969, has peppered the media with a continuing series of letters, studies, and complaints, especially in matters related to the political predilections of its organizers, Reed Irvine and Abraham Kalish.[63] Another conservative group, the Institute for American Strategy, published a book-length critique of CBS News's coverage of national defense issues.[64] The Media Institute, an even more sophisticated media monitor backed heavily by business, conducted, among other studies, an in-depth critical examination of network television's coverage of the acute oil shortages of the early 1970s.[65] Other monitor groups represent feminists, fundamentalist Christians, liberal Christians, Jews, Arab Americans, lesbians and gays, oil companies, and anti-abortionists, among others.[66]

There can be little question that the scrutinizing and public critiquing conducted by these and other media monitors have contributed to the credibility problem that has become almost endemic in the past twenty years. Not least of the contributors is the American press itself. Michael J. Robinson, a political scientist who specializes in media studies, documented media coverage of the news media. He studied the *Washington Post,* the *Wall Street Journal,* the newsweeklies—*Newsweek, Time,* and *U.S. News and World Report*—plus the three networks. He found extensive coverage of media foibles, especially by one medium of another, during the winter and spring of 1983. "I discovered that the press is a tough critic of itself," Robinson said at the beginning of an article[67] which found that coverage of media failures outnumbered coverage of successes by a ratio of 3 to 1. He concluded:

> The 93 news stories analyzed . . . also suggest that the press is not so monolithic as the term "media" implies. Establishment publications enjoy disassociating themselves from network journalism; network news enjoys distinguishing itself from local TV news.
>
> And, finally, these findings help explain why it is that journalism has so rarely been popular with the public. If the news media cover themselves this negatively, the public will tend to believe what it sees, hears or reads about the press, whatever the reality of the press happens to be.
>
> Some reporters may find all of these findings and conclusions as chilling

proof that the press has been destroying its own credibility. But most defenders of a free press should recognize public skepticism toward the media for what it is—proof the First Amendment works.[68]

The media consumer has his or her own role to play in media criticism. Timely, well-placed letters to the editor or on-the-air replies on broadcast stations, can be citizen expressions of the ethic of stewardship, of citizen responsibility for oversight of the exercise of the First Amendment. Although there has been little serious scholarship on the nature, frequency, and influence of such expressions, editors and news directors can attest to their impact.

One cannot safely recommend media criticism as part of an ethic of stewardship without acknowledging the need to improve the quality of such criticism and to raise some difficult questions. Some academics have demonstrated excellence in media criticism.[69] But many more such efforts are needed if, as seems likely, the news media evaluation is to have an increasingly important role to play in society.

We need to know more about who does media criticism, and who doesn't, and why. We need to understand more about how good and effective media criticism gets done. Which methods are reliable? Which ones are risky, and how can the pitfalls of unfairness to journalists themselves be avoided? What standards should there be in media criticism, and how can their observance best be promoted? What types of media transgressions best lend themselves to treatment in journalism reviews, as distinct from internal memoranda or individual conferences? How can one, if at all, effectively measure the impact of criticism? Are the believers in such criticism, including the author of this chapter, correct in their assessment of its potentially beneficial effects? If there are harmful effects, can these be identified and minimized? Are these harmful effects part of the price that must be paid for the First Amendment itself?

Lest these questions be regarded as "academic" or trivial, it should be noted that media leaders themselves are becoming restive under the cumulus cloud of ethical suspicion that the 1980s have cast above them. *United Press International Reporter,* a newsletter, partially reprinted a talk given by Brian Hogben, group general manager (editorial) of News Limited newspapers and magazines in Australia, who said: "What we really need to do is to demonstrate that bad journalism places an offender's job in jeopardy. We need to show our personal professional disapproval of bad journalism. It is not something like halitosis which etiquette demands we do not mention. We need to tell bad journalists face to face that we don't like what they do."[70]

CHAPTER EIGHT

Government and the News Media

Substituting Ethics for "Adversarity"

No prescriptive concept has enjoyed wider usage within the news fraternity in recent years than the notion of the media's so-called adversary role. Like a long-submerged directional buoy, it lurched to the surface toward the end of the 1960s at a time when both the government and the Fourth Estate had come upon troubled waters. No one in the press or government had ever sought or thought there could be an idyllic relationship between the two. Instances of conflict from Teapot Dome[1] to the U-2 episode[2] remained fresh in memory. But the 1960s and 1970s loosened the structures of civility and custom that had usually prevented open animosity and had obviated any need by journalists for a militant, central metaphor with which to define their role.

When John F. Kennedy successfully urged the *New York Times* not to publish all it knew of preparations for the Bay of Pigs invasion—and then later reflected, after the invasion's failure, that the *Times* should have published—it was an invitation to the press to be more aggressive.[3] When the Cuban missile crisis created a debate over whether government had a "right to lie," many in the news media took it as a challenge. Others saw it as a warning that Dr. Goebbels might well have been reincarnated as a sort of diabolic, hard-line Dale Carnegie, that what had passed for occasional duplicity by government had been elevated to a matter of high principle.[4] As if such single events had not been enough, the movements for civil rights, student power, and economic equality deepened the controversy, as the media's coverage came to be seen as a political force in its own right.[5] Next, the bitter collisions of journalists and officialdom over the coverage of the Vietnamese War epitomized the new, almost abrasive salience of the media in matters of state. In the 1960s, how better to describe the developing relationship than as adversarial? In the early 1970s, the conflicts generated by the press's pursuit of Watergate wrongdoings gave further legitimacy to use of the word *adversarial* to describe the relationship between government and the media. Many in both camps embraced an adversarial role as a prescription for the press. And the news media's exclusion from the initial protective military operation in Grenada made it clear that the 1980s would provide ample experience to rationalize use of what had become a staple phrase in the journalistic vocabulary. Although no doubt the phrase had been used previously, a Stanford University professor and former Washington correspondent named William L. Rivers provided the critical mass of acceptability in a book called *The Adversaries.* It grew from an idea that came to Rivers while writing an earlier book, *The Opinionmakers,* a survey and analysis of the Washington press corps. The thesis of the second book, Rivers wrote, is that "there is an ideal relationship for government officials and journalists everywhere, and that the relationship should be that of adversaries."[6]

The popularity of the phrase among journalists has been widespread. Fred Graham, an attorney and widely respected network broadcast journalist, served as rapporteur for the Twentieth Century Fund Task Force study on government and the press. In a preface, Graham declared unequivocally that "relations between government and the press have always and inherently been of an adversary nature."[7] Graham quoted Rivers: "if anything is clear about press-government relationships throughout our history, it is this: in theory, America's leaders have wanted a free and independent press as a check upon government; in practice, they wanted no such thing."[8] At a 1972 forum of some of the nation's top scholars, journalists, lawyers, and others, Professor Ithiel de Sola Pool of M.I.T. said "An image housed in the psyche of many journalists is that of themselves as St. George and the government as the dragon. In current jargon that is called the adversary relationship of government and media. Most Washington reporters believe it." William Small, network news and wire service executive and author, quoted his friend and senior colleague Eric Sevareid invoking the Sevareid Stipulation: "We will consider alteration of our adversary relationship when two things begin to happen—when political leaders complain they are overpraised and when they admit policy mistakes of a serious nature. That will be the day."[9] Journalists are not alone in accepting the adversary view. Stephen Hess, a scholar and aide to Presidents Eisenhower and Nixon, said: "In short, the public is best served in government-media relations—as in jurisprudence—by each side's recognizing its adversary role."[10]

The argument to be made here is that describing the news media as an "adversary" of government is a harmfully incomplete statement of the facts and a perniciously poor choice of nomenclature. An adversary is an opponent. A "role" as an adversary clearly implies a systemic posture of opposition. Reporters, in fact, do not consistently oppose the government. Often, probably most of the time, there is either neutrality or cooperation, according to common sense as well as scholarship on the subject.[11] There is a real sense in which an uncritical embrace of an "adversary relationship between the press and government" forecloses the critical thinking needed in moral reasoning. There is a sense in which an adversarial posture becomes an ideology that prevents the sensitive interpretation and application of the principles of humaneness, truth telling, justice, freedom/independence, and the stewardship of free expression. These principles are implicitly, and in most cases explicitly, at stake in the adversarial episodes of this chapter.

Professor Pool once went so far as to claim that, to some degree, the adversary concept can be looked at as what psychoanalysis describes as a "reaction-formation." Thus, the adversary notion "is a reaction to the very compromises and concessions that he [a journalist] must make, a brave assertion that wards off guilt." He added: "It is the newsman's proof to himself and to society that he has not been bought. It is his way of saying, 'Look not at how I must cohabit with the system; for in fact I am its foe.' And so the adversary stereotype is reinforced, not undercut, by its remoteness from reality."[12] Although de Sola Pool's interpretation may seem farfetched, there must be cooperation between reporters and officials for the news media to fulfill their basic role of reporting and interpreting the news.[13]

It also is emphatically true that to be a truth teller, to be fair and audit the equity of government services and actions, a reporter must be consistently *skeptical* of officials. Such skepticism often (some would say always) *results* in tension and, perhaps ultimately, in an adversarial relationship with sources. However, the just reporter, the reporter seeking truth, does not wisely enter a news story with an adversarial, oppositional *intention*. "Adversarity" may *result* from his skepticism, a necessary tool of truth telling, but the adversarity is not, or should not be, the initial or sustaining motivation. Even after he or she has obtained what appears to be damaging evidence against a public official, to put on adversarial armor is to risk unfairness by closing one's mind. To be oppositional is to invite a mind set that is incapable of searching for alternative evidence or explanation, that may well fail to give the government its fair opportunity to reply, or fail to establish an adequate context in reporting.

To make this point in no way impugns the intention or the ethical performance of those scholars and journalists who have embraced adversarity as a definition of role or description of behavior. It is to challenge the adequacy and risk of the terminology. Rivers himself qualifies his use of the term at several places. "Surely a proper adversary relationship is a delicate balance of tact and antagonism, cooperation and conflict," he writes.[14] In his final chapter, which includes a substantial contribution from William Blankenburg, limits of adversarity are defined. Thus, friction can be generated by incompetent as well as crusading journalism. Adversarity can likewise be the result of overbearing, insulting reporters. Government stories based on new disclosures are sometimes the result of competitive urges rather than solid news judgment. When differences arise between officialdom and the media, behavior can be guided by self-pride rather than by the public interest. Disclosure in certain contexts (invasion plans in time of war) have the power to unfairly cancel government decisions.[15]

The heavy qualifications necessary with the use of the adversary nomenclature crop up in the term's use by working journalists. Jerry terHorst, Washington correspondent and former press secretary to President Gerald Ford, once said: "A truly free press does not have an obligation to support government policy; indeed, it has an obligation to refrain from support. . . . The press need not be hostile, but it must remain an adversary—willing to test, investigate and challenge governmental decisions."[16] How can one *not* be hostile to an adversary? How can one show tact and *cooperation* to an adversary, an opponent? Even if possible, these behavioral qualifications are so heavy that they dilute both the descriptive and prescriptive power of the adversary concept.

Perhaps with some of the same objections in mind, other commentators have preferred different terminology when describing the relationship between media and government. William Small, himself a veteran of many collisions between the news media and the government, views the press's role as that of "auditor," with the responsibility to "give an accounting of what government does and to interpret its meaning."[17] In a penetrating essay Vincent Blasi, professor of law at the University of Michigan, argues that theories enunciated thus far to account for certain Supreme Court decisions under the First Amendment to the constitution have failed to make a "central place" for what he calls the "checking value." That value is reflected in the use of free speech, free press, and free assembly to check the abuse of power by public officials.[18] It was evident, Blasi argues, when widely publicized peace marches apparently helped induce President Lyndon Johnson's resignation, thereby forestalling escalation of the Vietnam War, when press disclosures seemed to prevent a full-scale expansion of the War into Cambodia, and, when the news media, cooperating with knowledgeable official sources, exposed widespread corruption in the Watergate affair.[19]

An impression should not be left that an objection to the concept of an adversary role is merely semantic quibbling. Words have impact. Neither the public, whose goodwill and forbearance are needed to sustain the First Amendment, nor the young people entering journalism, who need a clear sense of mission, are well served by misleading language. Nor can it be safely supposed that experienced journalists, flying under the adversarial banner, will themselves always keep the qualifiers in mind, will not drift into an oppositional posture when they intend to be skeptical.

Periodically leaders within journalism worry aloud about the adversarial stance. On one such occasion, Michael J. O'Neill, former editor of the *New York Daily News,* declared that it "is falsely coloring the information flowing to the public." In a speech to the American Society of Newspaper Editors, O'Neill said, in part: "We should make peace with the government. No code of chivalry requires us to challenge every official action. Our assignment is to report and explain issues, not decide them. In the final analysis, what we need most of all in our profession is a generous spirit, infused with human warmth, as ready to see good as to suspect wrong, to find hope as well as cynicism, to have a clear but uncrabbed view of the world. We need to seek conciliation, not just conflict, so that society has a chance to solve its problems. So that we need to overcome the great challenges we face in the 1980s."[20]

The reaction to O'Neill's argument against "adversarity" as a basic stance toward government seemed to confirm that as a concept it lacked clarity and consistency. Ralph Otwell, editor of the *Chicago Sun-Times,* called some of O'Neill's criticisms valid, adding: "But in this day of big government and big business, I think the press has an obligation to be as aggressive . . . as possible. I would not describe that as an adversarial role." Robert Haiman, executive editor of the *St. Petersburg Times,* said: "Certainly, wherever arrogance and hostility have replaced skepticism and tough-mindedness there's work to be done. The press and government should not be enemies, but a spirited, adversarial relationship conducted with civility in search for truth has served us pretty well." Fred Taylor, executive editor of the *Wall Street Journal,* said: "I am uneasy when Mike assaults the press' adversary relationship with government without emphasizing that . . . the press should be highly skeptical of government." In the opinion of Joseph Shoquist, managing editor of the *Milwaukee Journal,* O'Neill's was an "idealistic talk" which "portrayed a world of newspaper journalism not as it is but as it should be." He added: "I think the [adversarial position] between government and the press is necessary . . . and healthy if we use good judgment. Government will judge us as an adversary no matter what position we take and we would be naive to think otherwise." Jon Katz, managing editor of the *Dallas Times Herald,* said he is "reluctant to give up the role of an insensitive questioner of government."[21]

If one listens carefully to editors the message most often heard, whatever their choice of words, is that they do not wish their reporters to take the adversarial term literally, to become outright foes of the governments they cover. They do want persistent, skeptical questioning, arms-length relationships, and knowledgeable searching for truth. They want reporters who neither expect nor need admiration from government officials but who, by their professional skill, fairness and deportment, command respect. They want reporters who understand their obligation to serve as a check on government, whether that check is exercised by exposure of wrong-doing, incompetence, or stupidity, or by supplying the public with the knowledge it needs to do its own checking. Most would hold that, in the nature of things, the checking function must be accompanied by news coverage that informs and interprets the meaning of governmental actions; the latter function is inseparable from, if not a prerequisite to, the former.

Neither adversarial nor even the less prejudicial "skeptical" reporting is a rich or broad enough term to encompass the principles embodied in journalism's codes and the values at stake in the interplay of media and government. Perhaps journalists, who arguably are more open and active in self-criticism than any other profession, need to take the next step and shed the vernacular of their occupation. Perhaps they need to discuss their work in ethical terms to which others, sources as well as consumers, can relate. Writes professor of government Michael Walzer: "When men and women can't talk about moral questions—when they imagine all such talk to be unscientific, a sign of weakness and sentimentality—then they simply live off the accumulated stock of older decisions and understandings. Or they function without the controls of tradition and common discourse, and fall prey to the crudest kinds of moral extremism."[22] Perhaps journalists, without discussing them frequently or searchingly enough as such, have taken for granted the principles of humaneness, truth telling, justice, freedom/independence, and stewardship. Perhaps they need to take the counsel of John Stuart Mill that such received values and beliefs need vigorous and precise discussion lest they lose their "effect on character and conduct."[23]

However, even if one believes that journalists are renewing the wisdom of their craft/profession and are not living off inherited under-standings, and even if one argues that, in their fashion, most journalists try to heed principles, the argument made here is that changes still are needed in the way ethics are considered. Specifically, changes are needed such that journalists not only touch the bases but name, exam-ine, weigh, and compare the bases as they pass. It is a simple proposal, one certain to slow the news game somewhat on occasion, but one that could bring a new focus and clarity to decisions involving ethics and to subsequent debates about those decisions.

Had internal debate and discussion of ethics been more thorough, precise, and vigorous, how might some of the more important ethical issues between government and the media have looked different? Hindsight can be invoked for insight.

When Erwin Knoll, editor of the *Progressive,* first began coping with the prickly problems associated with freelancer Howard Morland's efforts to tell the secret of the H-bomb, he and the magazine's attorneys found disturbing information in the Atomic Energy Act. Publishing "restricted data" would be an offense with severe penalties. With little or no visibility of the practice, reporters and editors confronting similar questions had for years merely cleared their copy with the federal censor in the old Atomic Energy Commission, now the Department of Energy. That prospect was repugnant to Knoll and, at a critical point in the controversy, the *Progressive* flatly refused the Department of En-ergy's offer to rewrite Morland's article to make it acceptable to the government.[24]

However, the issue arose in the first place because Morland, checking the technical accuracy of his article, sent a portion of it to a scientist who, in turn, passed a copy along to George Rathjens, a government consultant and political scientist at MIT. Rathjens, despite Knoll's objections, sent the Morland material to the Department of Energy. Meanwhile, the magazine's attorneys, having learned of the vague but potentially heavy penalties under the act, pressed Knoll to forward to the government an updated copy of the article. Knoll said the lawyers "felt that if the government understood the nature of the piece, and especially that all the materials were in public domain, that it was inconceivable the government would take any action to block publica-tion."[25] The magazine forwarded the later version of the article—a move Knoll later was to call a mistake.[26] The government, after reading the article, tried to persuade Knoll to kill it or have it rewritten. When the magazine refused, the resulting federal court injunction represented a grievous case of prior restraint. It ended only when, in defiance, the material was published elsewhere and the government eventually dropped its case.

Looking back on the episode with the perspective of several years, Knoll said he and his colleagues "debated for days" whether to forward the revised Morland article, the one that ultimately triggered the injunction, to the government. "I would do everything differently. I would not allow myself to be caught up in the legal process at all. I would just publish, period," he said. As for the quality of the debate, he said "it wasn't good enough, because under the circumstances nothing would have been good enough."[27] He thought he was dealing with a situation which was unprecedented. In fact, however, *Scientific American* had been threatened by the government in 1950 to alter an article by Hans Bethe, a noted physicist who had helped in the construction of the first H-bomb and who knew that his article did not contain nuclear secrets. Yet, the times were different, and the magazine censored the article while it was going to press. Significantly, Knoll did not know of the *Scientific American* episode. Had he known, he said, he would not have sent the Morland article to the Department of Energy.[28] Knoll said he was "amazed" of first learning of the earlier incident through the *New York Times*. Gerard Piel, publisher of the magazine, agreed in the face of an injunction to delete several sentences, and government agents actually oversaw the burning of 3,000 copies of *Scientific American* which had already been printed. "Strict compliance with the commission's policies," Piel had argued, "would mean that we could not teach physics."[29] That Knoll did not know of the *Scientific American* episode, and did not have it in mind as a negative example at the time of his debate over what to do in the *Progressive* case, is not a reflection on Knoll. It is a barometer, in part, of the lack of strong tradition of ethical dialogue in journalism for such a major episode not to have become part not only of Knoll's but of the profession's repertoire.

Frameworks of principle can be useful in structuring this dialogue. In discussing the *Progressive* case and other episodes using the eclectic framework outlined previously, the purpose is not to speak ex cathedra but to illustrate how a set of principles may be used in discussing ethical issues in media-government relations. With some such continuing framework, the possibility exists that differences can be better clarified, that missing information can be identified, that reflection can be refined, and that whatever knowledge or wisdom emerges from important cases can be made cumulative.

Howard Morland was straightforward in describing his objective: "The point of my article is that the myth of secrecy is used to create an atmosphere in which public debate is stifled and public criticism of the weapons production system is suppressed. I hope to dramatically illustrate that thesis by showing that what many people considered to be probably the ultimate secret is not really a secret at all. The information is easily available to anyone who wants to acquire it."[30] As *Progressive* publisher Samuel H. Day, Jr., put it: "The weapons, not the 'secrets,' were the prime target. . . . We wanted to raise the level of public consciousness about America's continuing preparation for nuclear war."[31]

Howard Morland and editor Knoll could argue that they intended no harm and could not be charged with directly or indirectly violating the principle of humaneness. Their intention, in fact, was described in just the opposite terms, to protect human life by curbing nuclear proliferation. But their opponents did argue, as plausibly, that the effects of their article could potentially be harmful. Neither side in a debate over humaneness would have convincing evidence, and prominent physicists split over the risks of publication. Predicting harm would require assessing "possibilities," not probabilities.

As for truth telling, the *Progressive* conceded that Morland made a few technical errors.[32] But even critics of the magazine, and the government by its intervention, seemed to underscore the basic accuracy of Morland's work. True, the writing was suffused with an animus to nuclear weaponry. But it did not pretend to be other than an article of opinion, and the magazine could argue that the fidelity of its facts on nuclear matters would alone vindicate it with respect to the principle of truth telling. But some of the magazine's critics argued that its *opinions* were false. Wrote Jeremy J. Stone, director of the Federation of American Scientists: "It is false that the public needs, as the *Progressive* asserts, to know the details at issue in order to work effectively for a comprehensive test ban. It is false, as Howard Morland writes in the *New York Times,* that one needs to know how the bomb is configured to discuss intelligently the implications of bomb storage in Hawaii. The original class of arguments for the socially redeeming value of the details was malarkey. They were comparable to saying that a study of the environmental implications of the automobile industry required the public to know how spark plugs are inserted."[33]

The principles most at issue are humaneness, justice, freedom, and stewardship. By censoring, the government denied the *Progressive* its freedom to publish. That was an unjust act, the magazine contended. But the government itself argued that the magazine was unjustly putting the public and national security in jeopardy by publishing. Not even the supporters of the *Progressive* would argue that the prospect for favorable action from the United States Supreme Court was bright. When the

Pentagon papers case was decided, 6 to 3, the 1971 majority included justices William O. Douglas and Hugo L. Black, both of whom had since left the court. The newer mood of the high court gave no encouragement to First Amendment supporters. Taking a case of such magnitude to the Supreme Court could be a breach of stewardship, in that it could risk a ruling adverse to the media.

But are *any* important First Amendment cases ever raised at a "good time?" As Ben Bagdikian argued, "Every time an infringement of the right of expression is accepted, either because some of the press feels more comfortable in alliance with authorities, or because the fight seems too difficult, it adds legitimacy and power to the revisionists of the First Amendment and to the larger growth of secrecy in society."[34] And, in filing a friend-of-the-court brief for *Scientific American,* Yale Professor Thomas Emerson argued that the constitutional ban on prior restraint is "inherently incapable of accommodating exceptions, adding: "Once an exception has been recognized, all the government has to do is to allege that a certain contemplated publication falls within the exception. The court then issues a restraining order so as to allow the government to present its case. A hearing is held and the court decides whether the matter falls within the exception. Appeals to higher courts follow. This process is itself a form of prior restraint. . . . The scope of the exception is thus determined by the government's claim and the exception has swallowed up the rule."[35]

Faced, then, with this summary of the principles and facts surrounding the principles, how might one weigh and weight those most at issue? That Morland could bring together from public or near-public documents the fundamentals of the construction of an H-bomb did not necessarily mean that the article would have been of little assistance to a nation aspiring to the nuclear club. Harm is distinctly possible, though not clearly probable. The First Amendment guarantees a free press, not one that will never inflict harm, accidentally or unintentionally or in stubborn pride for its own rights. Moreover, those who do not defend the press's *right* to be irresponsible may one day find *themselves* without the actual right to argue against what they believe to be irresponsible.

Certainly Morland could not be safely accused of inhumaneness—an *intention* to inflict palpable physical harm or irreparable psychological harm. One could argue effectively, however, that the nature of the harm possible as a result of his article is too grave to risk—even though he and the magazine should not be denied the freedom to publish it. As a steward of the First Amendment, one could argue for the *Progressive's right* to publish, even as one disagreed with its decision to do so in the way it did. One could support the magazine's legal position, and none-theless argue that the article, as written, could cause harm—not only to people but also to the standing of the First Amendment and the media's already troubled standing with the public. Exercising restraint would seem to be an act of stewardship, all things considered. Under this interpretation, the *Progressive* could publish legally but not ethically.

Although cases of prior restraint by government strike at the heart of the free press/government relationship, they occur only infrequently as the context of ethical dilemmas. Far more common and insidious are the problems that are associated with what Washington correspondent James McCartney once called the "vested interests" that reporters have in their beats. "Some reporters have been so closely allied to specific political figures that their copy, for all practical purposes, could be read as handouts," McCartney wrote.[36] Thus, for example, Pentagon report-ers, ever needful of copy and access, snuggle close to the armed services. Likewise, reporters assigned to Capitol Hill find reason to spare their prime sources of news. Thus, in 1975, a long-ignored drink-ing problem of one of Washington's most powerful lawmakers cata-pulted into view. Rep. Wilbur Mills, D-Ark., chairman of the House Ways and Means Committee, wound up in Washington's Tidal Basin early one morning after a drinking escapade with a stripper exposed his alcoholism. Reflection led one psychiatrist, L. D. Hankoff, to conclude in a public letter to the *New York Times:* "the media has [*sic*] appar-ently failed over a protracted period to report some of the obvious evidences of Mr. Mills's condition. The public might have been better served to have had some glimpses into his functioning prior to the more explosive recent events. I do not advocate a gossip-column approach to the lives of prominent figures but I do wonder if information regarding his condition might have been judiciously reported by the press ear-lier."[37] The question Hankoff raised is whether the press, by time-honored, there-but-for-the-Grace-of-God-go-I custom, sacrificed its ca-pacity as a truth teller by having been so close to a valuable source—in short, by having lost its freedom and independence. The prevailing general rule in the Washington press corps is that the drinking habits and sexual relationships of public officials are private matters unless they affect the performance of official duties. Documenting the impact can certainly be a challenging and delicate task. In the case of Mills and others, the Washington press corps showed little concern until the indiscretions leaped flagrantly into the headlines.

McCartney, writing in the early 1960s, noted what may be termed a structural dimension to such ethical issues. "The increasing complexity of national news, and of news everywhere, has made specialization virtually inevitable. Frequently, only an expert reporter is in a position to understand, let alone report, the news. Yet the problem of developing vested interests becomes more acute when reporters specialize."[38] It was McCartney's view that "snooping general reporters in Washington lead the pack in developing news stories."[39] The tradition of the independent journalist, thinking critically on public issues, persons, and problems, is a valued one within the profession. But it is a tradition under stress. Thus, when scholar Stephen Hess surveyed some 183 print and broadcast journalists in Washington at the beginning of the 1980s, almost 57 percent described "pack journalism" as the most serious problem.[40] "Pack journalism," clearly a pejorative term, is the practice of covering the same events as other reporters, with the implication that a reporter would do better by her or his readers by independently foraging for news or trends of significance. The term also can be taken to mean collective decision making based on shared information, which can sometimes be viewed as cheating. More generally, pack journalism can lead to shared misinterpretations and collective laziness. A laundry list of the evidence of "pack journalism" can easily be compiled: decades of shared perception that the South's (and the North's) treatment of the nation's blacks was not the kind of injustice worthy of sustained, in-depth coverage—a posture that left the nation unprepared;[41] a "group think" mentality that obscured the meaning of the Gulf of Tonkin resolution, which effectively broadened the White Houses's capacity to wage war in Vietnam largely unchecked;[42] prlonged delay by many Washington correspondents in recognizing and investigating the significance of the Watergate burglary;[43] chronic neglect of the bureaucracy and regulatory agencies in Washington in favor of more glamorous, less complicated news;[44] and an almost systemic failure to pay proportionate attention to regional, state, and local issues affected by Washington policy and politics.[45]

The ethical snares which the government reporter's occupation and his own humanity set for him include not only the biased perceptions of the adversarial posture and the self-interested perspective of the beat reporter who snuggles too close to sources or colleagues. There also is the beguiling temptation of expedience. While there are many manifestations of this vice, none is more common, especially in Washington, than the overreliance on unidentified sources. Such sources make reporting easier and news manipulation easier, too. In his study of journalism along the Potomac Hess found that somewhat more than two-thirds of the journalists he polled said that reporters "make it too easy for sources to go on background," a condition of interviewing in which a reporter is permitted to use information without identifying its source.

When asked if the public gains from backgrounders, 71 percent said it gains; 16.9 percent said it loses; 9.3 said it gains *and* loses, while only 2.7 percent said it neither gains nor loses.[46] A similar ambivalence shows up among editors, 81 percent of whom once told a pollster-scholar that they believed unnamed sources are less believable than those clearly identified. Yet, 87 percent said the use of leaks is, on balance, a good practice.[47]

The testimony favoring the use of anonymous source material is illustrated most dramatically by Watergate, even though *Washington Post* reporters Bob Woodward and Carl Bernstein did say they took the precaution to verify most of such information with two different sources. But the Watergate episode, resulting in the removal of a president from office, obscures the more common practice of anonymous background briefings, leaked government documents, whispered bureaucratic stilettos aimed at governmental rivals or infant policies, not to mention leaks of damaging information on candidates during political campaigns. The harm done by such cloaked sources can be considerable. Roger Morris, reviewing the media coverage of a debate over the proposal to build a neutron bomb, noted: "The press largely failed to investigate, analyze, or sometimes even to tell the who, what, where, when, and why of a national security story with wide implications for defense and foreign policy. Reporters became instead the undiscriminating spokesmen for bureaucrats in Washington and Western Europe, whose leaks were designed to enlist public support in a clandestine policy struggle with the president."[48] John D. May, an Australian teacher of politics, criticized the standardized way in which journalists "allude, often in the guise of doing 'straight' reportage, to what is believed, estimated, expected, perceived by—well, by nobody in particular, by everybody, by unidentified and yet implicitly credible witnesses, by ghosts," adding: "In this world, envisioned by German metaphysicians of the nineteenth century, ideas operate independently of any merely human agency and repose in ghostly nonpersons who do not work in visible offices and do not have telephones—or, in any event, cannot be reached for comment."[49] In fairness, it should be noted, reporters themselves sometimes hold back information deemed damaging to national security. This discretion by journalists was once described, in an article on leaking, as follows: "We've gotten to the point where reporters are behaving more responsibly in handling classified material than government officials." That quote, however, was attributed to "the head of one intelligence agency" who had "marveled" at such journalistic restraint.

The unnamed source is a problem that some media organizations have tackled with rules—rules which implicitly express a concern for the principles of truth telling and justice. For example, Paul Janensch, executive editor of the *Louisville Courier-Journal and Times,* listed the following guidelines:

1. Use an unnamed source only if the information is significant, only if the source absolutely refuses to go on the record, only if the information can be corroborated and only if there is no alternative.
2. Say in the story why the source insisted on anonymity such as fear of loss of job.
3. Don't let an unnamed source attack someone personally.

Added Janensch: "From time to time we violate, or at least bend, one of these guidelines. When we do we talk about it."[50]

In "talking about it," through Janensch's column, letters to the editor, and articles opposite the editorial page, the *Courier-Journal* fosters a concern for ethics; it thereby furnishes a prototype for ethical dialogue within the news business.

To the list of journalistic sins in covering government—adversarial bias, beat influence, self-interest, and easy-way-out expedience—there should be added a fourth, which Bob Greene, assistant managing editor of *Newsday,* frankly calls "greed."[51] Whereas self-interest operates via such practices as pack journalism and cooptation by sources, greed, as such, springs from deeper personal wants and desires, illustrated by the need for "scoops."

The wish to be first is not an exclusively journalistic desire. Politicians want to win elections; research scientists want to discover first, if possible, a new explanation of the physical or natural world. The most competitive athletes and salespersons have passion for setting records. Of course, none of these wants is in itself "bad." Society can benefit thereby. However, in these fields, as well as in journalism it often requires courage, temperance, a sense of justice, and wisdom to contain personal ambition, and to keep the desire to be first in constructive channels. A case in which this was not done—former CBS correspondent Daniel Schorr's handling of a secret congressional report on American intelligence—will illustrate the need for thorough and precise discussion of ethics, especially in the field of media and government relations.

Schorr, in more than twenty years as a correspondent for CBS News, developed a string of exclusives any one of which might be regarded as a notable career achievement. He was the first to disclose that the CIA had at least toyed with the idea of assassination of foreign officials hostile to U.S. interests. He also disclosed that data bearing on plots to kill Castro had been withheld by both the FBI and CIA from the Warren Commission, which had been appointed to study and report President Kennedy's assassination. The fact of CIA financing of elections in Italy was another of Schorr's scoops, as was the revelation that the United States had armed Kurds along the Iran-Iraq border and then abandoned them.[52] During a distinguished career, he collected a variety of critics, including Lyndon Johnson, who once called him a "son-of-a-bitch"; Richard Nixon, who ordered him investigated by the FBI on the pretext he was being considered for a federal position;[53] and colleagues in the news business, one of whom accused him of "rewriting history" in explaining certain aspects of the leaking of a congressional report of the House Intelligence Committee, chaired by Rep. Otis Pike, D-N.Y.[54]

Schorr's quest for scoops included an episode in which a former Air Force colonel, L. Fletcher Prouty, told Schorr on the "CBS Morning News" on July 11, 1975, that Alexander Butterfield had been the CIA's man in the White House, with the function of "opening doors" there for the CIA. There was no simultaneous reply from Butterfield—the Nixon staffer who had revealed the existence of the secret tape recordings that eventually provided the critical evidence that drove Nixon from office. Ultimately Butterfield and others were reached to effectively deny the accusation, but not before Schorr, joined by most of the news media, had circulated a false accusation reminiscent of the press's shoddy performance in the McCarthy era.[55] Schorr expressed regret over the Prouty episode, adding: "I wish we lived in a risk-free profession. But you can't win them all." He said he meant a risk to himself, and that the Prouty episode would trouble him "for a long time."[56]

In late January 1976, Schorr and a reporter for the *New York Times* managed to inspect a copy of the report of the House Intelligence Committee headed by Rep. Otis Pike, D-N.Y. Later it developed that Schorr not only inspected it and took notes, but actually obtained a copy of it. He was first out with the substance of the report, which showed among other things that the CIA had failed to foresee the 1973 Yom Kippur War and the 1968 Tet offensive and that Henry Kissinger had impeded the congressional investigation of intelligence operations. When Schorr realized that he apparently had the only copy of the report, which the House of Representatives voted not to release, he said he explored with his company's management whether any of its subsidiaries wanted to publish it. When no quick affirmative answer was forthcoming, he approached the Reporters Committee for Freedom of the Press.[57] Schorr proposed to donate to the committee any proceeds that might result from commercial publication.[58] The committee put Schorr in contact with its attorney, Peter Tufo, who also held a membership on the board of New York Magazine Company, owner of the *Village Voice,* an outspokenly anti-establishment weekly. Schorr's agent, Dick Leibner, then entered the picture, attempting unsuccessfully with Tufo to interest two paperback houses. But agreement was reached to publish the report, in full, in the *Village Voice.* Because the weekly had recently published an article critical of Schorr and because the CBS correspondent wanted to preclude any hint of the identity of his source, he gave up his original idea of writing an introduction to the report.[59] However, *Washington Post* reporter Laurence Stern verified that Schorr was the source of the leak and so reported publicly the next day, despite Schorr's denial. Looking back on the episode, Schorr said: "once you start down a certain line, the steps by which one thing leads to another come very swiftly, and suddenly you're totally wrapped up in it. You want *your* copy published and not somebody else's. You find yourself saying, 'By God, I don't care if this appears in Pravda as long as it appears.' In the end you're amazed at how far you've come from what you originally wanted to do."[60] He argued that he could not bring himself to suppress in full a report that had been paid for with taxpayers' money.

Schorr has been criticized for his actions on several grounds. First, although he approached CBS about having its subsidiary, Popular Library, publish the Pike report, he did not clear with his superiors at CBS News his plans to publish the report elsewhere.[61] Second, he lost control of the report, allowing it to be published in a weekly with a strong point of view, thus raising questions about his and, by association, CBS's impartiality. Third, although the Reporters Committee for Freedom of the Press ultimately disassociated itself and announced it would not accept any proceeds from publication,[62] Schorr did not keep the committee abreast of publication developments at a time when their mutual agreement apparently was still in effect. This put the committee in an untenable position when news media asked it to comment on its own role in the affair.[63] Fourth, there was the question of whether Schorr had, as a *New York Times* editorial charged,[64] sold official secrets. Although Schorr argued that the *Times* had done precisely the same thing when a *Times* subsidiary published the leaked Pentagon Papers,[65] the *Times*'s editorial page editor, John B. Oakes, claimed Schorr's act differed significantly in that it represented "selling to a third party." Oakes claims such an action was wrong, "no matter how lofty the cause."[66] Fifth, for a period of hours Schorr allowed his CBS supervisors in Washington to believe that another CBS correspondent may have leaked the document to the *Voice*.[67] Schorr later explained—

in Orwellian tones—that he had done so only to gain time to devise "a general plan for shedding my ill-conceived anonymity."[68] Sixth, Schorr is faulted for having attempted to hide his role as the leaker of the report once it became known that he had, in fact, leaked it. Schorr admits that was "a spectacularly bad" judgment.[69]

Within the media, at least, little of a critical nature was said about Schorr's role in the denouement of the Pike report controversy. In fact, his performance was praised. Subpoenaed by the House Ethics Committee, Schorr declined to identify his source or to hand over his copy of the report, saying: "To betray a confidential source would mean to dry up many future sources for many future reporters. The ultimate losers would be the American people and their free institutions. But beyond all that, to betray a source would be to betray myself, my career and my life. To say that I refuse to do it is not quite saying it right. I cannot do it."[70] The committee lacked a majority to cite Schorr for contempt. If it had information on its own to dispute Schorr's argument that national security had not been damaged, it did not present it at the hearing. Schorr, who had been suspended from his duties during the controversy, resigned from CBS. The network, in the immediate wake of the controversy, had promised Schorr severance pay as well as two years' salary. *Time* magazine disclosed the agreement was withheld from the public at the time because it was felt it might prejudice Schorr's case with Congress, which both CBS and Schorr wanted to win. When it was won CBS offered to take Schorr back, but Schorr declined because his lawyer, Joseph Califano, advised him it was merely a ruse by which the network would shed its obligation to pay the generous settlement, and perhaps Schorr himself, later. Schorr kept the money and left.[71]

The critics and commentators on media performance certainly cannot be faulted for ignoring the Schorr affair. Nora Ephron's *Esquire* account[72] brought to light hidden facts and made explicit ethical judgments. Laurence Stern, whose *Post* story first identified Schorr as the source of the leak, gave the case needed visibility in the *Columbia Journalism Review*.[73] Schorr's reply to Stern in *CJR* amplified several major points.[74] Bob Kuttner's account in *(more)*, the now-defunct journalism review,[75] was searching and, like Stern's article, raised serious ethical questions. In retrospect, however, journalism still did not gain from these major articles an in-depth or codified discussion of the ethical principles involved. Nor were there any apparent attempts to derive from the Schorr experience rules based on principles, rules— such as those by the *Courier-Journal* on confidential sources—that might provide at least some guidance to future recipients of classified documents or to journalists caught in circumstances in which they are forced to choose between competing principles.

In fact, a careful reading of the four articles shows that at least three contain what amount to pleas for further discussion, in effect, for a tradition of detailed ethical dialogue. Wrote Ephron: "There are a number of interesting peripheral issues here—the question of whether Schorr broke the ground rules in Xeroxing the report, the question of whether CBS or Schorr owned the report, the question of whether Peter Tufo informed Schorr of his conflict of interest—and I'm sorry I don't have the space to go into them."[76] Although they are clearly not the paramount issues, they certainly need precise discussion. And, ironically, Schorr himself listed, in his *CJR* reply to Stern, a series of largely unexplored issues, among them:

1. Where is the line to be drawn between national security and freedom of the press, and who decides?
2. Are leaks a legitimate subject for government or congressional investigation?
3. Who decides what should be appropriately disseminated, as between press and government? As between reporter and employer?"[77]

Stern, in *CJR,* called the Schorr affair "a complex morality play from which each of the interested parties could extract the message it wanted to hear."[78] However, no one in American journalism compared what the interested parties extracted from the play, or whether or how those messages could fit within a framework of principle.

Kuttner, apparently alone among the commentators on the Schorr affair, could see new truth being added to public dialogue by the publication in the *Voice* of what amounted to the bulk of the Pike report. Kuttner said an eighty-page section on how the investigation was obstructed "is a thoughtful, literate narrative, undoubtedly staff director Searle Field's cri de coeur of the frustrating months fencing with Henry Kissinger over access to classified materials." Added Kuttner: "It is the most fascinating case study I have read on just how the Federal police and espionage agencies successfully thwart Congressional supervision. So far it has been almost totally ignored."[79] If Kuttner's interpretation is correct, the media majority was wrong in dismissing the Pike report as containing nothing new or valuable that had not already been printed or aired. And thus Schorr's defense, at least on grounds of the principle of truth telling, had an adequate basis.

As for justice or fairness, Schorr can clearly be faulted for letting stand, even for a short time, the impression that another colleague might have leaked the report to the *Village Voice*. Schorr could correctly say that he had made an initial attempt to let his employer publish the full account of the Pike report. Apparently, however, he did not press his case there. Nor did he use persuasive, moral imagination to invent a way (say, a documentary on Kissinger's resistance to the investigation) to air the fresh material in the Pike report that remained unbroadcast. Certainly, he had an obligation, from the justice principle, to let his employer know of his attempts to publish the report elsewhere, but he did not.

Schorr lost control of the reort, and thus the independence and freedom to decide its fate. By this miscalculation, and by denying he was the source of the leak even after it was clear his role had been verified, Schorr's stewardship of his craft/profession left something to be desired, at least in those particulars. If CBS had flatly refused to broadcast or publish the remainder of the report, and if he still believed publication of the report was paramount, he could have resigned his position and arranged publication as a free man.

On the other hand, when subpoenaed before the congressional committee, steward Schorr rightly refused to divulge his source of information, especially since no case, persuasive or otherwise, was presented on behalf of such a disclosure. Despite personal and professional resentment toward Schorr among many of his colleagues, the media supported him strongly in his confrontation with Congress, thus remaining faithful stewards in this important instance.

The foregoing treatment of the Schorr affair within a framework of principle is certainly not proffered as a "last word" on the episode. It is meant as a sketch of how such a case might be considered were a stronger tradition of more explicit dialogue to develop in journalism. Developed fully, and published in monograph form along with critiques, dissenting comments, and comparisons to other cases, it might help develop the ethical sensitivity most committed journalists seek.

CHAPTER NINE

Journalism's "Tragedy of the Commons"

Investigative reporting helped alter the ethos of American journalism in the 1960s and 1970s. While practiced, in fact, only by a few, its visibility cast a new, romantic aura over a profession whose entrepreneurial talents had lain largely dormant in the 1940s and 1950s. A few examples highlight the new assertiveness of the later decades.

- Louis Kohlmeier of the *Wall Street Journal* won a Pulitzer Prize in 1964 for assiduously documented stories revealing how Lyndon and Lady Bird Johnson amassed a fortune in their government-regulated television business, disclosing the relationship between their private and public lives.[1]
- Drew Pearson and Jack Anderson in 1965 exposed, among other things, the mishandling of campaign funds by Senator Thomas J. Dodd, D-Conn., for which he was censured by the Senate in 1967.[2]
- Throughout the late 1960s and the 1970s, the late Jerry Landauer of the *Wall Street Journal* uncovered conflicts of interest by lawmakers, foreign bribes by corporations, and unjust tax loopholes, as well as failings in the media's own performance in covering "Koreagate."[3]
- Derring-do, shoe leather, and shrewd intelligence led to a Pulitzer Prize and a new national investigative reporting career for Seymour Hersh with his 1969 exposure of an army massacre of innocent civilians at the Vietnamese village of Mylai.[4] He subsequently reported for the *New York Times* the first story on massive domestic spying by the CIA.
- Early in 1969, *Life* magazine had helped force the resignation of Supreme Court Justice Abe Fortas, a Lyndon Johnson appointee, by disclosing Fortas's questionable relationship with the family foundation of financier Louis E. Wolfson, who later was jailed for stock manipulation.[5] The meticulously researched article by

Pulitzer Prize–winning reporter William Lambert showed that while Fortas had not been hired to fix Wolfson's case, the justice's name had been "dropped in strategic places" during eleven months in which Fortas kept a fee (later returned) given by the foundation for work which Fortas ultimately concluded he was too busy to perform.

- In the early 1970s, the exposure of Watergate by *Washington Post* reporters Bob Woodward and Carl Bernstein and others in the Washington press corps[6] placed investigative reporting at the very center of national attention.

But the movement was by no means confined to the national print press. For example, intensive investigation by the *Lufkin* (Texas) *News,* circulation 12,000, brought congressional and presidential attention to a Marine recruit's death by pugil-stick at Camp Pendleton, Calif., spurring reforms in training methods.[7] By the mid-1970s, a nucleus of committed journalists banded together to form Investigative Reporters and Editors (IRE), which meets nationally and regionally to develop and promote the craft, publishes a magazine, and organizes special seminars on issues of interest to practitioners.[8] Significantly, it placed its national headquarters at the University of Missouri School of Journalism, one of the most prestigious journalism schools in the world.

This "institutionalization" of investigative reporters' attention to their own professional interests had begun earlier in the 1970s. Then law enforcement agencies began seeking and the courts began issuing subpoenas for reporters' notes on a significant scale. Grand juries began pumping reporters to disclose their confidential sources. Stories on the Black Panther Party and Students for a Democratic Society were particular targets. Following an informal organization meeting in Washington's Georgetown section, some of the leaders in the reporting movement—J. Anthony Lukas of the *New York Times,* Jack Nelson of the *Los Angeles Times,* and Fred Graham, then of the *New York Times* and later of CBS News—chose the name Reporters Committee for Freedom of the Press. It has since developed into a legal resource for journalists and a monitor and critic of what it deems to be incursions into First Amendment rights.[9] The committee's first press release foreshadowed the nature of its concern. Subpoenas and forced testimony, the reporters said, threaten "the delicate process through which news is often gathered and disseminated to the public," with the likelihood of destroying "whatever trust newsmen have developed among sources who can provide information not otherwise available to the general public."

Creation of the IRE marked a formal effort by investigative journalists to codify and develop their skills. Formation of the Reporters Committee was an attempt by reporters as a group, to justify and defend themselves in the practice not only of investigative journalism but also any reporting in which government and media views of the law conflict. The existence of both represents more than an expression of occupational self-interest, though both are very much involved in self-defense and self-promotion. But these groups also are practicing a form of stewardship of journalism's truth telling function. Simultaneously, they seek to preserve journalism's freedom and independence, and its ability to report on a society many of whose institutions, like the media, proclaim justice as a value.

This chapter will discuss the special role investigative journalism claims for itself in the American political system. It will examine the status and ethical implications of such a role. It will explore whether ends sought by investigative journalists justify the means sometimes employed to gather stories. To understand this classic dilemma, ethical theory will be consulted. Ways will be suggested to attack, if not resolve, such stubborn and difficult problems. Finally, note will be taken of the view held by some influential journalists that a new form or mode of enterprise journalism is needed to reflect the complexities of a new world, one far more complicated than either the muckrakers dreamed or current practitioners have admitted.

Like journalism in general, investigative journalism at its ethical best can be identified as expressing Lockean values—empiricism and rationality in public discourse, government by consent of the governed, a government of laws rather than of men, and limitations on governmental power. A celebrated project which served almost all those values appeared in the *Philadelphia Inquirer* in 1973 when its specialists in documentary investigation, James Steele and Donald Barlett, examined the criminal justice system in the City of Brotherly Love.[10] With the programming help of Philip Meyer, a pioneer in using computers to gather and interpret the news, Barlett and Steele fed into the computer some 100,000 bits of information on more than 1,000 persons accused of crimes. Convictions, they found, varied between judges with and without backgrounds as public prosecutors, and between those convicted depending on whether they were white or black. These and similar findings were available to make public discussions of the courts more rational and, presumably, the administration of the courts as well. The use of the computer represented a new technique to expand the truth telling capacity of journalism. It was used in the cause of a more just and more humane court system, one that would respect the freedom and independence of citizens. And by sharing their techniques with colleagues in Investigative Reporters and Editors, Barlett and Steele showed themselves to be active stewards of their craft, just as would any jurist who worked to make courts more just.[11]

Other examples of a neat fit between Lockean values and the practice of investigative journalism are easy to find. Gene Miller, a reporter's reporter for the *Miami Herald,* twice won a Pulitzer Prize for dogged reporting that led to the freeing of citizens wrongly sent to prison.[12] Reporters Sydney P. Freedberg and David Ashenfelter of the *Detroit News* won a Pulitzer for exposing the navy's coverup of information on the deaths of sailors aboard ship, and their stories led to changes in U.S. Navy procedures.[13] Fortas's case is clearly in point as holding up a standard that judges must avoid even the suspicion of wrongdoing. And Watergate, although many have lost sight of the essence of the scandal, represented an attempt—exposed with the help of the press—to thwart the administration of justice.

However settled a role these examples might indicate for the investigative journalist, the acceptance is qualified. No clearer sign can be found of this qualification than the criticism of investigative reporting from within not only the ranks but the temple itself. Virginius Dabney, editor of the *Richmond Times-Dispatch* for a third of a century and a former president of the American Society of Newspaper Editors, looked back at his profession from the vantage point of the 1980s and deplored the excesses of investigative reporting. "I know of cases," he wrote, "where reputable men's careers were blasted by investigative reporters using highly questionable methods; I know of two executives hounded from their positions and a third gravely and unnecessarily embarrassed. The techniques that were used included quoting from unnamed 'sources' that couldn't be verified, slanted and unfair reporting of specific events and failing to give facts essential to understand a situation properly."[14] Veteran editor Michael J. O'Neill, in his speech to the 1982 convention of ASNE, said that "if we had not been so busy chasing corrupt officials," the press might not have missed the truly big domestic and foreign stories of the recent past, such as the black migration from the South, the genesis of the Vietnam War, and the women's liberation movement. He added: "In some cases, investigative reporting has also run off the ethical tracks. Individuals and institutions have been needlessly hurt when the lure of sensational headlines has prevailed over fairness, balance and a valid public purpose."[15] Marian Sulzberger Heiskell, a board member of the *New York Times,* told United Press International editors that investigative reporting may have lost perspective. "What I fear is that investigative stories may become

TABLE 9.1   **Investigative Techniques**

	Approve (%)	Disapprove (%)	No opinion (%)
Unnamed sources	42	53	5
Hidden cameras and mikes	38	58	4
Paying informers	36	56	8
Reporter misidentification	32	65	3

so voguish, so full of glamorous appeal for reporters and editors, that the practice may often be pursued simply for its own sake," adding: "The sharp edge of revelation will be dulled if we overdo it."[16]

These criticisms, more than matched by non-media leaders in American society, have not undermined the basic public support for investigative reporting. At the beginning of the 1980s, George Gallup asked a cross section of Americans 18 and older: "As you probably know, the news media—TV, newspapers, and magazines—often do what is called 'investigative reporting'—uncovering and reporting on corruption and fraud in business, government agencies, and other organizations. In general, do you approve or disapprove of investigative reporting by the news media?" The response showed 79 percent approved, 18 percent disapproved, and 3 percent had no opinion. Moreover, 66 percent said they would like to see more such reporting.[17]

However, when the poll went on to query the 1,508 adults about their opinion of the methods sometimes used by investigative reporters, a more critical portrait came to the surface (see Table 9.1).[18]

Interestingly, there are apparently variations in attitude toward investigative reporting in different parts of the country. The *Chicago Sun-Times,* which conducted a survey in February 1980 during one of its investigative series, found an overall approval rating of 77 percent, similar to Gallup's 79 percent nationally. But more Chicagoans approved than disapproved of the use of unnamed sources (55 percent to 38 percent), hidden cameras (60 percent to 35 percent), hidden microphones (54 percent to 40 percent), and the failure of reporters to identify themselves (60 percent to 35 percent). Paying for information as a journalistic practice split the respondents exactly evenly, with 45 percent disapproving and 45 percent approving.

In judging these methods respondents are implicitly saying how much they value certain ethical principles. Thus, for example, the accuracy of information obtained by checkbook, unless verified before publication or broadcast, could be tainted. It could represent a reporting shortcut that compromises truth telling. And using unnamed sources can be unfair if it forecloses adequate response by accused persons.

Many factors could explain the relative tolerance of Chicagoans for these methods. The Windy City has a history not only of municipal and other corruption but of civic crusading and free-wheeling daily journalism. Chicago, after all, is the inspirational birthplace of Ben Hecht's immortal *Front Page,* with its hero, the legendary reporter Hildy Johnson, who would stop at almost nothing to "get the story." Some of the country's most widely known investigative journalists—such as the late George Bliss of the *Chicago Tribune*[19] and Art Petacque of the *Sun-Times*[20]—earned their laurels there, sometimes by unique, daring, or unorthodox methods.

Whatever the prevailing attitudes in Chicago,[21] it is clear from the Gallup survey that nationally a majority of the populace doubts these methods and finds them unacceptable.

Journalists might rationalize these findings in several ways. First, the public can be regarded as "fickle," accepting the benefits of investigative reporting without the appropriate empathy that might come from thinking carefully about the problems investigative reporters face. But this merely deflects attention from the moral issue by asking for more solicitude than other professions expect or get. Second, the results can be ignored as not representing the "true feelings" of the public; the argument can be made that if greater thought *had* been given, the results would have been different. This is disingenuous and also ignores the stated expressions of public opinion in response to a properly conducted poll. Third, the journalist can merely persist in his opinion that such methods sometimes need to be used, arguing that he or she has the superior wisdom to discern when these are or are not justified by the circumstances. This can be regarded as hubris, pure and simple, a manifestation as old as Plato of the belief that nobilities have privileges denied others in judging the public interest.

Implicit in the findings of the public opinion polls is a need by the attentive public for a dialogue on the ethics of the methods journalists employ, particularly the methods of investigative reporters. In view of the media's hostile reaction to U.S. Supreme Court decisions curbing media prerogatives[22] and in light of libel jury verdicts that reach crippling proportions,[23] such a dialogue could serve more than academic purposes, especially since public opinion does have at least some influence on court decisions and is critical when it comes to media credibility.

IRE and the major news organizations have been prodigious holders

of panels, forums, and conferences on ethics in investigative journalism. Journalism reviews have treated ethical issues on a case by case
basis. National television shows have been staged using Socratic methods to explore media ethics. What has not emerged is a consistent focus
that will advance the understanding and application of the criteria that
now seem to be emerging as a consensus approach. As previously
quoted from Bob Greene of *Newsday* and others, these yardsticks are
that unethical means, such as deception or role-playing, are never
justified unless (a) all moral means to gather a story have been ex-
hausted or weighed and found wanting and (b) the story itself is in
response to a "compelling public urgency."[24]

Too often these standards are no more than ritually invoked, if at all.
Little in journalism tradition fosters explicit and open discussion of
means/ends questions both before and after publication, yet it is sorely
needed. In the late 1950s a young reporter, new to town, was asked to
check out reports that a state assemblyman in a large midwestern city
was conducting a gambling operation in a neighborhood bar as part of
his reelection campaign. The reporter and his wife visited the bar,
participated, and collected a few gaming prizes, with little thought that
the story could have been gathered by direct observation. Although this
can be chalked up to the reporter's inexperience at the time, there was
no subsequent criticism of his methods by peers; the supposed purity of
intent within his published story was judged sufficient explanation of
why he had violated the law himself.[25]

Almost twenty years later, examples can be found of this casual
approach to decision making. In a southern town one Christmas in the
late 1970s, a nightclub operator steered customers to a source of inex-
pensive but supposedly high quality perfume: Chanel No. 5 at $8 for a
two-ounce bottle. A reporter, investigating, visited the nightclub and set
up a purchase, telling the nightclub owner his real name but giving a
fake occupation. Chemical analysis of the perfume proved it to be
bogus. The reporter said the nightclub owner reacted: "That's not fair.
You didn't tell me you worked for the newspaper!" And the reporter
explained himself: "True, and it probably wasn't 'ethical' but it may
have saved scores of unsuspecting citizens from buying fake perfume at
that nightclub and, as it turned out, at other places as well."[26] In the
body and headline of the article, which was identified explicitly as a
discussion of ethics, the assertion is made: "In most cases, the end
justifies our means."[27] In the article itself, there is precious little discussion of this bold and questionable assertion, and no statement of any
consequence contradicting it. There is not even a discussion of whether
actively faking one's occupation is a moral compromise justified by so

small a return as sparing a customer from the purchase of fake perfume. It would seem a disproportionate sacrifice.

The difficulty is precisely that the ends of journalists cannot safely be said to *usually* justify means. To make such an assertion is to trivialize or foreclose giving serious, principled thought to each case. That some, perhaps many, journalists can make these decisions so lightly shows a need for a consideration of basics.

Garrett Hardin, professor of human ecology in the department of biological sciences at the University of California at Santa Barbara, has depicted the planet earth as a commons loaded with cattle. Herdsmen in the hinterland all graze their stock on the commons. Each can individually calculate the utility of adding one more head. Since each herdsman gets all the proceeds from that head, the utility of adding it can be considered as one. By contrast, the negative effects are widely shared. If "logic" is followed, all herdsmen keep adding stock until the commons is depleted and all their livestock eventually die or are sold. This was Hardin's "tragedy of the commons."[28]

If cattle represent investigative stories gathered through lies or deception, and if public trust is the grass on which they graze, perhaps the dilemma facing the media can be seen more graphically. A reporter, not perceiving that his own particular deception actually erodes public trust, feels freer to use deceptive means. Trust, the basis of human dialogue, erodes. Under this circumstance, perhaps the reasoning of Immanuel Kant can then be seen as more than the pontifications of an antiquarian Boy Scout. Perhaps, after all, there is something to the notion that a maxim should not be acted upon if it cannot be willed as a universal guide to action. Thus, journalists can foresee the ultimately self-defeating nature of the maxim that seems to underlie the unquestioning use of deceptive means: "Tell the truth, except when doing so hinders one's immediate self-interest, the interest of one's employer or colleagues, or unless telling an untruth appears to serve what we journalists alone define as a compelling public interest."

Journalists howl, and howl loudly, whenever someone in public life is audacious enough to assert a similar prerogative. Thus, Arthur Sylvester's claim, as assistant secretary of defense for public affairs, that the government had a right to lie to save its citizens from nuclear war during the 1962 Cuban missile crisis, generated a fire storm of congressional and media criticism that continued when he refused to retract his remarks in a way that might satisfy his critics.[29]

No attempt to establish stricter standards in investigative reporting can fail to ask why deception or lying can be wrong. One way to begin is to consider the opposite view, that there is nothing wrong with lying in itself. The utilitarian philosopher Jeremy Bentham asserted: "Falsehood, take it by itself, consider it as not being accompanied by any other material circumstances, nor therefore productive of any material effects, can never, upon the principle of utility, constitute any offense at all."[30] Quickly or casually invoked deception or role-playing by some journalists is often undertaken in the spirit of Bentham, with the individual performing his own calculus of greatest good for the greatest number, or public interest.

Another view, represented by Kant and Augustine, is that all lying is wrong in itself. Stating as true to another what is known to be false constitutes lying. As such it denies one or more persons access to truth, which is not a commodity that is or should be appropriated as exclusively one's own. Others need it to exercise the freedom and rationality that just societies claim for all persons. To lie is to deny the personhood of those to whom one lies.

While sharing the view of lying as wrong and as a denigration of personhood, modern ethicists such as Charles Fried qualify the Kantian assertions by saying that all lying "is wrong *unless* excused or justified in defined ways."[31] As an example of an excused lie, Fried cites the classic and oft-quoted hypothetical case of an assassin inquiring about the whereabouts of his intended victim. Revealing to the assassin that the person he seeks is in one's basement would clearly be wrong because the assassin would be receiving information to which he is not entitled. *Chicago Tribune* columnist Bob Greene, when he let stand the erroneous impression that no wiretaps were on his telephone, allowed police to trace the call of and apprehend "Moulded to Murder," a mentally ill man whom psychiatrists judged to be on the verge of killing innocent people. In both the classical hypothetical case and the "Moulded to Murder" case, there is a clear indication not only that a greater wrong was averted but that information was withheld from a person not entitled to it by reason of the wrong intended.

A helpful distinction can be made between passive deception, a usually acceptable option, and the kind of aggressive deception, such as role playing, which can in effect be lying. Passive deception occurs when the reporter in his work appears as a citizen would—at a restaurant to dine (and write a review), at a mechanic's shop to repair his car (and test the honesty and adequacy of consumer services), or to a political fund raiser to hear the pitches (and examine techniques and note promises made). Ray Brennan, attempting to establish that a hospitalized Chicago hoodlum was not actually ill, was asked by a nurse at the hospital whether he was a friend of Mr. Sam de Stafano. Evasively but truthfully, he said, "I've known him for many years." Later, after observing de Stafano's robust behavior—occasionally from behind a newspaper he kept as a shield near his face—Brennan began to document his story. The convict was soon back in jail. Brennan walked the outer edges of passive deception but did not then lie, that is, assert something to be true knowing it to be untrue.[32] However, when Brennan pretended over the telephone to be the new office manager of the Kefauver Crime Committee, thereby gaining eventual access to a secret transcript of hearings, he actively lied, and was even indicted.[33] Impersonating—especially impersonating a police officer or someone with formal powers over the citizenry—has come to be a taboo. It is usually against the law.

A more normative classification than the spectrum from "passive" to "active" deception is use of the terms "benign" and "invasive" deception. Benign deception would be all those measures which merely allow a reporter to gather information. These measures do not alter the news gathering context and do not invade the rights of a subject in the news. Among such techniques are simply not volunteering one's identity, conducting passive, "eyeball" surveillance of a person's public movements, and wearing sunglasses, a toupee, or a wig to avoid detection from among a public audience. In all of these situations, a reporter is prepared to admit his identity, if pressed. Arguably, a reporter could claim to be using benign techniques by accepting a job within a "target" organization about which he was conducting an investigation. However, in such a case the reporter must be prepared to admit his identity if asked in a background check of employment. Invasive deception would be all those measures, such as role playing, in which a reporter's identity is actively misrepresented or falsified. This would include posing as an applicant for a new job while concealing one's employment by the media, or masquerading as a patient in a mental institution or nursing home.

Sissela Bok, in her modern classic on lying in public and private life, makes several major points that journalists who are tempted to use ruses, deception, or lies should ponder. Among them are:

- The practice of lying comes dressed in many varieties of sheep's clothing, and lies are excused supposedly because they avoid harm, produce benefit, assure fairness, and even foster a faith in truthfulness! But beware of easily invoking these excuses, most of which will not stand critical examination.[34]
- Liars and deceivers tend to "overestimate the forces pushing them to lie."[35] Moreover, the "need" to lie often expands beyond the scope of lying originally intended.[36]

- Crises in some professions are not rare but frequent; thus ethical dilemmas constantly face doctors, lawyers, journalists, police, and soldiers. Yet "there is, in fact, rarely a clear professional standard or open discussion of the unspoken standards in professional organizations."[37]

After critiquing the deceptions practiced by Woodward and Bernstein in the Watergate investigation, Bok concludes:

It can be argued that, in order for this exposure to be possible, deception was needed; but what is more troubling than the lies themselves is the absence of any acknowledgement of a moral dilemma. No one seems to have stopped to think that there was a problem in using deceptive means. No one weighed the reasons for and against doing so. There was no reported effort to search for honest alternatives, or to distinguish among different forms and degrees of deception, or to consider whether some circumstances warranted it more than others."[38]

In fairness to Woodward and Bernstein, it should be acknowledged that, at least after the fact, there was an admission of wrongdoing, for they wrote of themselves: "They felt lousy. They had not broken the law when they visited the grand jurors, that much seemed certain. But they had sailed around it and exposed others to danger. They had chosen expediency over principle and, caught in the act, their role had been covered up. They had dodged, evaded, misrepresented, suggested and intimidated, even if they had not lied outright."[39]

The argument made here is that, when considering the use of deception as a technique, there should be deliberation before the fact by reporters and editors, and the dialogue, where possible, should be both explicit and comprehensive. Moreover, in addition to dialogue within the particular news institutions, there should be proceedings within the profession at large which attempt to establish general standards to guide the dialogue within particular news organizations. In cases where no other honest, nondeceptive means can be found, and after moral argumentation has established what the journalists regard as the existence of a "compelling public interest and urgency," there can be resort to a kind and degree of deception appropriate to the evil to be exposed or the wrong that is to be righted. However, the news organization should, when reporting the results of its investigation, report the debate over means and over moral justification with the same clarity and comprehensiveness as it would one of the stories in its investigation.

The rationale is that if the profession and the news organizations within it voluntarily assume a responsibility for internal and external debate, deceptive means are more likely to be minimized than under the current ad hoc practice in which ethical dialogue remains either too private or only superficially public and in which the skills of moral imagination and comprehensive ethical discourse are underdeveloped and decidedly undervalued by the profession.

The basis in ethical theory for such elaborate mechanisms of justification can be found in the writing of Kant and in the works of neo-Kantians such as John Rawls. In his slender but powerful volume *Perpetual Peace,* Kant says that no maxim is morally worthy of use in public affairs if it cannot be asserted and defended publicly.[40] Rawls proposes tests of publicity, similar in spirit to the procedure here proposed, as part of his definition of a just society and as a constraint on any moral principle.[41] Applied here, the notion is that if journalists have a maxim or principle to guide their decisions about when to use and not use deception, the proposition should be stated and defended publicly, or they risk forfeiting full public acceptance of their watchdog role.

To be meaningful, a public defense must include the views of representatives of those who could be deceived—that is, members of the public, government officials, representatives of private industry and labor, and religious and nonprofit groups. These could be present at a properly organized and representative forum at which a major professional organization—say the American Society of Newspaper Editors or the Radio-Television News Directors Association—opened for discussion its statement of principle on the use of deceptive means. Then, after hearing the views of those in attendance, the professional organization could later formally adopt such a general statement, perhaps as a part of its existing code of ethics. The public, affected by the adoption or rejection of such a statement, would have been consulted and its views considered. The organization itself could vote later at its own convention whether to adopt, reject, or modify it.

How might such a general statement, meant to inform the membership's handling of the deception question, read? Recapitulating the position stated in this chapter and in Chapter 4, it could read as follows:

> The American public and the journalists within it are beneficiaries of the First Amendment, a right guaranteed in the social contract, whose fullest and clearest expression is the U.S. Constitution. The principles that should govern the behavior of individuals and institutions which are parties to the social contract are humaneness, truth telling, justice, freedom, and stewardship (responsibility). Citizens will have the freedom, subject to due process of law, to define what responsibilities they will voluntarily assume when confronted with probable infractions of the social contract by public officials and by private persons whose positions and activities affect the public interest.

Journalists are citizens who deem it their responsibility to report as newsworthy incidents that can be established as infractions of the social contract. In their work, journalists should rely on truthful, open means, avoiding lies and deception. When such truthful, open means have been tried and found wanting, and honestly judged as insufficient to verify and report the probable violation of the social contract, journalists and their editors should debate whether the likely violation is serious enough to morally justify the deceptive means thought capable of verifying the violation.

Before resorting to such means, the probable violation must be judged to be: First, systemic or nearly so—that is, pervasively rather than selectively or occasionally present. Second, urgent—that is, requiring immediate attention in the public interest. Third, in need of media attention before it can be properly exposed and corrected. Fourth, substantive—that is, it violates one of the principles of the social contract in such a way that a faithful adherent of the contract would clearly adopt deceptive means to expose it. Fifth, the news organization must report fully its attempt to use truthful, open means, the reasoning behind its choice of deceptive means, and its moral justification of why such means were deemed necessary.

Investigative reporting, as in the truly rare resort to deceptive methods, can require of journalists that they choose between clearly competing principles, such as justice and truthfulness. Indeed, investigative journalism may require this more frequently than other journalistic specialties. Deceptive methods translate to a subordination of truthfulness to whatever other moral principle, such as justice, is sought to be served by the deception. Because principles are values, the resort to deception is a value judgment. The public justification procedure just described is an attempt to help journalists weigh such choices carefully and still preserve their credibility with the public.

To justify active deception in reporting methods, for example, an unjust violation of the social contract must be systemic, urgent, substantive, and incapable of rectification without deceptive means and without media exposure. Expecting, in addition, that media report fully to the public about the deception and the reasons for it will maximize the chances that such deception will be used only in cases in which there is a vital public interest at stake.

Nothing quite so explicit or as inclusive is followed by contemporary news media, but the best in current practice can be seen as foreshadowing a trend toward the "tests of publicity" implicit in Kant and explicit in Rawls.

For example, the *Chicago Sun-Times* described in detail the precautions it took and the methods it used to report payoffs to a state law enforcement agency as they occurred, to avoid legal entrapment, to never solicit a payoff, and to reap no material gains from the operation. The health and safety of patrons were protected by having all violations corrected, even after payoffs. The newspaper even made a start at explaining why it had resorted to undercover means. The beginning of a letter of transmittal forwarding the series to the Pulitzer contest read in part:

> The Mirage project was the result of years of complaints from small businesses about the systematic day-to-day corruption they had to endure in Chicago. The callers said they were being harassed, especially by city and state inspectors—building, fire, health, revenue and on through the long list—who have the power to shut down a business if they are not kept happy with regular payoffs.
> But if the businessmen hinted strongly at a system of government by envelope, almost none would step forward to cooperate in an investigation. The fear was that City Hall would retaliate. And it was a legitimate fear; a few who had the courage to go on record were harassed out of business within months.[42]

These few sentences suggest that other means may have been tried. But they do not document the truthful, open means actually attempted, and of retaliation actually carried out by City Hall and police, who, if honest, would be expected to remedy wrongs committed by inspectors. Nor were readers themselves given thorough explanations of means that were tried and failed or detailed arguments of moral justification. Perhaps they were regarded as unnecessary. However, in what was perhaps the most elaborate use of undercover techniques in American journalism, the *Sun-Times* met many, though not all, the tests here proposed. Nonetheless, some remain unconvinced that the wrongs exposed by the *Sun-Times* and righted by subsequent official action—and they were extensive[43]—justify the massive deception used. Others defend the *Sun-Times* and argue it should have won a Pulitzer prize.[44]

As explained in Chapter 5, the process of ethical judgment is an act of valuing, and valuing occurs at several levels. It can be argued, for example, that actively deceiving might permit greater proximity to the facts, placing a reporter closer to the truth than would second-hand, derivative methods. It can further be argued that such direct observation, in fact, is in the best interest of the "target subject" of the investigation. It is thus only a short step to the inference that the greater the harm a story might cause to a subject the greater the duty of journalists to observe truth directly, even if it means active deception. Hence, so the reasoning goes, it is in the best interest of all that the journalist actively deceive to gain the most direct access to the facts. The chain of reasoning has Orwellian features best checked by the rigorous use of a justification device such as that proposed above. Otherwise, the ends, the seemingly good consequences, will be seductively invoked to justify almost any means. By definition, to value truth and truthfulness must mean that one is willing to pay a price for them. Such a price may mean the loss or deferral of publication of a story, and, on occasion, a very good story. To the committed investigative journalist, the price can be paid with an equanimity born of the knowledge that patience, imagination, determination, and craftsmanship will usually uncover stories that truly need to be made public without resort to deceptive means.

Undoubtedly, the beginning of the 1980s, and even earlier, marked a reaction against investigative reporting. With rising libel judgments, with disenchantment from within the profession, with a sagging domestic economy that permitted little optimism and fewer resources for "extras," it was no surprise that the reaction set in. And no doubt the fruits of investigative work often came with a bittersweet taste. Under an article headlined, "Woodstein in Des Moines: Memories of a Reporter Who Hoped to Change the World," John Lancaster discussed his and the *Des Moines Tribune*'s investigation of a crew of laggard city housing inspectors and a wayward suburban police chief. He concluded:

> The fallout from the two investigative pieces certainly cured me of any tendency to see myself as a shaker of dynasties. Which is not to say that the effort was poorly spent. Chief Cooney will no doubt treat his men, and the citizens of West Des Moines, more delicately after seeing his darker side laid out in the newspaper. And as for the inspectors, they probably spend at least as much time glancing in their rear-view mirrors as they used to spend drinking coffee."[45]

Necessary as such qualifications and midcourse corrections are, the history of investigative reporting is too rich, and the spirit of searching inquiry too embedded in the soul of journalism, for it to evaporate in the aridity of post-Watergate reaction. The *New Yorker,* no intellectual slouch, noted in 1975 that the nation's economic, diplomatic, and political problems—intertwined as they are with those of other nations— "call for a new kind of news reporting, as yet undiscovered, which will answer the special needs of our era as brilliantly and as daringly as investigative reporting met the special needs of Watergate."[46] The call is echoed in many quarters.

Leonard Downie of the *Washington Post* cited the *New Yorker* column approvingly and went on to declare that "to accomplish such ambitious tasks, investigative reporting must mature beyond titillating exposés of individual wrongdoing and embrace expert analysis of complicated subjects and institutions."[47] Ben Bagdikian, one of the profession's foremost critics, has similarly written: "The fact is that investigative reporting need not be an unending litany of corruption and failure. Inevitably, much of it will be. But as we become more knowledgeable, we also develop credentials for seeking out solutions to the ills that we find."[48] John Hughes, editor of the *Christian Science Monitor,* once wrote that "these days a newspaper must come up with the facts, the ideas, the alternatives, on which solutions to problems can be based."[49]

In a widely quoted essay Max Ways of *Fortune* depicts a complicated age in which the knowledge explosion is compounded by the fact that the power it brings is diffused into "the hands of millions of organizations and hundreds of millions of individuals." Not only does this complicate the gathering of news, Ways argues, but it requires, on the part of journalists, new habits of mind and new strategies for thinking about how groups interrelate. With a sense of urgency about the need for a new form of journalism, Ways stresses: "Every year we become more like strangers—and more like brothers."[50]

If a new form or sequel to investigative journalism is to be born, it will not leave infancy and certainly not attain maturity without a system of ethics. And not just any system of ethics will do. Guidance is needed not only for individual and group decisions on right and wrong in professional practice. It also is needed for a richer perspective on the issues raised as individuals, groups, and nations compete and try to cooperate with one another in a world that even, and perhaps especially, the wise do not profess to fully understand.

CHAPTER TEN

Ethics, the Media, and the Law

Certainly one measure of a society's strength is the degree of justice and civility with which it settles disputes between its citizens. The more severe disputes are those over civil rights. Perhaps the most severe of these contests, in turn, are those in which society's own designated instruments of the law—police, prosecutors, defense attorneys, and judges—find themselves in judicial combat over their respective roles or performance. And when their disputes center on a party such as the press, which enjoys a constitutional protection, the public's stake in the outcome could scarcely be much higher. The past twenty-five years have witnessed a series of such collisions at the bench. The Supreme Court's decisions have affected such fundamental matters as the definition of prior censorship and of libel against a public official or public figure, the obligations of journalists with respect to the giving of court evidence, and the circumstances, if any, under which court proceedings may be closed to the media and the public. The timely tracking, analysis, and critique of these decisions is an exercise in journalistic stewardship of the highest importance. Journalists need to know the current status of and trends in media law.

By contrast, the purpose here is to make clear the sense in which ethical issues lie behind many such court cases. Moreover, court decisions often create, or leave open, ethical issues for the journalist, quite apart from the legal limits they may attempt to define. This chapter will illustrate ethical issues involved in court cases in the areas of prior censorship, libel, forced cooperation with law enforcement, and mandatory versus voluntary guidelines on the coverage of court proceedings. An attempt will be made to show the relationship between ethical sensitivity, principled moral reasoning, and the larger relationship between the media and the court system in a constitutional democracy.

The 1971 decision by the *New York Times,* the *Washington Post,* and other newspapers to publish the so-called Pentagon Papers usually has been noted more for the legal scenario that ensued than for the ethical judgments that preceded publication. Even a brief examination of the case, however, will show that ethical judgments affected the course of the controversy and that the concluding Supreme Court judgment shed as much light on ethics as on the ultimate legal question of whether prior restraint of publication is ever permitted by the First Amendment.[1]

In successfully preventing the *Times* and *Post* from publishing for fifteen days, the government of the United States had accomplished an unprecedented limitation of the press's freedom. True, the court ultimately overturned the preliminary injunction that the papers had agreed to respect during the historic litigation. Yet, the case clouded if not eroded the legal status of the ban on prior censorship. It did so because the attorneys for the newspapers did not rest their appeal on an argument that the First Amendment prevented any prior censorship. They conceded that under certain rare and grave circumstances such censorship might be justified. They argued merely that the government had not proved such censorship necessary in the case of the Pentagon Papers. By a margin of six to three, the court sided with the newspapers, leaving them free to publish but likewise vulnerable to the vagaries of a legal future made somewhat uncertain by their major concession, by the absence of a unanimous ruling, and by the lack of standards any clearer than the 1931 ruling in *Near versus Minnesota,*[2] which overturned a Minnesota gag law.

The existence and ultimate publication of the Pentagon Papers, known officially as "History of U.S. Decision-Making Process on Vietnam Policy, 1945–1967," were as much an act of conscience by two government officials as a brilliant exposé by journalists. Defense Secretary Robert McNamara, initially an apostle but later a saddened penitent of America's Vietnam policy, had ordered the compilation of an objective history of how decisions were made to enter and escalate American involvement in the war. Antiwar activist Daniel Ellsberg, a former military officer and supporter of the war, leaked this massive study to the *Times* and, later, to the *Post* after another recipient of Ellsberg's copy of the papers, Senator J. William Fulbright, D-Ark., chose not to make the classified documents public himself.[3]

Legally, the question confronted by the court was whether the president, as commander-in-chief and as the primary conductor of foreign policy, had inherent powers, in the absence of a statute, to seek an injunction to halt what he deemed to be a grave and immediate danger to national security. Ethically, when the journalists on the *New York Times* fully understood the significance of the Pentagon Papers, the primary issue was truth telling versus humaneness, or the avoidance of direct harm. They wanted to share with the public the new information they had found, a major, historic "scoop" detailing how successive administrations deepened American commitment in Vietnam. It was a commitment, the papers showed, which the executive branch had engineered, often without consultation with congress and the public, and, on occasion, by deception and deliberate withholding of information. Also, the papers showed that intelligence analyses that dissented from American Vietnam policy were disregarded.[4]

Yet, the journalists were not unmindful of security considerations; they were not heedless of potential harm. In his thorough account of the case Sanford Ungar noted: "The *Times* reporters and editors, relying on their experience in journalism and government, searched for material they thought might be considered dangerous to national security— battle plans, secret weapons, ongoing negotiations. But they found almost nothing in that category."[5] They specifically removed notations and any text that might have allowed a foreign power to determine either that the United States had cracked its coded messages or how quickly it had done so.[6]

Truth telling in the Pentagon Papers case also involved more than devising the best plan to summarize the 3,000 pages of narrative and 4,000 pages of appendices, or 2.5 million words.[7] Thus, Ben Bagdikian, an editor who garnered the papers from Ellsberg for the *Post,* had among his responsibilities the careful analysis of the specific cases advanced by the government before the courts, which charged there were breaches of national security. Recalled Bagdikian: "Either the claimed secret document had already been released to the public by the government (the majority of cases), or it was information that was original reporting by the press with the clippings later classified by the military, or it was material issued publicly by Moscow, Peking or Hanoi and therefore already known to adversaries."[8]

When the case reached David Bazelon, chief judge of the U.S. Court of Appeals, the government rested its case on what it claimed was an example so secret that it could be presented only within the chambers of the judge himself. After bringing the example to court contained within three separate envelopes in a locked briefcase, the government made its revelation. It was a decoded message, contained in the Pentagon Papers, of a North Vietnamese order to its naval units in the Gulf of Tonkin in August of 1964. Said the government: if this message were made public, the North Vietnamese would know that the United States was capable of intercepting and deciphering their military communications. As it turned out, however, the *Post* had succeeded in persuading the legal entourage to permit one reporter, George Wilson, into the judge's chambers. With a quickness and sureness that impressed both sides around the judge's desk, Wilson opened a green vinyl zippered bag and brought out a copy of the 1968 hearings on the Tonkin Gulf episode before the Senate Foreign Relations Committee. There he located the decoded message in a published transcript. The government itself had made it public in an effort to prove that U.S. ships had been deliberately attacked by the North Vietnamese. "Wilson had the book shown to the judge," Bagdikian recalled, adding: "It may have been the single act, more than any other, that helped win the Pentagon Papers case, possibly because there was a superb reporter who knew the system almost as well as the officials (and in this case, better)."[9] The point emphasized here is that, as illustrated by the *Post* and *Times,* ethical judgment required the exercise of prudence, imagination, sensitivity, intelligence, and reportorial memory. There was, in it, a blend of craftsmanship and morality.

But the story is only half told because one needs to consider whether there were other alternatives available to the *Times* and the *Post*. As stewards of free expression, they would have wanted to avoid any constriction of the Supreme Court's interpretation of their First Amendment rights. The late Alexander M. Bickel, the Yale Law School professor who defended the *Times* in the Pentagon Papers case, claimed that the press's freedom was extended "in that the conditions in which the government will not be allowed to restrain publication are now clearer and perhaps more stringent than they have been."[10] On the other hand, it was constricted, in Bickel's view, in the sense that "freedoms which are neither challenged nor defined are most secure."[11] Because Justices Byron White and Potter Stewart implied that punishment after the fact was an option and because a significant minority opposed the ruling, the argument appears much stronger for the view that freedom was diminished. At a minimum, the press would have been better off had it found a way to publish without going to court.

Herb Klein, the Nixon White House's director of communications, opposed the prior restraint action.[12] He said that the First Amendment confrontation might have been avoided had the newspapers either sought the release of the papers through the Freedom of Information Act or directly consulted with government officials to double check the newspapers' own judgments about national security violations.[13] Even if, as could be expected, the government had resisted any disclosure, the newspapers would have behaved as most had done in the past when handling classified information—that is, by checking the extent of its sensitivity. The press, in that event, still would have been free to publish, to exercise its own judgment. It could have done so with greater security in the wisdom of its own behavior and, perhaps, without risk of prior restraint litigation had the government agreed to declassification.[14]

As Klein suggested, neither side trusted the other.[15] In addition, if the *Times* or the *Post* had signaled their possession of the papers by consulting with the government, Ellsberg could have given them to the competition, and the *Times* would have lost its scoop. To preserve its scoop, in fact, the *Times*, while preparing its series, ordered its reporters not to contact any of the authors of the papers or participants in Vietnam policy making. "That was a kind of reporting and writing alien to them, and they became in effect prisoners of their own source material," wrote Ungar.[16] That competitive considerations also influenced the *Post,* which published second, seemed vividly clear from *Post* editor Richard Harwood's recollection: "Our main concern was not the public's right to know, it wasn't that we ought to tell people about this dreadful war in Vietnam. We had one basic consideration, and that was here was a hell of a news story and we were getting our ass beaten."[17]

Clearly, the *Times* and the *Post* were energetic and yet adroit truth tellers who weighed the potential risk of their actions, minimizing harm by prudent screening of any information that could possibly violate national security. However, they might have spared their profession even the semblance of a loss of freedom had their sense of stewardship been strong enough to risk losing a scoop. Voluntarily postponing publication for a bit longer could have had an added advantage. It could have made it "perfectly clear" that the Nixon administration—and not they—were unjust in their handling of a right, freedom of the press, which belonged to the public, too. The extra time and the consultation it would have allowed with the compilers of the Pentagon Papers and former Vietnam policy makers undoubtedly would have enhanced the quality of the reporting, the truth telling, of an enormously complicated set of documents.[18] The attentive public would have been better informed and the norm against prior censorship would probably have been left more secure.

Ethical and professional judgments likewise pervade most libel suits, which are far more common in the courts than prior censorship cases. In fact, the latitude for such judgments in certain cases was broadened significantly by the courts in the 1960s when the Supreme Court established guidelines on what must be proved in a libel case. In the landmark case of *The New York Times* vs. *Sullivan,*[19] the court said a public official must show that a publication or broadcast medium acted with knowledge that what it printed or broadcast was false or with reckless disregard of whether it was false. This is what the court called "actual malice." In subsequent decisions, this protection was expanded to include "public figures"—for example, retired army general Edwin Walker, whose role in rioting accompanying the racial integration of the University of Mississippi was the topic of an AP dispatch that contained an unintentional error.[20] These subsequent decisions,[21] extending press protections in major ways, seemed to be countered somewhat in 1974 in the case of *Gertz* vs. *Robert Welch*,[22] which held that private persons in libel actions need to establish only "negligence" plus damages by a publication or broadcast station. The "swing back" toward more protection for individuals also seemed apparent in *Time, Inc*. vs. *Firestone*,[23] which upheld socialite Mary Alice Firestone's libel suit on grounds that she was a private person and that the magazine was not protected in falsely reporting she had been divorced on grounds of adultery.[24]

Despite these judicial caveats, those news media which view investigative reporting as their role rely heavily on the letter and spirit of the *New York Times* vs. *Sullivan* ruling, in which Justice William Brennan enunciated the "actual malice" rule as a protection for public debate that is "robust, uninhibited and wide open." In moral terms, this ruling means that in reporting on public officials and those who are truly "public figures" the news media have a wide berth. Inadvertent errors, misjudgments, unintentional misstatements, incomplete truths, and even untruths are permitted the news media as long as they do not *knowingly* publish false and defamatory statements or show a *reckless* disregard for whether they are true or false. Clearly, however, prudent journalists will know that most often the judgment of "actual malice" rests with juries. In their own self-interest, reporters will report and editors will edit carefully and responsibly. The ethical journalist will do so because that is the right course, not necessarily because doing so offers self-protection.

The stewardship involved in the responsible exercise of the First Amendment often puts to difficult tests the competence, consistency of news judgment, and wisdom of the most prestigious newsrooms. Such appeared to be the case in the *Washington Post*'s attempt to show that William Tavoulareas, president of Mobil Oil Co., used his corporate influence to "set up" his son Peter, then twenty-five years old, in the shipping business. The stories, which brought a $2 million libel jury judgment against the *Post*, could be taken as implying that Tavoulareas had somehow broken the law. The *Post*'s own extensive coverage of the trial and extensive commentary on the proceedings brought to light several facts that ultimately made jurors question the *Post*'s judgment in the case, even though its widely respected executive editor, Benjamin Bradlee, called it "a textbook case of how a responsible newspaper should act."[25]

In 1974, after the Arab oil embargo, Mobil anticipated that Saudi Arabia would begin giving preference to Saudi ships in the movement of Saudi oil and would extend more generous financing to such ships. Thus Mobil formed the Saudi Maritime Co., Samarco, with Saudi interests as partners, to benefit from preferred treatment (although the preference never materialized). Atlas Maritime Co., a management firm, was formed to actually manage the affairs of Samarco. To head Atlas, Mobil and the senior Tavoulareas recruited George D. Comnas, formerly a veteran Exxon executive and then managing director and board chairman of a Greek shipping firm, a firm that employed the younger Tavoulareas. Peter Tavoulareas became a partner in Atlas, and a millionaire in the process. Federal law does not forbid companies with relatives in such situations from transacting business with one another. But companies from both without and within must guard against favoritism. And Mobil chairman Rawleigh Warner, Jr., as the *Post* reported, assured stockholders the senior Tavoulareas did not participate in "any decisions" in the business between Mobil and Atlas.

In its initial story,[26] the *Post* reported that the Securities and Exchange Commission had reopened an investigation of the Mobil/Atlas ties. It also quoted "a source close to the Tavoulareas family and those familiar with the formation of Atlas" as saying the senior Tavoulareas was involved in a number of decisions affecting Atlas, including the inclusion of his son as an equity partner. The initial *Post* story also included Tavoulareas's denial that he had urged his son's inclusion.

Although there were other issues in the libel trial, the question of whether Peter Tavoulareas was "set up"—to use the arguably loaded words of the *Post*'s headline—turned out to be central. But the *Post* appeared to be hurt even more by the fact that, as three jurors told the newspaper after the trial,[27] the newspaper's key source on Atlas business dealings, George Comnas, was not called to testify.

Other developments appeared to detract from the *Post*'s case. These included the SEC's decision, after an eighteen-month investigation, to take no action against the Mobil/Atlas relationship,[28] and a memorandum in which a *Post* copy editor, Cass Peterson, said that although she was impressed by the scope of research by *Post* reporter Patrick Tyler, she was "still left with an overwhelming sense of So What? . . . It's impossible to believe that Tavoulareas alone could put together such a scheme for the sake of his son's business career, or that he wanted to."[29] Additional harm was done by the testimony of Sandy Golden, a freelance writer who tipped the *Post* to parts of the Tavoulareas story, that Tyler had once said, "It's not every day you knock off one of the Seven Sisters," a reference to Mobil's place among the top seven international oil companies.[30] Golden said Tyler once suggested it would be neat to have a disaffected in-law "rifle" Tavoulareas's safe—a remark Tyler said was facetious. There was also testimony that Peter Stockton, a house subcommittee investigator, gave the *Post* a summary of Comnas's statement to the subcommittee in return for "some publicity"[31] and an agreement by Tyler to highlight the views of Stockton's boss, Representative John Dingell, D-Mich., in a separate story. Finally, it was dislosed that despite many past efforts to reach Tavoulareas for comment directly, the *Post* reporter had failed to try to reach him in writing the second Tavoulareas story. It had quoted a letter by Representative Dingell to the SEC that said that William Tavoulareas may have given "false and misleading statements" to federal investigators in 1977 when questioned about Atlas.[32]

Washington Post attorney Irving Younger was able not only to show extensive involvement in Atlas's affairs by William Tavoulareas but to raise serious questions about the propriety of the Atlas arrangement by two Mobil directors and a former Mobil executive.[33] Then William Tavoulareas himself took the stand and said Comnas was the initial source of the idea that Peter take an equity share of Atlas. The senior Tavoulareas did admit that Peter's inclusion probably was an effort by Comnas to curry favor with him. But these revelations were not enough to persuade the jury. The counter evidence, as *Newsweek* magazine suggested, "may have given the impression of something less than a dispassionate search after truth"[34] by the *Post*. On the other hand, many attorneys thought that the *Post* had taken great pains to obtain what Bob Woodward, one of the *Post* editors on the story, called "the best obtainable version of the truth."[35] There was surprise that William Tavoulareas, whom Judge Oliver Gasch ruled to be a "public figure," could be found to have been libeled by the *Post*, which appealed the case. Gasch overturned the jury's decision. Some took this as a complete vindication of the *Post*.

However, C. T. Hanson, a contributing editor of the *Columbia Journalism Review,* found the Tavoulareas stories to be exceptions to the *Post*'s "frequent, generally admirable exposés of official misdeeds." Although Hanson acknowledged the stories represented a legitimate attempt to scrutinize big business as carefully as the *Post* has investigated big government, there were three problems: "(1) it turned out that the evidence that Peter had been set up by his father was far from conclusive; (2) the suggestions of illegality turned out to be tenuous or unfounded; and (3) the articles did not make clear how the public or Mobil's 270,000 shareholders had been hurt, if at all."[36] In another trenchant interpretation of the proceedings, Steven Brill, writing in the *American Lawyer,* blamed the surprising result on the jury's failure to understand the judge's instructions concerning "actual malice," and on a would-be lawyer jury foreman who stubbornly took the plaintiff's side. "More than that," Brill wrote, "it's a story of why the courthouse is a bad place to resolve questions of journalistic fairness, especially when the judge fails to focus issues for the jury and when defense counsel brilliantly masters his case but makes enough mistakes of language and strategy that he performs as if he were lecturing to lawyers rather than to a group of five white and blue-collar working people and a foreman who thinks he's a lawyer with clients, the Tavoulareases, to acquit."[37]

Tavoulareas himself took to the stump to answer critics of the decision in a 1982 speech to the Society of Professional Journalists/Sigma Delta Chi. He dismissed as "nonsense" the suggestion that the verdict represented "an attack on all journalists' ability to carry out their responsibilities," and concluded: "If leaders in journalism continue to demand virtual immunity for irresponsible reporting, if they continue to refuse to condemn the practices which have caused the reduction of the media's credibility with the public, and if they refuse to consider a process for developing voluntary standards of behavior, then the day will come when the press will no longer be free."[38]

Although it is easier to second-guess than to perform without error in the goldfish bowl of a prestigious national newspaper, no doubt the *Post* itself could wish in retrospect that the public could have seen its reporters and editors as they saw themselves in the Tavoulareas case— as diligent stewards of the rights of free expression. On April 9, 1985, a divided three-judge U.S. Court of Appeals panel reinstated the jury's verdict against the *Post,* only to have a full appeals court vacate that opinion pending further argument. Appeal of the case continued.[39] However, the *Post* might never have had to fight the expensive legal battle at all had its reporters and editors exercised greater prudence and sensitivity in gathering and presenting the story.

Although individual libel cases with larger awards to plaintiffs have been highly visible in recent years, another category of cases—disputes over confidential sources—has had a greater impact on the relationship between the media and law enforcement. The decade began with a close, five to four, Supreme Court decision, *Branzburg* vs. *Hayes,*[40] holding that a journalist may not use the First Amendment to refuse to give a Grand Jury information sought for a criminal prosecution. In

1978, in another key case, the Supreme Court let stand a contempt conviction that had sent *New York Times* reporter Myron Farber to jail for forty days for refusing to turn over his notes in the murder trial of a New Jersey doctor who had been indicted, in part, as a result of a series of articles written by Farber.[41] The New Jersey Supreme Court, whose decision against Farber the *Times* appealed, ruled in essence that the Sixth Amendment to the U.S. Constitution, which assures a fair trial and compulsory access to evidence, should prevail. The state court rejected the *Times*'s invocation of the First Amendment argument and said it had no obligation to weigh or to balance the societal interests represented in the two constitutional amendments, adding: "The obligation to appear at a criminal trial on behalf of a defendant who is enforcing his Sixth Amendment rights is at least as compelling as the duty to appear before a grand jury."[42]

However reluctant the New Jersey court to balance between the First and Sixth Amendment, members of the Supreme Court have actively resorted to a form of balancing in judging the media's claims under the First Amendment. In doing so, they have in certain circumstances attempted to weigh society's interest in the proper working of the judicial system against the press's obligation to serve the public through a steady flow of the news its readers need to judge public affairs. True, the court's majority opinion in the Branzburg case struck down any claim to an absolute privilege by a reporter not to testify. But in a concurring opinion that provided the decisive vote in the Branzburg case, Justice Lewis Powell made clear that the court's intention is that "no harassment of newsmen will be tolerated." He asserted:

> If a newsman believes that the grand jury investigation is not being conducted in good faith, he is not without remedy. Indeed, if the newsman is called upon to give information bearing only a remote and tenuous relationship to the subject of the investigation, or if he has some other reason to believe that his testimony implicates confidential source relationships without a legitimate need of law enforcement, he will have access to the court on a motion to quash and an appropriate protective order may be entered. The asserted claim to privilege should be judged on its facts by the striking of a proper balance between freedom of the press and the obligation of all citizens to give relevant testimony with respect to criminal conduct. The balance of these vital constitutional and societal interests on a case-by-case basis accords with the tried and traditional way of adjudicating such questions.[43]

When translated into reporter privilege statutes in twenty-six of the states, and especially into case law decisions, this balancing has generally meant that a government must persuade individual courts that it has a "compelling need" for the reporter's information, that the information goes to the heart of the case, that a reasonable effort has been made to obtain it elsewhere but that there are no alternative means to obtain it "less destructive of the First Amendment rights."[44]

An empirical analysis of 129 subpoena cases reported in two major journals from 1977 through 1980 showed that state courts upheld subpoena requests in almost six of ten cases, compared to almost four of ten cases in the federal courts. Reporters were forced to testify in 58 percent of the criminal and 43 percent of the civil cases. State shield laws figured in only 6 percent of the 129 cases, a fact which seems to suggest, in the opinion of researcher Achal Mahra, that these state laws have been "ineffectual."[45] Most judgments in privilege cases are made at the lower court level, and most of these were upheld when appealed. However, of the fourteen lower court cases that were reversed on appeal, twelve were decided in favor of the journalists.[46]

The status of the law and the cumulative experience under it can at best provide only a general framework for a journalist's ethical stance in specific cases. Because intricate sifting of the factual context is extremely important in ethical judgments, the reporter's privilege cases are especially difficult inasmuch as journalistic secrecy prevents access to facts needed in ethical dialogue. However, that does not preclude a close consideration of the general issue.

A steward of free expression in a democratic society benefits from a rule of law and a system of formal justice that uphold and protect free expression. A steward will recognize that the court system will not always decide in his or her favor. Until or unless it becomes fundamentally destructive of free expression, prudence will dictate that he or she abide by the court and/or accept its penalties with whatever grace can be mustered. That is what Myron Farber and the *New York Times* did.

But such a summary observation begs the question of how a reporter should behave to honor his own obligations as a citizen and yet to minimize court interference with free expression. First, confidential sources can be used without identifying them as such in a published or broadcast story. That happens when the confidential source is used to lead the reporter to a source or a document that *can* be publicly quoted or identified. This is the most frequent and legitimate use of a so-called confidential source. Often it can forestall fishing expeditions by prosecuting attorneys, or by defense attorneys hoping for a mistrial on grounds that a client has been denied evidence by a balky reporter.

Second, not all relationships with confidential sources need result in absolute pledges of confidentiality. Bruce Locklin, an investigative reporter for the *Bergen* (N.J.) *Record,* asks his sources to sign affidavits that stipulate that the source's name "won't be in the resulting article, but that the source may be disclosed in the event of subsequent litigation."[47] Bob Greene, assistant managing editor of *Newsday,* will return to a source to whom confidentiality has been pledged and ask for permission to disclose it in court. If granted, he will give the name. Greene estimates that 60 percent of his sources will agree to go public if Greene finds himself at risk of going to jail.[48] For those who refuse to go public under any circumstances, Greene will "go all the way," protecting their confidentiality. However, the device of conditional confidentiality is another way to minimize costly court fights and reporter jail terms, to say nothing of the public ill will often generated by a refusal to testify.

Third, reporters can minimize interference with free expression by being ethical in their dealings with news sources and the public. That seemingly "Sunday schoolish" injunction is the advice of a respected law professor, G. Robert Blakey of Notre Dame University, who traces some of the anti-media trend in court decisions of the 1970s to judicial reaction to "loosey goosey" investigative reporting of the Watergate era. Before an audience of investigative reporters, Blakey outlined those decisions and declared:

> If you want the law to develop in this area where it gives you a broad definition of malice, a broad definition of public official, and a broad definition of public figure . . . and of qualified privilege, you have to do three things. You have to be accurate. You have to be fair. And you have to be trustworthy. And you have to be perceived as being those three things by the legal community, the political community. If you continue to be perceived as being inaccurate, unfair, and untrustworthy, this law is going to continue to develop in ways you will find it difficult to do the job that I think you ought to be doing."[49]

Finally, however, there are circumstances when a reporter must rely on a confidential source and accept the ultimate penalty, jail, for honoring a promise. The statement of principles of the American Society of Newspaper Editors states: "Pledges of confidentiality to news sources must be honored at all costs, and therefore should not be given lightly. Unless there is clear and pressing need to maintain confidences, sources of information should be identified."

There are similar statements in most other codes, such as those of the Society of Professional Journalists/Sigma Delta Chi, the American Newspaper Guild, and the Associated Press Managing Editors. It is widely, and correctly, believed that unless reporters are willing to go to jail to protect confidences, the flow of information to the public on vital public questions will dry up. The minority in the Branzburg case declared, in fact, that would be the result of that 1972 decision. Wrote Justice Potter Stewart:

> After today's decision, the potential informant can never be sure that his identity or off-the-record communications will not subsequently be revealed through the compelled testimony of a newsman. A public-spirited person inside government, who is not implicated in any crime, will now be fearful of revealing corruption or other governmental wrongdoing because he will now know he can subsequently be identified by use of compulsory process. The potential source must, therefore, choose between risking exposure by giving information or avoiding the risk by remaining silent.[50]

The experience of Myron Farber and others sent to jail would seem to signal that the risk to a source may be less than Justice Stewart implied. And the experience of Greene would indicate that pledges of conditional confidentiality are not unworkable. To summarize, a defensible posture would then be to aggressively avoid pledges of confidentiality unless forced to by the tests of "no other way" and "compelling public urgency." Even then, consideration should be given to a possible need for the information as well as the identity of a source to assure an individual's fair trial. When such is the case, try to give only a pledge of conditional confidentiality. Pledge absolute confidentiality only in those cases in which the resulting news story clearly and unequivocally serves ends such as freedom and justice which are protected by the social contract. A willingness to go to jail is likely to be a sound test of the ethics of such a judgment.

Perhaps the oldest and most pervasive issue that fuses ethical and legal questions is the controversy over how especially newsworthy trials can be open without restriction to the news media and still preserve the fairness guaranteed by the constitution. Because the issue involves a dispute over two constitutional rights, it is not one likely to be settled permanently, as its long history makes clear. For example, the 1935 trial of Bruno Richard Hauptmann for the kidnapping and murder of the infant son of Colonel and Mrs. Charles A. Lindbergh marked what journalist John Lofton called one of the "most mercilessly publicized crimes of the century."[51] There seemed little doubt to the close observers of the spectacle that its outcome was influenced by the saturation coverage before and during the trial. The latter generated eleven million words over the news wires.[52] There were many subsequent sensations which received considerable coverage. But it was not until 1961, in *Irvin* vs. *Dowd,* that the U.S. Supreme Court declared for the first time that a lower court conviction should be reversed on grounds of prejudicial publicity.[53] In one newspaper alone, the *Evansville Courier,* twenty-five of fifty-nine pre-trial stories written after the arrest of Leslie Irvin, an ex-convict, mentioned his confession of six murders.[54] Said Justice Tom Clark, in reversing his conviction: "With his life at stake, it is not requiring too much that the petitioner be tried in an atmosphere undisturbed by so huge a wave of public passion and by a jury other than one in which two-thirds of the members admit, before hearing any testimony, to possessing a belief in his guilt."[55] In a similar decision the very next year, the Supreme Court said the Louisiana high court erred in declining to give its blessing to a change of venue ordered to counteract prejudicial publicity. News coverage, the court ruled, had "fatally infected" the trial of Wilbert Rideau, charged with kidnapping, robbery, and murder.[56] In 1965, the swindling conviction of Billie Sol Estes was overturned by the Supreme Court in a five to four ruling that in effect held that live television stripped the infamous Texas operator of his rights to a fair trial.

It was against this background of increasing concern for the Sixth Amendment rights of individuals that the Supreme Court in 1966 decided the case of Dr. Sam Sheppard, the Cleveland society dentist accused of murdering his wife in 1954. The pre-trial and trial coverage included many items not admitted or documented on the witness stand. Among these were accusations that Sheppard had deliberately obstructed the murder investigation, that he had lied under oath, that he was sexually promiscuous, and that Sheppard had been named as the father of a child of a woman convict. The court placed heavy emphasis on the available powers, unexercised by lower courts in the Sheppard case, to protect individuals from invasions of their constitutional right to a fair trial.[57]

The judicial fat was in the fire. The American Bar Association by 1968 had formally adopted the so-called Reardon Report. Based on the work of a commission of lawyers and judges headed by Justice Paul C. Reardon of the Supreme Judicial Court of Massachusetts, it set forth specific types of information that should not be released before and during trials. Newspaper editors, publishers, and radio-TV executives protested, and months of acrimonious debate ensued.[58] The voluntary nature of the guidelines seemed not, in itself, to solve the problem. In fact, their volitional nature ensures that ethics and professional judgment will be as important as judicial mandates in the free press versus fair trial controversy.

Indeed, the judicial mandates of the years immediately following the ABA's adoption of the Reardon Report kept both jurists and ethicists more than fully occupied. In 1976 a Nebraska judge, acting under the pressure of a trial involving gruesome family murders and sexual assaults, ordered members of the media and others who had attended a pre-trial hearing not to report anything they had heard about the accused, Erwin Charles Simants. He likewise ordered them to obey the supposedly voluntary Nebraska Bar-Press Guidelines. The Nebraska Supreme Court eschewed enforcement of the guidelines but backed the court-ordered suppression of any reports by the media of confessions or admissions made to police. Later, the U.S. Supreme Court overturned that court order as prior censorship. However, as the National News Council noted, "the entire experience convinced many in the press that there was danger in pursuing cooperative efforts with bench and bar for the mutual exercise of self-restraint."[59]

The skepticism was compounded in 1978 when the Supreme Court, in an ambiguous five to four decision in which there were five written opinions, upheld the closing of a pre-trial hearing on a motion to suppress confessions allegedly given involuntarily by suspects charged with second-degree murder. In its appeal, ultimately denied by the Supreme Court, the Gannett Company claimed an independent right of the media for access to pre-trial proceedings under the First, Sixth, and Fourteenth Amendments.[60] The predictable media anger at the decision may have been less important, in the long run, than the judicial response to it. Within fifty-two weeks of the decision in *Gannett* vs. *DePasquale,* judges sought to close court proceedings in thirteen federal courts and 259 state courts involving a total of 272 cases. A study by the Reporters Committee on Freedom of the Press showed that fifty-eight of the cases involved trials and post-trial actions—and thirty-eight of the fifty-eight were actually closed,[61] even though Gannett had dealt only with pre-trial proceedings.

This serious misreading by the lower courts of the Supreme Court ruling in the *Gannett* vs. *DePasquale* case was largely responsible for the Supreme Court's action in the landmark case of *Richmond Newspapers, Inc.* vs. *Virginia.* Although the high court did not reverse Gannett, it did insist that the previous ruling applied only to pre-trial proceedings. Writing for the majority, Chief Justice Warren Burger asserted that trials were a type of public forum which the public and the media were entitled to witness, discuss, and report under the First Amendment. Stopping short of establishing a First Amendment "right of access" across the board, he nonetheless identified the public trial as a type of proceeding to which the public should be given access. He said that just as a government may impose reasonable time, place, and manner restrictions upon the use of its streets in the interests of such

objectives as the free flow of traffic, so may a trial judge, in the interest
of the fair administration of justice, impose reasonable limitations on
access to a trial."[62] But these limitations, the chief justice said, cannot
deny or "unwarrantedly abridge . . . the opportunities for the communication of thought and the discussion of public questions imme-
morially associated with resort to public places."[63] Only a vigorous
exercise of stewardship made such a protective ruling possible. In short,
freedom of expression can only survive in a society in which the
capacity for ethical commitment is abundant and alive.

The tension evident in the relationship of the news media to the court
system is mirrored in John Rawls's statement of the two principles of
justice for institutions. "Each person," under the first principle, "is to
have an equal right to the most extensive total system of equal basic
liberties compatible with a similar system of liberty for all." In Rawls's
schema, "liberty can be restricted only for the sake of liberty." In cases
of restrictions, there are two conditions: "(a) a less extensive liberty
must strengthen the total system of liberty shared by all; (b) a less than
equal liberty must be acceptable to those with the lesser liberty."[64]

These portions of Rawls's theory, at a minimum, have the virtue of
providing a sharp focus for discussing the ethics involved in the press/
bar debate. If the liberty of the press is restricted, does the restriction,
in fact, "strengthen the system of liberty shared by all?" If a reporter's
refusal to testify is honored by a court in a specific case, and another
citizen's similar request is denied, on what grounds can this "less than
equal liberty" be acceptable to the public? The questions call for
evidence, debate, and dialogue. To take a specific instance, the Supreme
Court in *New York Times* vs. *Sullivan* set as a general rule that public
officials could not collect for libel unless it could be proved that the
news media knowingly printed or broadcast a falsehood or acted with
reckless disregard for the truth of a story. Despite significant later
qualifications by the courts of this holding, it still provides a measure of
protection for the news media which other segments of society, without
benefit of owning a newspaper or broadcast station, do not enjoy. It is
an advantage underlined by the constitutional protection given the
press, the only such private institution so "constituted."

If this constitutional protection given the press, is meant for all, as
many media codes of ethics stipulate, then Rawls's second principle of
justice acquires a special force. It states that social and economic
inequalities "are to be arranged so that they are both: (a) to the greatest
benefit of the least advantaged . . . and (b) attached to offices and
positions open to all under conditions of fair equality of opportunity."[65]

Do the news media's special powers and constitutional protection work for the least advantaged? Do all have equal opportunities to compete for positions of leadership in the news media? These questions, too, call for evidence, debate, and dialogue. They call for a tradition of media criticism that itself is open to all and nurtured with "freedom and justice for all" in mind.

CHAPTER ELEVEN

Social Science and Journalism Ethics

Just as the vital organs of a living creature are not all visible to the naked eye, so the dynamics of ethical life are not all separately and simultaneously evident to the student of ethics. And just as the anatomist declares the unity of an animal even while he dissects and classifies, so must an ethicist attempt to show the whole of the subject even while identifying its separate, dynamic, and interactive elements.

This chapter depicts one person's version of key building blocks for ethics in journalism. The normative model is that of a five-stranded spiral, a quinate helix. Each of the strands is a dynamic process, related to the others. Although most of the material in each of the strands has appeared in previous chapters, the new material will be presented such that it serves basically to tie together the old. The attempt is not to reify a model, but to unify the related ideas of previous chapters while setting forth the work of scholars whose findings help congeal the model.

THE DEVELOPMENT OF MORAL REASONING

This first process, although only alluded to earlier, is fundamental. While classical ethics has contributed little to understanding the steps by which humans develop ethical capacity, modern psychology has contributed much.

The moral development psychologist whose work has commanded by far the most attention is Lawrence Kohlberg, who for a quarter of a century has been relentlessly building on ideas first developed in his doctoral dissertation at the University of Chicago in 1958. Influenced heavily by child psychologist Jean Piaget, Kohlberg defined moral growth in stages.[1] To Kohlberg, the stages represent not increases in the volume of cognitive learning but qualitatively different ways of thinking about right and wrong. Kohlberg says his data, based largely on interviewee reactions to structured questionnaires, show the stages to be invariantly sequenced or ordered. Each stage successfully absorbs and puts to work the cognitive experience of its predecessor.

Kohlberg's first stage corresponds to an egocentric posture. Rules are followed to avert punishment by authorities. Stage 1 persons hardly differentiate between their own and authority's perspective, so complete is their orientation to obedience. Stage 2 persons differentiate their own from others' interests; "doing right" is a system of reciprocity in which their own self-interest is thereby protected. Each person has a right to pursue his or her own interests, and rules are meant to govern concrete conflicts.

In Stage 3 the awareness of others remains concrete rather than abstract, but there develops an ideal of walking in the other person's shoes. The desire to act and to be seen as acting, in this spirit, is strong. Rules and authority figures are looked to for guidance. Stage 4 differs from Stage 3 in the systemic view of rules and of the authority figures that make, abide by, and mediate those rules. To a Stage 4 person, adherence to rules accounts for the coherence of society itself. Conscience demands that one meet obligations, not merely satisfy the need to win approval of authorities.

Stage 5 represents the individual's entry into a "post-conventional" or principled mode of moral reasoning. Rather than merely mechanistic rules "holding society together," there is a deeper commitment to a social contract (based on a set of explicit values such as equality, justice, and freedom) that precedes friendships and familial allegiances. Calculations of what is best for society are based on "the greatest good for the greatest number." Persons at Stage 5 are keenly aware of and feel the tensions between legal and moral perspectives. In Stage 6, the distinguishing characteristic is the preference for individually chosen ethical principles, which are seen as the basis for just laws. The person in Stage 6 has the capacity to be civilly disobedient should laws conflict with principle. There is a strong and personal commitment to rationality and to ethical values that are universal. People are ends, not means, in the perspective of the Stage 6 person.

Kohlberg also postulated a seventh and still higher stage—reachable only after attaining Stage 6, and based on a cosmic, transcendental orientation rather than one devoted to humanistic universals such as justice.[2] In this stage wisdom leads to a view of oneself as an integral part of the cosmos. Although this is clearly a religious perspective, Kohlberg does not specify any particular religion or ethical orientation. Indeed, examples of persons cited as at Stage 7 include Spinoza, a Jewish philosopher; Teilhard de Chardin, a Jesuit paleontologist; Martin Luther King, the civil rights leader; and John Dewey, an apostle of pragmatism.

In summary, in Kohlberg's scheme, if a person runs the gamut of moral development, the progression is from an obedience to authority to an internalization of society's rules and, finally, to a state in which the individual freely chooses and commits to principles and values. But he is not saying that all persons at the higher levels will always behave in a correspondingly ethical way. Rather, he is delineating in his stage by stage schema the evolution of a capacity for moral reasoning. And he argues that Stages 5 and 6 *are* higher forms, even if human beings at these stages do not always measure up to their capacities. Kohlberg himself attempts to make clear the subtle distinction:

> To act in a morally high way requires a high stage of moral reasoning. One cannot follow moral principles (stages 5 and 6) if one does not understand or believe in them. One can, however, reason in terms of such principles and not live up to them. A variety of factors determines whether a particular person will live up to his stage of moral reasoning in a particular situation, though moral stage is a good predictor of action in various experimental and naturalistic settings.[3]

Major critical questions have been directed at Kohlberg's work. What makes him so sure that acting from fear of punishment is less moral than acting from an allegiance to abstract principles? And even if his empirical research describes reality accurately, he appears, clearly, to be "inferring an ought from an is," a risky enterprise. Even if Kohlberg's basic idea of the existence of stages is correct, are they necessarily invariant? Isn't moral reality more subtle and variable than he proposes?

Whatever the limitations of Kohlberg's methods or conclusions, his work seems substantial enough to give certain fairly clear messages and challenges to journalists, editors, and journalism educators. First, it is difficult to see how news organizations can be run in a reasonably ethical way with persons below Stage 4 or 5. While no one expects an editor to administer Kohlberg's questionnaires as a personnel screening mechanism, the trained journalistic eye and the sensitive journalistic ear should be committed to spot—certainly on the job, if not in interviews and employment records—the capacity for meeting ethical obligations that transcend self. Second, it is clear that peer standards can be sufficiently strong so as to have a deleterious effect on, say, an editor's effort to upgrade the ethical standards of a newsroom whose members had collectively slipped into a set of shoddy practices. To break the lockstep of ethical mediocrity, a tradition of ethical dialogue in the newsroom might well be not only useful but mandatory. Young reporters need no longer quietly imitate the worst practice of peers if authorities commit themselves to examine ethical choices openly.

Eventually the standard to imitate is not the lowest denominator of peer emulation but the highest denominator of carefully defined policy, policy reviewable in confident and open conversations with superiors and colleagues. Third, if Kohlberg is correct in his assertion that ethical behavior can be taught, then editors and educators have an opportunity rather than a problem on their hands in the current concern over ethics. At a minimum, they need to reflect on what Kohlberg can tell them about how ethical capacity develops.

THE PRACTICE OF CRITICAL THINKING

Except in its most rudimentary forms, journalism requires a capacity for self-detachment, deliberative thought, and reflective scrutiny of events, people, and circumstances. Such critical thinking inheres in the mechanics of serious news work as well as in the ethical and value judgments made in gathering and disseminating news, information, and opinion useful to the citizenry. Although this point may be assumed or asserted with some frequency, it is too seldom demonstrated as fundamental to ethical decision making and moral reasoning in journalism.

There are several attractive definitional schema of critical thinking. One used especially widely is that of educator Benjamin S. Bloom.[4] In his view, cognitive activity scales upward through increasingly complex critical thinking capacities. Bloom and his colleagues identify a hierarchy of capacities, briefly described as follows:

Knowledge: Grasping facts, information, terms, and classifications.
Comprehension: Understanding ideas such that they can be translated and interpreted.
Application: Using concepts and ideas instrumentally.
Analysis: Breaking down a problem in terms of its constituent elements and showing their relationship to one another.
Synthesis: Creation of an article, plan, proposal, or solution with elements organized to meet an objective.
Evaluation: Assessing events, ideas, or phenomena by reference to criteria internal as well as external to those phenomena.

To illustrate Bloom's taxonomy of cognitive skills at work, an episode of journalistic enterprise will be summarized with the taxonomy in mind. The episode was chosen because of the availability of a written account of a reporter's thought processes, because it raised serious ethical questions, and because it is memorable for both its factual content and social and political significance.

On the morning of November 13, 1969, the front pages of thirty-six metropolitan newspapers in the United States headlined a freelanced story about a young American army lieutenant accused of murdering at least 109 Vietnamese civilians during a search-and-destroy mission in a Vietcong village, Mylai. Reporter Seymour M. Hersh had managed to obtain an interview with the accused, Lt. William (Rusty) Calley, and relentlessly pieced together the grim story that won him the 1970 Pulitzer Prize for international reporting.[5]

Tipped by a civilian source, Hersh, a former Pentagon correspondent for the Associated Press, learned the whereabouts of Calley's lawyer, George Latimer, hundreds of miles away in Salt Lake City. Sensing that the matter was too sensitive for a telephone interview, Hersh made an appointment to see Latimer in person. At the time he lacked outside support for his travel expenses (later he obtained a $2,000 grant from the Philip Stern Fund for Investigative Journalism), but the gutsy Hersh flew to Salt Lake anyway, talked with the attorney, promised to confer with him before publishing anything on the case, won his confidence, and was allowed to see the formal court-martial charges against Calley.

Back east again, Hersh continued to pursue his goal of an interview with Calley, at that time under house detention at Fort Benning, Georgia. His legwork included talks with three formal sources: the army's prosecution office, Calley's military-appointed lawyer on base, and a captain into whose custody Calley had initially been entrusted. His conversations with these sources were carefully orchestrated so as to forestall their predictable reactions—attempts to head Hersh off by passing the news of his presence on to a higher authority.

Like the ferret he was and is, Hersh encountered and picked the brains of dozens of soldiers, including a telephone operator, busted a private working as a mail sorter, a sleeping GI, and some of Calley's drinking buddies. Ultimately he succeeded in dining with and interviewing Calley himself and in writing the story. In doing all of this, Hersh clearly demonstrated all the cognitive skills on Bloom's list:

Knowledge.

By discovering an array of contextual facts, from the shockingly high estimate of Vietnam civilians slain to the army's plans for the court martial.

Comprehension.

By his shrewd insights into the psychology of military personnel that allowed him to advance in his pursuit of Calley without hindrance from the army.

Application.

By the exercise of applied imagination, such as (to use one example) locating a telephone number for Calley in the "new listings" section of an old, discarded base telephone directory.

Analysis.

By identifying several conditions the meeting of which would maximize his chance of finding and interviewing Calley. These included winning the trust of Calley's chief civilian lawyer, minimizing the knowledge of his presence on the base, correctly reading the self-interest of the sources involved, and persistence in the face of imperceptible progress.

Synthesis.

By writing a story which verified the dimensions of the Mylai tragedy yet treated evenhandedly not only Calley and his attorneys but also the military lawyers preparing the case against him.

Evaluation.

By determining the existence of conditions that freed him from the strict observance of a journalistic norm against showing a news story to a source (in this case, Latimer) before publication. The result was a factual, truthful account of the army's plans to try an officer on charges of inhumane conduct—in fact, murder of innocent civilians—during war. Explained Hersh:

> This [the reading of a story to a news source] normally is a frowned-upon practice in journalism and rightly so, but I knew two things would impress Latimer: the fact that the story was written objectively (all my years with the Associated Press had given me that ability); and the fact that none of the quotes I had from Calley involved specifics about what he had or had not done that day. To this day, I have not written all that Calley told me; he is entitled to make his own defense at a time of his own choosing.[6]

Interpreted within the framework of principles outlined earlier, Hersh's evaluation of the situation allowed him to acknowledge the principle of humaneness, in securing a news story in which that value was central. He told as much of the truth as he dared, giving due weight to Calley's rights to a just trial. Although he might be accused of risking the loss of his freedom and independence by showing Latimer the story, the central principle of truth telling was better served by that precaution, under the circumstances.

The foregoing account might be criticized on the grounds that it is needlessly self-conscious about matters of thorough, careful reporting, matters which should be self-evident and taken for granted. Yet, as the following critique of another aspect of Hersh's reporting will argue, it is just such an awareness and conscious scrutiny of their work that journalists need.

THE CULTIVATION OF ETHICAL DIALOGUE

If a classical text were needed on which to base the practice of ethical dialogue, none would serve better than Mill's essay *On Liberty*. It speaks clearly to a situation in which full discussion of the rightness or wisdom of a particular journalistic practice is suppressed by management ignorance, fiat, or custom. To silence reporters and editors by any of the foregoing—Mill would argue—is to assume infallibility by whomever makes the ultimate decision, or, worse, to follow the path of least resistance.

A lone reporter or editor may in fact know the best resolution of an ethical dilemma, or he or she may have a portion of the truth, and that portion may be the very part necessary for emergence of the whole truth. Yet the seemingly wisest course needs, itself, to be open to attack: otherwise journalistic conventions (such as the one to which Hersh made an exception) may be allowed to prevail as prejudices. Finally, continuing with the application of Mill, if a truth is held as a prejudice, it might well lose its effect on the character and content of professional behavior. Thus, critical thinking both before, during, and after sensitive journalistic enterprises, is in the spirit of Mill.

To be specific, Hersh's public account of how he broke the Mylai story should have provoked a major discussion of the methods he used to track down Calley at Fort Benning.[7] For example, Hersh at Fort Benning wore a suit and carried a brief case, and traded on the impression he was an attorney or an official. Thus, marching into a mail room where he knew there was a disgruntled, busted private named Jerry with access to information on the whereabouts of Calley, Hersh boldly got what he wanted. He recalled:

> I left my car, motor running, in the parking lot directly in front of [the mail room], grabbed my brief case, straightened my tie, and walked in. "I want to see Jerry outside in my car in two minutes flat," I said crisply and angrily to the first sergeant sitting near by. The sergeant giggled happily (one could hear him thinking: "What has that dumb son of a bitch done now?") and went off. I walked back to my car, and two minutes later Jerry appeared, looking apprehensive. I motioned him inside, and told him

whom and what I wanted. Gee, he was sorry, but he didn't know anything much about Calley. In fact, there was a big batch of undelivered mail waiting for the lieutenant now. The only way Jerry could find out anything would be to steal Calley's personnel file. There was a long pause.

"Well?" I said.

"I'll try, Mister."

In less than five minutes he returned with a short information sheet the battalion commander kept on each officer. The sheet included a local address in Columbus for Calley.[8]

To Hersh's credit, one can note that he never lied about his identity as a journalist when asked, and that he volunteered that identity regularly during his search for Calley. But in some instances, as above, he actively sought to pass for other than a journalist, in short, to deceive without actually verbalizing anything that was factually, demonstrably, deceptive or false. The effect, however, was the same. It would be difficult, using the criteria of a vital and compelling public interest outlined in Chapter 9, to justify the deception. The existence of the Mylai charges had already been verified by Hersh, and it was just a matter of time before his shoe leather at Fort Benning would have paid off without the deception. Perhaps worse, although Hersh did not specifically ask the once-busted private to steal or enter a personnel file without permission, the effect was the same. Considering the unjust stakes for the hapless Jerry were he caught, one cannot but wonder whether Hersh might have been better advised to invest in more shoe leather and straightforward questioning. As it was, Hersh induced Jerry to risk another career penalty. Jerry was a total stranger who owed Hersh nothing and whom Hersh owed, at least, the duty to do no harm.

Sensitivity to ethics has increased in the years since Mylai. One could argue that there is more dialogue on media ethics than ever before. The nation's two nationally circulated magazines of media criticism—*Columbia Journalism Review* and *Washington Journalism Review*—frequently pose questions involving ethics. The networks periodically feature media analysis on programs such as ABC's Viewpoint and CBS's "60 Minutes." Professional journals and the annual meetings of media organizations frequently feature panels and programs on ethics. News organizations, in these journals and at these professional gatherings, are reminded of the advantages of codes of ethics, especially for those who participate in the drafting of them. Certainly the news coverage of major controversies, such as Army General William C. Westmoreland's libel suit against CBS News,[9] the 1983 Tylenol killer tragedy,[10] and the 1984 New Bedford, Massachusetts, gang-rape trial, generated a dialogue of sorts on the ethics of journalism. Yet, much more—and more precise—dialogue is needed, especially within media organizations.

ETHICAL DIALOGUE WITHIN NEWS ORGANIZATIONS

Although the developments listed above are healthy, most of them are general, after-the-fact expressions of ethical concern. Yet only when ethical sensitivity filters naturally into the workaday world of journalism will standards be raised. For example, the New Bedford gang-rape trial began sizzling on the ethical griddle because of carelessness rather than calculated concern for ethics. The issue was the ignoring of the traditional ban on the disclosure of the names of rape victims. A pool electronic news camera simply broadcast the proceedings to four outlets, including the national Cable News Network, while the judge assumed, incorrectly, that equipment was on hand to "bleep out" the victim's name. Although the bench and bar can assume some of the responsibility for the gaffe, the news media's culpability is clear. "As it happened," wrote the *Hartford Courant*'s Bruce DeSilva, "the naming of the alleged victim . . . came about with virtually no thought of the consequences."[11]

Other lapses both less and more widely known make the point as tellingly:

- Two *Los Angeles Times* reporters almost found themselves in contempt of court after being caught trying to listen to a closed-door San Diego court proceeding. The newspaper apologized and the judge took no further action.[12]
- The *Honolulu Advertiser* suspended a freelance columnist who testified he took $500 in return for a favorable article on the dairy industry.[13]
- R. Foster Winans, once author of the *Wall Street Journal*'s "Heard on the Street" column, lost his job and ran crosswise with the law after it was disclosed he held interests in the stocks discussed in his column.[14]
- Even though the gossip columnist for the *Boston Herald* said it happened, former President Carter was not refused seating by an elite Boston restaurant for failing to wear a coat and tie.[15]

It is worth noting that these journalistic sins, of admittedly varying gravity, were identified and published, along with scholarly accounts of other ethical issues, by the Society of Professional Journalists/Sigma Delta Chi in a special 1984 report on ethics. That in itself is a barometer of increased ethical sensitivity. Yet, the breadth and nature of the offenses indicate that much more needs to be done, and at a deeper level. This was what Louis D. Boccardi, executive vice-president of the Associated Press, seemed to have in mind in reminding editors they could no longer account for widespead public disaffection with the news media merely by reiterating the public's propensity, psychologically, to slay the messenger that brings bad news. Noting the pervasive influence of the news media in society, Boccardi urged that journalists reexamine "those things that we know are at the heart of this issue of public support of our role and see whether there is a message we can safely heed." Getting down to cases, Boccardi said:

> It is no longer enough for us all to busy ourselves with defenses of the status quo. Yes, when a judge threatens to throw us out of a courtroom, we should fight like hell. We belong there. But do grand jury minutes or leaked indictments belong in our news columns? I think not, but there they appear.
>
> When American mothers and fathers learn of the death of their Marine son, their grief is part of the story. It is part of the nation's agony, and we must tell it. But must we be at their side with our camera when the marine major breaks the news? I think not, but we are.
>
> When the whistleblower turns to us to expose government wrong-doing but demands anonymity, we should welcome him or her and expose. But should we let high officials use our news columns to argue anonymously for their policies or to attack their political foes? I think not, but we do.
>
> Do we delight in sometimes petty investigative stories while more fundamental issues go under-reported? Not always, of course, but too often.
>
> When human error lets an inaccuracy slip into our stories, what else can we do except correct it as soon as we know? But must our credibility forever be hostage to small errors that loom large to those few readers who themselves know the facts of the case? I think not.
>
> When a reader complains about too much bad news, do we dismiss the thought as a dreamer's longing for a world that is not? Or should we not reexamine standards which, on some days, seem to foreclose from our audiences any suggestion that anything, anywhere is being done right by anybody? The question is not an idle one about sugar coating reality. It is a question that challenges our ability to make our news products reflect the world of our reader's experience.[16]

Not everyone will agree with all of Boccardi's points, or the priorities he may seem to have on issues in the field. Nor is it obvious what specific practices might best remedy the offenses Boccardi and others articulate as they preserve their own integrity as journalists while at press. What does seem apparent is that the ethical dialogue mounting throughout the profession at large needs to be cultivated and focused closer to home, in news organizations.

One of the first to have developed this insight was Philip Meyer, former Washington correspondent and corporate executive with Knight-Ridder newspapers, now William Rand Kenan, Jr., professor of journalism at the University of North Carolina School of Journalism. After a wide-ranging survey research project conducted at the request of the Ethics Committee of the American Society of Newspaper Editors, Meyer, among other things, attempted to identify "an ethically efficient news operation." He concluded that it is one which provides "an environment where decision makers have the time, the support, and the emotional capital to discover what they really value."[17] Using a definition of ethics offered by Wayne A.R. Leys, Meyer said the ethically efficient news operation will be one that allows and supports its decision makers as they "straighten out the relationship between what is valued for its own sake and what is not." More specifically, Meyer said an ethically efficient newspaper might show:

1. Some degree of freedom from knee-jerk responses. People who always follow the conventional rule may think they are being ethical when in fact they are being thoughtless.

2. Mutual respect between editor and publisher. If the newspaper is ethically efficient, the editor and publisher will know it, and they will like each other for it.

3. High staff morale. News people are in this business for psychic income as much as any other kind. Nothing can destroy morale as much as a perception that the place is being run without regard for moral values.[18]

In another study related to the ethics of journalists, conducted at the Indiana University School of Journalism with a Gannett Foundation grant, a cross section of the country's journalists was asked which of the various sources listed below had had a significant influence on the development of their own ethics. Their responses, part of a broader study by the School's Bureau of Media Research,[19] were as follows:

Source of Significant Influence	Percentage of Respondents
Day-by-day newsroom learning	88.3
Family upbringing	72.3
Senior editor	60.8
Peers	56.5
Journalism teachers	53.2

Senior reporters	51.9
University teachers	49.5
Religious training	34.7
Publishers/general managers	24.6
High school teachers	24.0

Clearly, to be effective, ethical dialogue must include the members of the newsroom and take account of the newsroom's day-by-day encounters with issues of principle and value.

THE SHARPENING OF ETHICAL DIALOGUE

To sharpen ethical dialogue in the profession at large and within news organizations is to make clear how ethical reasons affect journalists' choices and behavior.[20] Sharp ethical dialogue seeks to:

- Identify the principles(s) and/or probable consequences considered and how they are weighted in reaching a decision.
- Assess the stakes of the parties affected by ethical choice: sources, public, the journalists involved, peers, and the profession at large.
- Minimize the chance that choices are based on mere personal impression, style, or whim.
- Show, in cases of conflicting principles or ambiguous forecasts of consequences, what values guide ethical choice.
- Create, in truly major cases, a record on which others can draw and reflect, so as to make the benefits of dialogue cumulative.

Because commentators at present seldom have access to the full range of facts and intentionality of the sources and to decision makers, case studies in ethics done retrospectively can only rarely satisfy most or all of the above. However, Hersh's article on how he broke the Mylai story comes close, and is invoked again to illustrate the points just made. Journalism needs more such richly detailed accounts.

The Mylai massacre represented a frightful violation of the principle of humaneness. To tell as much of the truth as was then available about that violation, and to make sure at the same time that the accused Lieutenant Calley would be treated justly, required extraordinary care by a journalist. More than a mere set of court-martial papers needed to be inspected. Calley needed to be found and interviewed.

In acting on that judgment, Hersh used many standard reportorial techniques and several ingenious ones. Passive deception, allowing persons on the military base to make their own most natural inference as to his identity, could be defended so long as it did no avoidable harm—that is, so long as it did not risk injustice or unfairness to innocents caught up in Hersh's quest for Calley. It can be argued that Hersh allowed his key source, Jerry, to make his own decision to obtain Calley's file. But, in fact, Hersh appears to have actively created a situation in which Jerry, already a busted private, risked further penalty to himself unless he cooperated. Having made an authoritative entrance demanding Jerry's presence, Hersh met with Jerry outside, "and told him whom and what I wanted."

On another point of principle, Hersh appears to have made a justifiable exception to a journalistic norm meant to protect reportorial freedom and independence. He agreed to check back with Calley's attorney, Georger Latimer. In fact, in a move that some might see as compromising his independence, Hersh read his story to Latimer before publication. "Latimer made one helpful addition to my story and, most importantly, stood behind it when the inevitable flood of newspaper calls came the next day," Hersh wrote.[21] Hersh not only had confidence in his own experience and ability to write a fair, accurate, and thorough story, he knew that he had the ability and fortitude not to alter the story in such a way as to compromise its integrity. Not showing a source a story is a rule of procedure, not a principle in itself; it is an operating norm meant to preserve and respect a principle. In truly exceptional circumstances—and the need to let the American public know that one of its army officers had been accused of mass murder was precisely such an exceptional circumstance—the norm could be waived. It could be waived because its substance was protected by Hersh's knowledge of the subject and his experience. The rule against allowing a source to read a story in advance is a good one because it recognizes that journalists must retain control of their work. Hersh maintained control, even though—and perhaps because—he did check back with Latimer. By contrast, such could not have been safely said about the neophyte college newspaper reporter, discussed in Chapter 4, who was sent to interview a distinguished academic whose specialty was totally unfamiliar to the reporter.

As defined earlier, a principle is a form of value, a guide that is not only prized in itself but also affects behavior. Sometimes, in fact—uncomfortably all too often—principles may appear to conflict, as did truth telling and independence in the vignette cited above. Hersh, in his retrospective account, wanted to tell as much of the truth about the Mylai massacre as he could. Moreover, unlike other journalists, Hersh elaborated, retrospectively, on his motivation for truth telling: "I hated the war in Vietnam and knew that the full story of its nature was not known to most Americans."[22] In one version, Hersh chose to value truth telling more than the principle of independence. By another interpretation, Hersh valued truth telling and observed the substance, if not the customary form, of independence.

In a narrow sense, it might be said that Hersh's justification of showing Latimer his story in advance indicates a "relativity" in the application of ethical principles. However, that term can be pernicious and pejorative in its implications. It is an accurate enough term if one means that, as in the foregoing example, a reporter should search to see if there are objective conditions that can genuinely justify an exception to a rule. It is inaccurate if it is meant to imply carelessness, subjectivity, or purely personal preference in decision making. In a very helpful discussion of values, Richard Morrill, president of Centre College in Danville, Kentucky, writes:

> Values give rise to those patterns of choice through which human beings are enabled to solve problems, to avoid impasses and impossible situations, and to create an open future. Values, then, are an expression of complementarity that can pertain between human conduct and the world. If there is a real world, then values are objective.[23]

It is well to note that having values and engaging in dialogue do not themselves guarantee ethical behavior, any more than the capacity for certain forms of rationality in moral reasoning, as highlighted by Kohlberg, does. As Morrill writes: "Even though a value marks a direction and sets real limits, it is best understood as inspiring conduct without determining all the particulars.[24] It seems logical to suppose that a news organization which stresses values—through its code, by rational dialogue, and by the exemplary behavior of its leaders—stands a better chance of encouraging ethical behavior by employees.

But journalistic leaders cannot themselves persuade practitioners to give fealty to a code, to discuss ethics sincerely, and behave ethically. It must come from the making of commitments by individuals. Few scholars have better understood the dynamics of the process of making commitments than William G. Perry, Jr., former professor of education and director of the Bureau of Study Counsel at Harvard University. His development "scheme" will be illustrated in a hypothetical journalistic context and its implications examined and critiqued.

Concerned in the 1950s that they should understand the similarities and differences of the personal development of Harvard students, Perry and his colleagues developed a study which systematically examined "the ways in which they [students] construed the nature of knowledge, the origin of values, the intentions of their instructors, and their own responsibilities."[25] It was a study of maturation but, more particularly, of intellectual and ethical development in young adulthood. Since many journalists are college-educated young adults, the potential relevance of Perry's scheme to journalism is clear.

Although the Harvard students of that era were no doubt a more homogeneous and certainly a more cognitively advanced group than the general population, the developmental scheme Perry conceived has shown remarkable usefulness to later generations.[26] In Positions 1 through 3 of Perry's developmental scheme, a person wrestles with a dualistic orientation to the world of knowledge and the world of values. Under the pressure of a certain set of experiences, the position is modified. In Position 1, the individual views the world in polar perspective—right and wrong, good and bad, with no grays tolerated. "Authority," in the form of parents, teachers, employers, is the fount of this wisdom, which is tangible, and can be accumulated by diligence and relentless labor. Translated into journalistic terms, there may be one and only one way, to a Position 1 person, to write a spot news lead. Use the 5 W's and the H: who, what, where, when, why, and how, all in the first paragraph. To our neophyte journalist—let's call him Peter—the more such stories one writes, the better.

But in Position 2, in the fullness of time, Peter happens across a spot news lead with several of the W's and the H relegated to subordinate positions of the story. Not only that, this particular story appeared in his very own paper! And there is a senior reporter who says he actually prefers to avoid using the 5W's and the H. Position 2 Peter subsequently encounters even editors who hold different opinions. Perhaps, he reasons, this newspaper has ill-prepared Authorities. Or, more likely, he reasons, Authorities want beginning reporters to determine for themselves the Right Answer of exactly when summary leads should be written and when they should not.

By the time Peter reaches Position 3, this dualistic posture of knowing and valuing is still perceptible. Yet his experience has been varied and extensive enough so that he has had to acknowledge the legitimacy of doubts and differences. But these must be merely temporary and exist only in those areas in which Authority has not yet found the Correct Approach. Thus, Peter was told *never* to allow a source to see a story before it was printed. Yet a famous weekly news magazine, he learned, had allowed a renowned surgeon to inspect a cover story prior to publication. Perhaps the practice is so new, Peter reasoned, that Authority has not yet devised The Rule to guide reporters in determining whether this is or is not appropriate.

At Position 4, the uncertainty and diversity of viewpoint, seen as temporary in Position 3, is now seen as pervasive. In fact, it is so widespread that Peter now has concluded that, even though Authorities have their own right and wrong, "everyone is entitled to his own opinion." Or, somewhat differently, Peter will give them what "They"— those Authorities—want. Thus, he knows that pledging confidentiality to a source is a procedure that the newspaper's rules say must be cleared in advance on investigative stories. He has his own judgment on the wisdom of that, but he will "give them what they want." He will "clear" such pledges with his editors, because Authority has told him and his colleagues that "it depends on a number of factors" whether such pledges are legitimate or wise.

At Position 5, Peter "perceives all knowledge and values (including Authority's) as contextual and relativistic and subordinates dualistic right-wrong functions to the status of a special case, in context."[27] Perry reports the transition to Position 5 is almost imperceptible to the person involved. For Peter, the transition might come, for example, after having observed for a considerable period the making of judgments on when and when not to pledge confidentiality to anonymous sources. Factors weighed included, preeminently, the importance of the story, the character of the source, the verifiable accuracy of the facts imparted, the potential consequences of the story, and the experience with the source on previous occasions. Having witnessed and weighed the interplay of these factors, Peter has come to know the meaning of "it all depends" and the variability of factual situations in which such pledges are or are not appropriate.

Peter finds himself practicing relativity of judgment in contexts other than pledges of confidentiality. In the case of source requests to see a story in advance, his "never" absolutism has been modified ever so slightly but ever so importantly to include situations in which the following objective factors have been weighed and found supportive: first, an extremely high probability of error unless there is some feedback from the source; second, a topic in the news volatile or technical enough that seeking "double corroboration" is reasonable; third, a pledge by the source to react only to factual errors; fourth, a positive assessment of the source's trustworthiness, and, fifth, an agreement by the source to accept the reading back of the story or portions thereof, rather than physical inspection of the entire article. He understands that these conditions seek to protect principles of freedom and independence valued by the profession, and he consults with his editors in such matters. Despite his embrace of such "relativistic" judgments, Peter acknowledges that judgments do have to be made. Ultimately, in cases of crucial importance, an editor or a publisher must take final responsibility.

But relativism is uncomfortable. With everything depending on context, with context shifting from day to day and week to week, Position 5 can be a vexing experience indeed. It can be, and is, lonesome. It is demanding and disorienting. One way to adjust is merely to drift from one situation to the next, as in the manner of the nihilist. But to do that is not only uncomfortable, but also personally demeaning.[28] As Perry says, it is to leave unanswered, somehow, the question, "Who am I?" One way to adjust would be to take advantage of shifting contexts to promote, say, career advancement. To Peter, unbridled relativism can lead to a number of "scoops," provided he can slip them by management more or less unexamined. To quote Perry: "Here a limited selfhood is achieved ("I am an opportunist"); the loss is to depth of feeling and to the social responsibility that springs from compassion."[29]

The response of Position 6 is to realize the need for a personal commitment to dissolve the disorientation. For Peter, it might seem natural to "become an investigative reporter." Perhaps, in truth, the decision should be to become an Investigative Reporter—that is, one who has made a deep commitment to a vocation within journalism that calls for modern expertness yet which has a tradition that stretches back into the nineteenth century.

Positions 7, 8, and 9 in Perry's scheme are periods in which the commitment foreseen as necessary in Position 6 is actually made and the responsibilities of commitment are assimilated, reflected upon, and nourished. In short, having made a commitment, Peter now "invests his energies, his care, and his identity."[30] Perry introduces into his scheme features that seem to make it realistic. Although Perry's positions succeed one another (one can't skip a position), the journey can be made again and again in various spheres and periods of one's life. And during each journey, one can temporize before entering the next position, retreat to the certainties of dualism, or escape into intellectual crannies such as mere technical virtuosity.[31]

As with Kohlberg, criticisms can be made of Perry. While Kohlberg provides an explicit "seventh stage" for a transcendental, religious orientation, Perry says religious commitment is one legitimate alternative in his Positions 7, 8, and 9. Although the key passage in which such an option is discussed carries a tone of tolerance, his actual language could be interpreted as limiting a person's freedom to persuade others to his or her point of view. Thus, Perry writes:

> If one later commits oneself to a faith in an Absolute, there is a criterion which reveals that this *Commitment has been made in the context of a relativistic world.* [Perry's italics.] This criterion is one's attitude toward

other people with a belief or a faith in a different Absolute. They cannot appear as alien, as other than human; one must, however paradoxically, respect them. In one sense they "must" be wrong, but in another sense, no more so than oneself. The moral obligation to convert them or to annihilate them has vanished.[32]

Certainly there is a difference between annihilating someone and believing one has an obligation to attempt to convert them by persuasion. This latter option seems to be ruled out by Perry as an illegitimate aspect of religious commitment.

Despite a clear depiction of a realistic cycle of development, Perry's scheme employs a vocabulary portions of which could be confused with a nihilistic version of "situation ethics."[33] However, the concept of commitment would seem to be an effective antidote to what many see as the instability and moral aridity of purely subjective, situational ethics. Commitment to principled reasoning, values inquiry, and ethical dialogue are essential ingredients of the normative model of journalism ethics outlined in this book. It remains to show how this model is compatible with the social philosophy that has sustained western journalism for more than two centuries.

CHAPTER TWELVE

Toward a Committed Journalism

In Philadelphia on January 17, 1980, leaders of the news media convened themselves in "The First Amendment Congress" to take stock of the standing of freedom of the press with the American public. They had hired the Gallup Poll to survey the citizenry. Its president, George Gallup, Jr., painted a mixed but, on the whole, grim picture.[1] Three in four Americans had no idea what the First Amendment is or does. Moreover, even among those with college backgrounds, six in ten could not identify the clause in the United States Constitution that protects not only the freedom of the press but of religion, speech, and peaceable assembly. Almost four in ten said current curbs on the press were not strict enough. Although there were positive findings (journalism careers were in favor with the young and local newspapers earned increasing confidence of their readers), Gallup suggested a need for action:

1. Still greater efforts by members of the media to maintain the highest principles of journalism, and a renewed dedication to helping future journalists develop the taste and sensitivity which a responsible press requires.
2. A major program of education—not only to increase awareness of basic freedoms, but to remind people of the long and difficult struggle behind the winning of these freedoms. Clearly it behooves those in the media to take a long hard look at what is going on in the classrooms of their communities.

Although Gallup's set of findings can be viewed as merely a familiar, modern lament about the status of the civic ethic in America, his conclusions have particular relevance to journalists and members of the public concerned about the ethics of journalism. A case can be made that not only must journalists and their publics understand how freedom evolved; they should also be aware of the origins of the ideas and institutions that were the precursors to free expression. As if those desiderata are not enough—and they aren't—there is a need for modern journalists to shed their antipathy to the kind of conceptual thinking

167

and philosophical dialogue that can enrich the ethics and the direction of their craft/profession.

The purpose of this chapter is to highlight some of the key events in the evolution of free expression and of the republican institutions that protect that freedom. It also will attempt to show the role of journalism ethics in a society whose political constitution vows to protect freedom and promote justice for all its members. Although the undertaking is uncomfortably large, it also is clearly unavoidable: a system of journalism ethics cannot be divorced from the strands of social philosophy which tie together the society's past and ask old questions of its future.

The relationship of Hebrew and early Christian thought to the evolution of western political ideas is obvious but, nonetheless, often unrecognized. The very idea of a higher law—the laws of God, as revealed to Moses—was consistent with the appeal to natural law on which the founding fathers based the Declaration of Independence and the Constitution. The Ten Commandments embody principles, such as the prohibition of bearing false witness, which are at the core of most ethical codes. Moses' definition of the good as obedience to the law (the Torah) contributed, through the centuries, to respect for the rule of law in a civil context. Later Hebrew prophets enunciated the virtue of righteousness, hence fostering the concept and practice of commitment. They also preached social justice, hence helping give public policy an enduring theme.[2]

The Greek city-state, the philosophy of which contributed so heavily to the western political tradition, emphasized the rule of communal law as well as a free society to which the citizen contributed and in which he participated intimately. The Hellenistic and later Roman empires of succeeding centuries ushered in a new era, influenced more heavily by religion, and especially by Christianity. With the demise of collective allegiance to a small city-state, religion stressed the worth of each individual, a one-to-one relationship with God, and the individual's kinship with all of humanity regardless of nationality. Christianity, with its emphasis on individual salvation and universal brotherhood, thus infused itself into the new political milieu of regional empires, and influenced them in turn.

However, neither the Greek city-state nor the Roman Empire, nor, for that matter, the later modern western states, were morally resilient enough to ban slavery. It was a "universal institution" in the ancient world, indeed, the basis of Greek agriculture.[3] Roman law exalted freedom and equality, but not for all, and slavery was specifically permitted.[4] It continued throughout the Middle Ages, the Age of Exploration, and well into the nineteenth century in America.

However morally lagging with respect to slavery, the ancients devised a mechanism of government the development of which had a profound effect on modern political institutions. Indeed, it shaped, to this day, the context in which American journalists gather and report the news from Washington and state capitals. The mechanism, of course, was the notion of checks and balances.

Aristotle (384–322 B.C.) had written of the virtues of mixed government, but his idea was that of the Greek city-state arrangement in which there was a mixture of various socioeconomic groups and classes. As Aristotle, in his *Ethics,* regarded the golden mean as the preferred course, so in his *Politics* he regarded as best a government with a large middle class, with extremes of wealth and poverty kept small. He differentiated monarchy, aristocracy, and constitutional government and saw the perversion of each in tyranny, obligarchy, and mob rule, respectively. The best government, constitutional government, represented a compromise to "unite the freedom of the poor and the wealth of the rich," both under the rule of law rather than the rule of men.[5]

When the Romans conquered Macedon, they deported a thousand Greeks who were among the elite of the city-state. Among these was Polybius (204–122 B.C.), a young public servant who ingratiated himself with the Roman ruling circles. As an insider, Polybius examined the Roman government at first hand and wrote *Histories,* a forty-volume account not only of what he saw but what he theorized. Carrying with him the ideas of Aristotle on mixed government, he adapted them to what he found in Rome. In the powerful Roman consuls he saw the monarchical, in the Roman senate the aristocratic, and in the popular assemblies the democratic elements.[6] Because each of these institutions could in fact serve as a reciprocal check on the others, the Romans had mixed governments, too. But unlike the mixture of economic classes in the Greek city-states, the Roman balance was of distinct political powers. Polybius's formulation of the separation of powers was picked up by the French aristocrat Montesquieu (1689–1755), whose *Spirit of the Laws* extolled its operation in England in the royalty (monarchy), the House of Lords (aristocracy), and the House of Commons (democracy).[7] The framers of the American Constitution embraced this concept, which had been a centerpiece of political theory for centuries.

If there is a special locale for political theorists in the afterlife, no doubt Aristotle, Polybius, and Montesquieu, among others, were there, together, smiling from 1972 to 1974. In those years, the separated powers of the oldest constitutional democracy on earth struggled with one another over whether to depose the chief-of-state. With the news media contributing to and benefiting directly from such authoritative competition, the House of Representatives (democracy), the Senate of the United States (aristocracy) and the Supreme Court grappled with issues surrounding the presidency (monarchy) of Richard M. Nixon. His egregious efforts to obstruct an investigation of a 1972 burglary at the Democratic National Committee headquarters prompted a major senate investigation and, subsequently, impeachment proceedings in the house. Both bodies plus special federal prosecutors and the Supreme Court forced Nixon to release secret tape recordings which ultimately documented his culpability. The governmental actors played their roles in the wake of exposés by the *Washington Post* and other newspapers. The news media fed information into the mechanisms created by the separation of powers and checks and balances doctrines, and the media were fed information by those competing mechanisms. The machines built of ancient design had separated wheat from chaff and a nation six years short of its two hundredth birthday could only marvel, with sadness but relief, that the system had met one of its gravest tests. It had forced Richard Nixon to resign his presidency—the only occupant of the White House ever to do so—based on evidence that he had exceeded his powers and had used them in an attempt to obstruct justice. The press had justified the constitutional framers' philosophy that freedom of the press itself would be a significant check on government.

The rule of law and the "checking structure" of American government are not the only historical legacies which contribute to the work of journalists in the present day. As rich a tradition is the active defense of free expression itself, a defense that preceded the existence of the rule of law and continues, today, two hundred years after adoption of the Constitution. Understanding the length and agony of the struggle to establish the right may help, as George Gallup, Jr., suggested, to freshen modern commitment to the ideal.

A little imagination could find a resemblance between the earliest martyr to free expression, Socrates, and the modern journalist. Forever asking questions (although usually more philosophical than factual), Socrates generated a range of emotional reactions to his calling and his presence. He provoked the anger of Anytus, whose son, under Socrates' tutelage, had defected from the father's polytheistic ways. Socrates inspired the ridicule of Aristophanes, who described Socrates' "thinking shop" as a place where one acquired the skill of proving oneself right, however wrong. And his too-vigorous pursuit of knowledge and wisdom provoked the fear of the powerful, who executed Socrates for teachings threatening to their leadership.[8]

In Greek and Roman societies and even in the Middle Ages, "free speech" was privileged, after a fashion. But it was not until roughly the thirteenth century in England that most historians mark the crude beginnings of the formal protections which alone could make freedom of expression a genuine social fact. In 1215, the now-celebrated Magna Carta crystalized the effort of feisty English barons to make King John explicitly recognize certain of their rights. Under pressure in a meadow at Runnymede, the king signed the famous document, which included the passage:

> No freeman shall be taken or imprisoned, or be disseized of his freehold or liberties or free customs, or be outlawed, or exiled, or any other wise destroyed, nor will we not pass upon him nor condemn him, but by lawful judgment of his peers, or by the law of the land.[9]

Antiquarian scholarship has interpreted the language of the Magna Carta as having meant something quite different to baronial eyes of the day then to our own. Thus "law of the land" meant trial by battle or ordeal; "liberties" were gifts of property from the king; and "peers" were those social equals who judged, for example, whether a defendant's grimace at red hot coals meant mea culpa.[10] Yet, as Irving Bryant wrote: "No matter what those terms [of Magna Carta] meant to the barons at Runnymede, to generations of Englishmen and to Americans setting forth their inalienable rights, they included a fair trial by an impartial jury."[11]

But that right became established only slowly, with the raising and re-raising of armies to enforce the Magna Carta, and the suffering of many, especially in sixteenth and seventeenth–century England. John Udall, a Puritan minister who wrote a book critical of the church hierarchy, died of prison hardships after an extended effort to defend himself and after his refusal to testify against himself. William Prynne, a lawyer who wrote a book condemning plays, masques, and dancing, was tried by the judge-and-jury Star Chamber in 1634. His book, entitled "Women Actors Notorious Whores," was published only six weeks before the Queen of England was to display her acting talent on stage. Even though written four years earlier, Prynne's book cost him two stands in the pillory, the loss of both ears, a find of £5,000, and life imprisonment. John Lilburne, the great leader of the Levellers, was the first to propose a written constitution guaranteeing human rights binding on Parliament and king. He refused to take an oath that would have forced him to testify against himself. The judges fined him £500, had him stripped and pilloried, and ordered him jailed. Later freed by the Cromwellian parliament, Lilburne was tried for treason and acquitted. Charles I, the "hated Catholic monarch," was beheaded after a sham trial by a commission named by a revolutionary Protestant parliament whose jurisdiction and procedures were as notoriously illegitimate as the judicial bodies Charles I himself had employed against religious and political dissenters.

The point of this hoary pageant of forgotten martyrs[12] is to underline the grotesque human drama that informed the social philosophers whose ideas shaped American and other political institutions, including press, to this day. The most influential such philosopher was the middle-class Puritan John Locke, physician, public servant, and statesman, whose *Two Treatises on Government* laid the intellectual basis for the Glorious Revolution of 1688–89, which overthrew the Stuart dynasty, brought the Protestants William and Mary of Holland to the throne and presaged the creation of the English Bill of Rights. In fact, the second treatise was the philosophical foundation for the American Declaration of Independence and the United States Constitution.

Locke held that "the state of nature has a law of nature to govern it, which obliges every one; and reason, which is that law, teaches all mankind who will but consult it, that, being equal and independent, no one ought to harm another in his life, health, liberty or possessions." These were the truths that the framers of the Declaration of Independence and the U.S. Constitution found, with Locke, to be self-evident, inalienable, given by their Creator. Although the governmental apparatus to ensure these rights was inspired by many sources—from Aristotle to Montesquieu—Lockean values guided, if not dominated, not only the government, but the socioeconomic and cultural environment of the new nation. These values were (1) the sanctity of the individual, not only in his legal rights but in the potential of his personhood; (2) the rule of law and the respect not only for equitable judicial procedure, but also fairness in the use of authority howsoever constituted; (3) government by consent of the governed, with freely elected representatives exercising a "fiduciary trust" for the citizenry and with clear, specific limitations on governments; (4) the right to accumulate property, not only for individual happiness but as a protection against intimidating incursions from governmental or private plutocracy; and (5) the rule of reason in human affairs, a faith that the human mind, if resolute and healthy, can find the truth needed not only for itself but for society.[13]

Classical liberalism, of which John Locke is considered the father, gained its preeminent economic theoretician, not so coincidentally, in 1776 when Adam Smith's *The Wealth of Nations* enunciated a laissez-faire capitalism that dovetailed with Locke's notions on the right to accumulate property. That Smith's laws of supply and demand were said to operate under the guidance of an "invisible hand" appeared to be in keeping with the mechanistic, Newtonian spirit of the times. It was as though Locke and Smith were at the philosophical controls of two giant, coordinated orreries, spinning and interfacing magically with one another, much as the Constitution's own checks and balances were intended to work.

The philosophic contributor to classical liberalism whose writings bear most directly on the press was John Stuart Mill (1806–1873), whose *On Liberty* (1859) is considered among the most elegant and systematic defenses of free expression in history. He extended the focus of liberal concern to the "tyranny of the majority," and, in an industrializing century, he identified pressured conformity by socioeconomic forces as inimical to liberty. So great was Mill's concern for diversity that he counted "the mere refusal to bend the knee to custom" as a contribution to the preservation or advance of liberty.[14] For he believed, circa late 1850s even, that "society has now fairly got the better of individuality . . . in our times, from the highest class of society down to the lowest, every one lives as under the eye of a hostile and dreaded censorship."[15]

Having such views, the argument by Mill for the maximum possible liberty is easier to appreciate and his reasons for advocating robust debate become more compelling. First, to suppress an opinion, Mill said, would require that one assume the posture that he or she is infallible. Second, the view suppressed might contain a portion of the truth—in fact, the very portion needed for the emergence of the whole truth. Third, if a "truth" is not contested, it will merely survive as a prejudice. And finally, if an actual truth is held merely as a dogma or prejudice, it will lose its effect on conduct and character.[16] Mill argued that the only occasions when society should interfere with individual liberty are instances of harm to the interests of others, an interest defined by due process of law.[17]

Although Mill was a utilitarian, he believed that judgments of utility should include not merely quantity of happiness but the quality of happiness as well. And he made clear: "I regard utility as the ultimate appeal on all ethical questions; but it must be utility in the largest sense, founded on the permanent interests of man as a progressive being. Those interests, I contend, authorize the subjection of individual spontaneity to external control, only in respect to those actions of each which concern the interest of other people. If any one does an act hurtful to others, there is a prima facie case for punishing him, by law, or, where legal penalties are not safely applicable, by general disapprobation."[18]

It is not difficult to see that the framework of principles outlined in Chapter 3 as one system of ethics for journalists is compatible in a general sense not only with the Judeo-Christian tradition, but with the social philosophy and cultural heritage of classical liberalism. The journalist should be a humane truth teller, heedful of the rights of others, doing his work fairly, attempting to promote justice where appropriate and possible within the limits of his craft/profession, and mindful that individual independence and freedom are possible only if journalism itself acts as a steward of free expression. But this ideal formulation must recognize certain realities. Undoubtedly, elements of classical liberalism have been alternatively eroded, modified, tempered, and (mercifully) fortified over the past two to three hundred years. Social, economic, political, and cultural traditions are radically different. No journalist who chooses to commit to the classical traditions should fail to understand the modern environment and the implications of such a commitment.

There are many persons for whom it is not only easy but essential to hold that inalienable rights to life, liberty, and the pursuit of happiness are an endowment from their Creator, a Supreme Being. In company with the ancient Stoics, who first made important the concept of a "higher law," some moderns still express fealty to a "natural law," which holds such rights to be self-evident, discernible by God-given reason. As a motive for respecting and fulfilling the human potential in the exercise of those rights, a theistic derivation of them can be powerful indeed. Certainly Thomas Jefferson's plucking with the idea left behind vibrations that are felt even today, vibrations which Abraham Lincoln once called the mystic chords of memory.

But by 1776 there also had been struck a series of counter, discordant notes that likewise are powerfully alive in modern western culture. Indeed, when David Hume died in 1776 he left behind a mighty symphony of skepticism to which philosophers and others are still forced to listen if they expect to understand what has happened to ethics in the nineteenth and twentieth centuries. These are the centuries when science came into its own as a value shared with the populace as well. Although contemporary scientists have not only qualified but rejected outright much of Hume's philosophy,[19] his radical empiricism has had an impact on science and, perhaps more lastingly and pervasively, on morals. To Hume, a statement that "lying is wrong" should be considered in the same way as an assertion, say, that "chlorophyll under the stimulus of sunlight helps produce plant food." Looked at objectively, the causal element in the first assertion—"lying," Hume would say— has not produced an external fact. What it has produced, according to

Humean analysis, is an internal impression, based on experience and acculturation, that lying is "wrong." In Hume's inimitable words: "The hypothesis which we embrace is plain. It maintains that morality is determined by sentiment. It defines virtue to be whatever mental action or quality gives to a spectator the pleasing sentiment of approbation; and vice the contrary."[20] To Hume, in matters of morals, reason served as little more than a weak sluice gate for channeling the emotions. Morals exist but they are prudential rather than Providential inventions, at least to Hume.

Although others—before and after Hume—argued effectively for the role of experience in ethics, it was Hume's work that apparently provoked the philosophic response that remains most influential in rebutting radical empiricism. Immanuel Kant, by his own word, awakened from "dogmatic slumber" by Hume's writing, countered with *Critique of Pure Reason*.[21] In it he argued, convincingly to many, that the senses were not the source of knowledge but mere tools of the mind. Reason turns perceptual data into concepts, which in turn organize and make experience useful in the form of laws, predictable sequences, and explained relationships. Theologians and the Prussian royalty were irate, for Kant's work held that God's existence was not provable by reason. Later, in his *Critique of Practical Reason,* Kant argued for faith as the means to establish God's existence. As for morals, they arose from an inner sense of duty, and from a good will, the only thing which is good without qualification. "Morality is not properly the doctrine of how we may make ourselves happy, but how we may make ourselves worthy of happiness," Kant declared.[22] Happiness comes from acting on *a priori* moral truths and by using one's God-given reason and will.

It is easy to say that Kant's influence was limited to philosophers and theologians. In fact, his viewpoint permeates western society and surfaces on many occasions. Take this passage from a 1984 address by Ray Cave, managing editor of *Time* magazine, at the University of Oregon School of Journalism:

> If you are a reporter, or an editor, how do you know when what you are doing is proper, or whether it has transgressed propriety and is infringing on the rights and privacy of others? I admit there are many difficult judgments to make in this regard. But I must also say that, in the six and a half years I have been managing editor of *Time,* on only two occasions did I find the issue totally confounding. My father once told me that in attempting to decide if a given action is right or wrong, you may think you do not know—you may even pretend you do not know—but you know. Follow that kind of guidance and you may lose a story now and then for

being over-cautious. But you will never lose faith in yourself as a journalist, in the true sense of the word journalist.[23]

But there are other positions between Hume's utilitarian prudence in matters of morals and the belief in *a priori* knowledge of right and wrong. Among these is Michael Polanyi's *Personal Knowledge*, a book on epistemology, in which he seeks to show the importance of individual commitment as an essential ingredient to the process by which scientists ruminate, hypothesize, search for, and attempt to describe truth. Though there are differences, the steps taken parallel reporting. With a hunch that a particular truth exists, the scientists, like the journalist, declares an intention to search to find it. It is a "universal intention" in the sense that it is honest and sincere. Whatever truth is found will be declared openly to the world, which is free to contest it. In reaching the conclusion of the search, "the freedom of the subjective person to do as he pleases is overruled by the freedom of the responsible person to act as he must."[24] It is an act of commitment. The same process is at work in the resolution of ethical issues, which involves gathering facts and making value judgements. Thus, William Perry acknowledges the influence of Polanyi[25] in conceptualizing his scheme of intellectual and ethical development, discussed in Chapter II. Polanyi's concept is equally applicable to finding a stance for ethical belief as for scientific truth. He writes:

> To accept commitment as the framework within which we may believe something to be true, is to circumscribe the hazards of belief. It is to establish the conception of competence which authorizes a fiduciary choice made and timed, to the best of the acting person's ability, as a deliberate and yet necessary choice. The paradox of self-set standards is eliminated, for in a competent mental act, the agent does not do as he pleases, but compels himself forcibly to act as he believes he must. He can do no more, and would evade his calling by doing less. The possibility of errors is a necessary element of any belief bearing on reality. The outcome of a competent fiduciary act, may, admittedly, vary from one person to another, but since the differences are not due to any arbitrariness on the part of the individuals, each retains justifiably his universal intent. As each hopes to capture an aspect of reality, they may all hope that their findings will eventually coincide or supplement each other.[26]

It is in the spirit of this passage by Polanyi that dialogue about the ethics in journalism—and about journalism itself—can proceed with the hope of cumulative, beneficent results. In the same vein, it is with that spirit that a journalist can accept belief in a modern version of the classical liberal tradition.

If ethics is more than mere personal taste or crass utilitarianism, if the tradition of defending free expression and republican institutions has an honored past and a most necessary future, is there then nothing problematic about the classical liberal inheritance?

Most certainly there is.

With its emphasis on individual rights and limitations on government, classical liberalism has often failed to develop a perspective that recognizes the common good, especially when doing so entails sacrifice or mutual restraint. This is doubly so when an issue involves—as it almost inevitably does—a congeries of competing interest groups knotted in combat over economic stakes. In such circumstances, republican institutions have too often judged their success not so much by standards of equity as by measures of whether equilibrium ensued. Because often the issues are complex and time consuming in their resolution, it is difficult for journalists to give them the degree of priority in public attention that their actual effect on the common good might well justify. If enough such deals are struck outside the glare of the commonweal, the potential exists for a Grand Tragedy of the Commons. The enormous United States governmental deficit, with its threat of national capital investment shortage and the vicious rape of family budgets via inflation, is a case in point. It is a deficit built of many shortfalls of taxes intended to pay for sundry projects, programs, and decisions. These might have developed differently had public officials and the press brought to them a perspective implied by the grand old term "commonwealth." A masterful analysis that underscores the points made above can be found in Theodore Lowi's modern classic, *The End of Liberalism*.[27]

A just society is one in which the well-being of many depends on equitable public and private judgments reached over a broad expanse of human activity. The domains include business, in all its variety; government, with all its many layers; science and health, with their many arcane corridors and seemingly unreachable crannies; and, not least, religion, with its potential for volatility as well as reassurance. Conversations in these sundry domains are too often conducted in specialized languages. Failure by the press to develop the competence to cover such fields is itself a breach of responsibility.

As if cramped perspectives and insufficient knowledge were not enough, classical liberalism has not bequeathed a commitment to the civic ethic to match the problems and opportunities at hand. For how many modern politicians could speak of their own countries as Pericles spoke of Athens?

An Athenian citizen does not neglect the state because he takes care of his own household; and even those of us who are engaged in business have a very fair idea of politics. We alone regard a man who takes no interest in public affairs not as a harmless, but as a useless character; and if few of us are originators, we are all sound judges of policy.[28]

No one expects, or even wishes, a return of the Greek city-state. Yet the ideal of public caring for and participation in public decisions remains alive; it is as real as the latest account of steps to build educational excellence, of communities acting on their wisest introspections, and of individuals fulfilling themselves by forgetting themselves in public service. It is as alive as the conscience and commitment of the few media owners and managers enlightened enough to match resources to the need for better and more penetrating news coverage.

In a word, if the inheritors of the classical liberal tradition wish to pass along their vineyard in a more productive state, they will need to prune excesses of individualism, spurn lethargy of intellect and cultivate, if ever so slowly, a richer perspective on their work as vine dressers. They will have to help invent not a theoretical definition of community but a genuine community. For journalism, this means a new patience and ability to portray the connections which, in fact, already link the constituent groups of society. It means reacting to the danger that unbridled journalistic careerism, loosed by the media's new awareness of its own importance, will undermine any possibility of journalistic fealty to a community, however defined. The fealty needed is not one blinded by ideology, but one bold enough to peel back layer by layer the films of ignorance, indifference, and deliberate stealth that often obscure the palpable community of interest that exists below the surface in local, national, and international settings.

If this species of "community journalism" requires a new form of courage, it also needs *not* to be encumbered by the hubris of a cadre of practitioners who believe they can write no wrong. For the world is a beehive that must be approached with a caution that balances journalism's energetic curiosity and idealism with a sense of ethics. International banking, global missile deployment, world poverty, cultural competition, and worldwide religious reawakening are stories, to name a few, that bespeak the need for news coverage informed by the Aristotelian Golden Mean.

The late Alexander Bickel, the Yale Law School professor who represented the *New York Times* in the Pentagon Papers case, wrote, in quoting Edmund Burke:

Theories were not fit to live with, and any attempt to impose them would breed conflict, not responsive government enjoying the consent of the governed. The rights of man cannot be established by any theoretical definition; they are (quoting Burke) "in balances between differences of good, in compromises sometimes between differences of good and evil, and sometimes between evil and evil. Political reason is a computing principle: adding, subtracting, multiplying, and dividing, morally and not metaphysically, or mathematically, true moral denominations."[29]

Bickel noted and approved Burke's declaration that society needed some "uniform rule and scheme of life." As Bickel said, "We cannot live, much less govern . . . without principles, however provisionally and skeptically held."

Reporters and editors, for their collective part, could do worse than heed the call of Burke and Bickel, which is the call of the classical liberal tradition placed in modern context. It is for a journalism of commitment and of humane truth telling. It is for a journalism watchful of its own ways but also alert to report injustice. It is for a journalism that respects its own independence, as well as that of others. It takes seriously its stewardship of free expression, and searches for better ways to report, and, therefore, help build the very community which can assure its own survival in a free society.

NOTES

1. Beyond a Socially Responsible Press

1. Michael Kirkhorn, "Reassurance, Boredom, Decency, Conversation," paper presented to the Association for Education in Journalism, Houston, Texas, August 1979.
2. Interview with Patrick Bova, National Opinion Research Center, University of Chicago, Jan. 9, 1985.
3. "Journalism Under Fire," *Time*, Dec. 12, 1983, p. 76.
4. "20 Years After Key Libel Ruling, Debate Goes on," *New York Times*, March 8, 1984, p. 1.
5. Edmund B. Lambeth, "The Elite Press and the Energy Crisis: An Examination of the Perceived Impact of the Press on Energy Policy Making," University Microfilms International, Ann Arbor, Michigan, 1976, pp. 203–210.
6. Robert L. Stevenson and Mark T. Greene, "A Reconsideration of Bias in the News," *Journalism Quarterly*, Spring 1980, pp. 115–121.
7. Lambeth, "Elite Press and the Energy Crisis," pp. 126–127.
8. Stevenson and Greene, "Reconsideration of Bias in the News."
9. Bill Green, "Janet's World," *Washington Post*, April 19, 1981, p. 1.
10. John Consoli, "1981 was a controversial year for daily newspapers," *Editor & Publisher*, Jan. 2, 1982, p. 8.
11. "Journalism Under Fire," *Time*, p. 79.
12. "SEC Investigates Charges of Traders Profiting on Leaks by Journal Reporter," *Wall Street Journal*, March 29, 1984, p. 3.
13. "SEC's Inquiry Widens As It Questions Broker, Others in Journal Case," *Wall Street Journal*, April 2, 1984, p. 1.
14. For the newspapers' own views on the episode in the context of the temptations financial reporters face on the job, see Harvey D. Shapiro's article, "Unfair Shares," *Washington Journalism Review*, July/August 1984, pp. 35–40.
15. Ann Tolstoi Wallach, "Is the Office Affair a Bed of Roses?" *Harper's Bazaar*, October 1981, pp. 78, 86, 90, 92.
16. For a single-volume treatment of the subject, see Bernard Roshco, *Newsmaking* (Chicago: University of Chicago Press, 1975).
17. This idea appears to have been first developed fully by Edward J. Epstein, *News from Nowhere* (New York: Random House, 1973).
18. See Gaye Tuchman, *Making News* (New York: The Free Press, 1978).
19. This view is perhaps most pronounced in J. Herbert Altschull, *Agents of Power* (New York: Longman, 1984).
20. Ibid., especially pp. 179–205.
21. *Washington Post*, June 12, 1977, p. B8.
22. Three of the most important books, each of which summarizes the literature on media power in different ways, are Herbert J. Gans, *Deciding What's News* (New York: Vintage Books, 1980); Doris Graber, *Mass Media and Modern Politics* (Washington, D.C.: Congressional Quarterly, 1980); and David L. Paletz and Robert M. Entman, *Media Power Politics* (New York and London: The Free Press, 1981).

23. Elisabeth Noelle-Neumann, "The Effect of Media on Media Effects Research," *Ferment in the Field,* a special issue of *Journal of Communication,* Summer 1983, Vol. 33, No. 3, p. 163.

24. H. Eugene Goodwin, *Groping for Ethics in Journalism* (Ames: Iowa State University Press, 1983), p. 306.

25. Commission on Freedom of the Press, *A Free and Responsible Press* (Chicago: University of Chicago Press, 1947).

26. These requirements are amplified in Fred S. Siebert, Theodore Peterson, and Wilbur Schramm, *Four Theories of the Press* (Urbana: University of Illinois Press, 1956), pp. 87–92.

27. Ibid., p. 95.

28. Altschull, *Agents of Power,* pp. 301–305.

29. John C. Merrill, *The Imperative of Freedom* (New York: Hastings House, 1974), pp. 85–98.

30. Siebert, Peterson, and Schramm, *Four Theories of the Press,* p. 71.

31. See especially William Ernest Hocking, *Freedom of the Press* (Chicago: University of Chicago Press, 1947).

32. Ibid., pp. 120–124.

33. Ibid., pp. 188–191.

34. Ibid., p. 183.

35. For a helpful essay on the problems in defining the "public interest," see Virginia Held, *The Public Interest and Individual Interests* (New York and London: Basic Books, 1970).

2. The Journalist and Classical Ethical Theory

1. Ethel M. Albert, Theodore C. Denise, and Sheldon Peterfreund, *Great Traditions in Ethics* (New York: D. Van Nostrand, 1980), pp. 60–65.

2. See Ayn Rand, *The Virtue of Selfishness* (New York: New American Library/Signet Books, 1964), and idem, *For the New Intellectual* (New York: New American Library/Signet Books, 1961).

3. Tom L. Beauchamp and Norman E. Bowie, *Ethical Theory and Business* (Englewood Cliffs, N.J.: Prentice Hall, 1979), p. 61.

4. William D. Boyce and Larry C. Jensen, *Moral Reasoning* (Lincoln: University of Nebraska Press, 1978), p. 36.

5. Ibid., p. 37.

6. Albert, Denise, and Peterfreund, *Great Traditions in Ethics,* p. 224.

7. Kant, *Fundamental Principles of the Metaphysics of Morals,* in Boyce and Jensen, *Moral Reasoning,* p. 48.

8. Albert, Denise, and Peterfreund, *Great Traditions in Ethics,* p. 228.

9. Jacques P. Thiroux, *Ethics, Theory and Practice* (Encino, Calif.: Glencoe Publishing Co., 1980), pp. 38–39.

10. Christopher Lasch, *The Culture of Narcissism* (New York: W. W. Norton, 1979), p. 21.

11. For a full account of the *Progressive* case, see Robert Friedman, "The United States vs. The Progressive," *Columbia Journalism Review,* July/August 1979, pp. 27–35; for a collection of differing views, see *Quill,* June 1979, pp. 21–32.

12. *Report of the Committee for Education in Business Ethics* (Skokie, Ill.: Fel-Pro, Inc., 1980), p. 6.

3. Toward an Eclectic System of Journalism Ethics

1. I first encountered the approach of articulating general ethical principles and setting them in priority in the works of John Rawls, W.D. Ross, and Jacques Thiroux. Although some of the principles used here are the same or similar in nomenclature to those used by the three named authors, as I use them they are construed somewhat differently and are set in a journalistic context. Their priority is likewise different.

2. See Clifford C. Christians, "Beyond Quandaries: A Plea for Normative Ethics," *Mass Comm Review,* Fall 1979, pp. 29–31.

3. Ten codes are collected in Bruce M. Swain, *Reporters' Ethics* (Ames: Iowa State University Press, 1978), pp. 111–134.

4. James W. Carey develops this argument in "A Plea for the University Tradition," *Journalism Quarterly,* Winter 1978, pp. 846–855.

5. See *Washington Post,* April 19, 1981, pp. 1, A12–A15, for Ombudsman Bill Green's special report on the Cooke case. See, also, "In the aftermath of 'Jimmy's World': A special report," *Bulletin of the American Society of Newspaper Editors,* July–Aug. 1981, pp. 3–29.

6. *University of Missouri Bulletin,* Vol. 30, No. 46, December 1919, p. 16.

7. An especially helpful book is Steve Weinberg's *Trade Secrets of Washington Journalists* (Washington, D.C.: Acropolis Books, Ltd., 1981).

8. Lewis Anthony Dexter, *Elite and Specialized Interviewing* (Evanston, Ill.: Northwestern University Press, 1970); Ken Metzler, *Creative Interviewing* (Englewood Cliffs, N.J.: Prentice-Hall, 1977); and Peter Johansen, "Interviewing," in Maxwell McCombs, Donald Lewis Shaw, and David Grey, eds., *Handbook of Reporting Methods* (Boston: Houghton-Mifflin, 1976), pp. 174–210.

9. Peter Johansen and David Grey, "Participant Observation," in *Handbook of Reporting Methods,* pp. 211–243.

10. Walter Lippmann, *Public Opinion* (New York: Macmillan, 1965), p. 228.

11. See Frederick T.C. Yu, *Behavioral Sciences and the Mass Media* (New York: Russell Sage Foundation, 1968).

12. Philip Meyer, *Precision Journalism* (Bloomington: Indiana University Press, 1973).

13. This suggestion was presented in a lecture at the University of Missouri School of Journalism by English journalist John Whale, and was cited by John C. Merrill, "Ethics and Journalism," in Merrill and Ralph D. Barney, eds., *Ethics and the Press* (New York: Hastings House, 1975), p. 10.

14. Swain, *Reporters' Ethics,* pp. 132–133.

15. *Washington Post,* March 22, 1975, p. A14.

16. See Note 5.

17. See Curtis D. MacDougall, *Interpretative Reporting* (New York: Macmillan, 1977), pp. 283–287.

18. Walter B. Jaehnig, "Journalists and Terrorism: Captives of the Libertarian Tradition," *Indiana Law Journal,* Vol. 53, No. 4, 1978, pp. 716–745, especially p. 729.

19. Clark R. Mollenhoff, *Investigative Reporting* (New York: Macmillan, 1981), pp. 357–360.

20. Henry H. Schulte, *Reporting Public Affairs* (New York: Macmillan, 1981), pp. 228–229.

21. John Hohenberg, *The Pulitzer Prizes* (New York: Columbia University Press, 1974), pp. 73–85.

22. John Rawls, *A Theory of Justice* (Cambridge, Mass: Harvard University Press, 1971).

23. Ibid., pp. 3–4.

24. Ibid., p. 7.

25. Charlene J. Brown, Trevor R. Brown, and William L. Rivers, *The Media and the People* (New York: Holt, Rinehart and Winston, 1978), pp. 217–219.

26. George C. Gallup, Jr., "Americans Favor Tough Controls on the Press," *Editor & Publisher*, Jan. 19, 1980, p. 7, and Jules Witcover, "A Reporter's Committee that Works," *Columbia Journalism Review*, May–June, 1973, pp. 26–43.

27. Warren Breed, "Social Control in the Newsroom," *Social Forces*, Vol. 33, No. 4, 1955, pp. 326–335.

28. See Edward J. Epstein, *Between Fact and Fiction: The Problem of Journalism* (New York: Vintage Books, 1975), pp. 3–18.

29. For a complete collection of documents on this case, I am indebted to my colleague Charlene Brown. Articles include "Hofstadter to sift the mind's secrets," *Indiana Daily Student*, Sept. 17, 1981, p. 6; "Correction," *IDS*, Sept. 22, 1981, p. 3: and "Policies need to be ironclad," *IDS*, Sept. 25, 1981, p. 4.

30. Rawls, *A Theory of Justice*, pp. 114–117.

31. Merrill and Barney, *Ethics and the Press*, p. 96.

32. *Congressional Record*, Feb. 13, 1972, pp. H817–H818.

33. Ibid.

34. Merrill and Barney, *Ethics and the Press*, p. 180.

35. William D. Boyce and Larry Cyril Jensen, *Moral Reasoning* (Lincoln: University of Nebraska, 1978), p. 51.

36. For a listing of mid-career programs and an explanation of how journalism schools and universities may sponsor them, see "The J-School and Mid-Career Training," *Journalism Educator*, Vol. 36, No. 2 (July 1978).

37. Jay Black, Ralph D. Barney, and G. Norman Van Tubergen, "Moral Development and Belief Systems of Journalists," *Mass Comm Review*, Vol. 6, No. 3 (Fall 1979), p. 15.

38. William G. Perry, Jr., *Intellectual and Ethical Development in the College Years* (New York: Holt, Rinehart & Winston, 1970).

39. Untitled sonnet by Edna St. Vincent Millay in volume entitled *Huntsman, What Quarry?* (New York and London: Harper & Brothers, 1939), p. 92.

4. Applying Principles to Cases

1. *Chicago Tribune*, Jan. 3, 1980, p. 1.

2. Ibid., Jan. 5, 1980, p. 1.

3. Ibid., Feb. 5, 1980.

4. Ibid., Jan. 7, 1980, p. 9.

5. The term "prima facie" is borrowed from W. David Ross, *The Right and the Good* (Oxford: Clarendon Press, 1930), p. 21. Like Ross, I use the term to mean principles that ought to be obeyed, other things being equal. On his list of prima facie obligations are (1) truth telling and promise keeping; (2) the responsibility to make reparations for injuries done another; (3) the obligation of repaying things done for one by others; (4) the requirement of justice; (5) the obligation to help others "in respect of virtue, or of intelligence, or of pleasure"; (6) the responsibility to improve oneself; and (7) the obligation not to hurt others and to try to promote their good.

6. Charles Fried, *Right and Wrong* (Cambridge and London: Harvard University Press, 1978), p. 21.

7. Frank McCulloch, ed., *Drawing the Line* (Washington, D.C.: American Society of Newspaper Editors Foundation, 1984), pp. 60–62.

8. See, for example, "Anderson column linked to death of Chicago editor," *Editor & Publisher,* July 16, 1977, p. 37, and "Spy Said He'd Kill Himself If Exposed, Then Did So," *New York Times,* April 2, 1976, p. 1.

9. This account is based on an article by one of the reporters of the *Sun-Times* involved in the coverage, Pam Zekman, "Behind the Mirage," *The Best from the Investigative Reporters and Editors Conference, 1980* (Columbia, Mo.: University of Missouri School of Journalism, 1981), pp. 19–20, and also on a book, Zay N. Smith and Pamela Zekman, *The Mirage* (New York: Random House, 1979).

10. *Bulletin of the Amercian Society of Newspaper Editors,* September 1979, p. 12.

11. Zekman, op. cit., p. 19.

12. *ASNE Bulletin,* p. 13.

13. From full draft column, by Douglas Hofstadter, for *Indiana Daily Student,* September 1981, p. 2.

14. Patrick Siddons, publisher of the *Indiana Daily Student,* in *ids in review,* Bloomington, Ind., Sept. 23, 1981.

15. From published column by Douglas Hofstadter, "Policies need not be ironclad," *Indiana Daily Student,* Sept. 25, 1981, p. 4.

16. Lawrence Roberts, "Crime and Punishment at the *Oregonian,*" *Washington Journalism Review,* October 1981, pp. 14–15.

17. John Rawls, *A Theory of Justice* (Cambridge Mass.: Harvard University Press, 1971), p. 41.

18. See Sissela Bok, *Lying: Moral Choice in Public and Private Life* (New York: Vintage Books, 1979), pp. 55–59, and p. 319, n. 9.

5. Values, Virtues, and Principles

1. Frank McCulloch, ed., *Drawing the Line* (Washington, D.C.: American Society of Newspaper Editors, 1984). Subsequent citations to page numbers in this volume will be given parenthetically in the text.

6. The Journalism Business

1. Bob Teague, *Live and Off-Color: News Biz* (New York: A & W Publishers, 1982), pp. 43–45.

2. Warren Breed, "Social Control in the Newsroom," *Social Forces,* Vol. 33, No. 4, 1955, pp. 326–335.

3. Ruth C. Flegel and Steven H. Chaffee, "Influences of Editors, Readers and Personal Opinions on Reporters," *Journalism Quarterly,* Winter 1971, pp. 645–651.

4. Mark Popovich, "Coordination in the Newsroom: An Analysis of the News Preferences of Reporters, Editors and Publishers," paper presented to the Theory and Methodology Division, Association for Education in Journalism Annual Convention, Seattle, Washington, August 1978.

5. Breed, "Social Control in the Newsroom," pp. 332–335.

6. Ibid., p. 329.

7. Edward J. Epstein, *News from Nowhere* (New York: Random House, 1973), p. 272.

8. Leon V. Sigal, *Reporters and Officials* (Lexington, Mass.: D. C. Heath and Co., 1973).

9. Ibid., pp. 65–100.

10. Ibid., p. 190.

11. Herbert J. Gans, *Deciding What's News* (New York: Vintage Books, 1980), p. 281.

12. Ibid., p. 42–69.

13. Ibid., p. 46.

14. Ibid., p. 51.

15. Chris Argyris, *Behind the Front Page* (San Francisco: Jossey-Bass, 1974), p. 1.

16. The role of *The New York Times* and other media during this period and the impact of this period on the relationship between the news media and government are brilliantly documented in the writing of another scholar who has studied the *New York Times.* See Paul Weaver, "The New Journalism and the Old," *Public Interest,* No. 35, Spring 1974, pp. 67–88.

17. Argyris, *Behind the Front Page,* pp. 1–33.

18. Ibid., p. 239.

19. Ibid.

20. Ibid., p. 242.

21. Ibid., Chapter 12, "Looking Back at the Experiment," pp. 228–237, and Chapter 5, "Evaluations of the Learning Seminar." pp. 110–137.

22. Ibid., p. 268.

23. See, for example, Max Ways, "What's Wrong with News? It Isn't New Enough," *Fortune,* October 1969, pp. 110–111.

24. Ernest C. Hynds, *American Newspapers in the 1980s* (New York: Hastings House, 1980), p. 142.

25. "Special Report," *Editor & Publisher,* Oct. 3, 1981, pp. 12–14.

26. William T. Benham, John Finnegan, Jr., and Patrick Parsons, "The Chain-Independent Debate Reassessed: Some New Evidence and an Interpretation," paper presented to the Association for Education in Journalism annual convention, Athens, Ohio, August 1982.

27. Walter Baer et al., "Concentration of Mass Media Ownership: Assessing the Current State of Knowledge," Rand Reports (R-1584 NSF) (Santa Monica, California: 1974), cited in Benham et al., "The Chain-Independent Debate Reassessed," p. 20.

28. American Society of Newspaper Editors, "The News and Editorial Independence: A Survey of Group and Independent Editors," April 1980, p. 8.

29. Judee K. Burgoon, Michael Burgoon, and Charles K. Atkin, "What's News? Who Decides? And How?" A Preliminary Report on the World of the Working Journalist, for the American Society of Newspaper Editors, May 1982, p. 6.

30. Ibid., p. 4.

31. Ibid., p. 10.

32. Ibid., p. 8.

33. See Edmund B. Lambeth, "The Lost Career of Paul Y. Anderson," *Journalism Quarterly,* Fall 1983, pp. 401–406.

34. Speech by Curtis MacDougall on the fifth anniversary of the publication of his book, *Interpretative Reporting* (New York: Macmillan, 1977), at the Association for Education in Journalism annual convention, Athens, Ohio, July 1982.

35. See Lester Markel, ed., *Background and Foreground* (Great Neck, N.Y.: Channel Press, 1960) and quoted in MacDougall, *Interpretative Reporting*, pp. 161, 164.

36. Donald McDonald, "Is Objectivity Possible?" in John C. Merrill and Ralph D. Barney, eds., *Ethics and the Press* (New York: Hastings House, 1975), p. 87.

37. Elmer Davis, "News and the Whole Truth," *Atlantic Monthly,* August 1952, p. 35.

38. Philip Meyer, *Precision Journalism* (Bloomington: Indiana University Press, 1973).

39. David Anderson and Peter Benjaminson, *Investigative Reporting* (Bloomington: Indiana University Press, 1976), p. 84.

40. Steve Weinberg, *Trade Secrets of Washington Journalists* (Washington: Acropolis Press, 1981).

41. See, for example, Bernard Roshco, *Newsmaking* (Chicago: University of Chicago Press, 1975), p. 122.

42. Bruce M. Swain, *Reporters' Ethics* (Ames: Iowa State University Press, 1978), pp. 88–95.

43. See "Nation's Journalists: We Need Codes of Ethics, But Don't Make Them Mandatory," *Quill,* July–August 1977, p. 9.

44. Swain, "Reporters' Ethics," pp. 93–96.

45. The episode at the *Binghamton,* (N.Y.) *Press* in 1959 involved the author as the young reporter, the late Stuart Dunham as the city editor, and the late Fred W. Stein as editor-in-chief.

46. Peter C. Townsend, "Unwanted Ombudsmen," *Columbia Journalism Review,* May–June 1981, pp. 7, 9.

47. Melvin Mencher, *News Reporting and Writing* (Dubuque, Iowa: William C. Brown, 1981), p. 419.

48. Ibid.

49. Breed, "Social Control in the Newsroom," p. 333.

50. Ibid.

51. Ibid., p. 331.

52. Presentation by Alan Parachini, *Chicago Sun-Times,* Regional Conference of Investigative Reporters and Editors, Indianapolis, Indiana, Fall 1978.

53. Hillier Krieghbaum, *Pressures on the Press* (New York: Crowell & Co., 1972), p. 172.

54. Ibid., p. 331.

55. Robert Cirino, *Power to Persuade: Mass Media and the News* (New York: Bantam Books, 1974), p. 133.

56. Anon., "Albritton Admits Error in Using Press Releases," *Editor & Publisher,* March 20, 1982, p. 82.

57. George Seldes, *Freedom of the Press* (Indianapolis: Bobbs-Merrill, 1935), pp. 62–76.

58. Goody L. Solomon, "Food Pages: Is the Heyday Over?" *Columbia Journalism Review,* January–February 1982, pp. 41–44.

59. Quoted in Lou Cannon, *Inside Reporting* (Sacramento, Calif.: California Journal Press, 1977), p. 89.

60. Anthony Smith, "Is Objectivity Obsolete?" *Columbia Journalism Review,* May–June 1980, p. 65.

61. Edward J. Epstein, *Between Fact and Fiction: The Problem of Journalism* (New York: Vintage Books, 1975), p. 17.

7. In Lieu of Licensing

1. This episode occurred during a visit by the author and his wife, Fran, with Seldes in Vermont and New Hampshire in July 1981. For an enlightening account of the Orozco murals, consult "An Interpretation of the Orozco Frescoes at Dartmouth," by Churchill P. Lathrop, professor of art emeritus, distributed by the library.

2. Review in *Journalism Quarterly,* Vol. 12, March 1935, p. 320.

3. Ibid., p. 321.

4. See Prof. Eric Allen's review of *Lords of the Press, Journalism Quarterly,* Vol. 16, June 1939, p. 179; Eric L. Vance's review of *The People Don't Know, Journalism Quarterly,* Vol. 20, December 1943, pp. 335–336.

5. *QS,* Newsletter of the Qualitative Studies Division of the Association for Education in Journalism, "Pioneer Press Critic, Famous Foreign Correspondent George Seldes, Honored with Second Professional Excellence Award; First in 90 years," Vol. 7, No. 1, Fall 1980, p. 6.

6. *Washington Post,* March 1, 1982, p. A-5.

7. This is a key point made in a discursive and scholarly tribute to Seldes by Everette E. Dennis and Claude-Jean Bertrand, "Seldes at 90: They Don't Give Pulitzers for That Kind of Criticism," *Journalism History,* Vol. 7, Nos. 3–4, Autumn–Winter 1980, pp. 81–86, 120.

8. See Robert V. Hudson, "Will Irwin's Pioneering Criticism of the Press," *Journalism Quarterly,* Summer 1970, Vol. 47, No. 2, pp. 263–271.

9. Ibid., p. 263.

10. For an insightful evaluation of Liebling, see Edmund M. Midura's "A. J. Liebling: The Wayward Pressman as Critic," *Journalism Monographs,* No. 93, April 1974, pp. 1–46.

11. See Bagdikian, *The Effete Conspiracy and Other Crimes by the Press* (New York: Harper & Row, 1972), and idem, *The Information Machines* (New York: Harper & Row, 1971).

12. Wilbert E. Moore, *The Professions* (New York: Russell Sage, 1970), pp. 4–22.

13. Ibid., p. 9.

14. Ibid., p. 14.

15. See John W.C. Johnstone, Edward J. Slawski, and William Bowman, "The Professional Values of American Newsmen," *Public Opinion Quarterly* 36, Winter 1972–73, p. 522–540; Penn Kimball, "Journalism: Art, Craft or Profession?" in *The Professions in America,* K. S. Lynn, ed. (Boston: Beacon Press, 1963), pp. 242–260; Dan L. Lattimore and Oguz B. Nayman, "Professionalism and Performance in Print Journalism: A Systematic Evaluation of Colorado Daily Newsmen and Newspapers," paper presented to Mass Media and Society Division, Association for Education in Journalism, Fort Collins, Colorado, 1973.

16. Ben Bagdikian, "Should Journalists Be Licensed?" *Chicago Tribune,* Dec. 27, 1981, and distributed by Knight-Ridder Newspapers, *Long Beach* (California), *Press Telegram.*

17. *Editor & Publisher,* Dec. 1, 1973, p. 7, p. 16.

18. Wayne Godsey, *Communicator* (Radio Television News Directors Association) September 1981, p. 32.

19. Ibid.

20. For example, see the March 1982 issue of the *ASNE Bulletin* which contains a special report, pp. 3–21, on credibility of the press.

21. Bruce M. Swain, *Reporters' Ethics* (Ames: Iowa State University Press, 1978), pp. 115–116.

22. Ibid., p. 113.

23. Commission on Freedom of the Press, *A Free and Responsible Press* (Chicago: University of Chicago Press, 1947), pp. 97–107.

24. Norman Isaacs, "Why we lack a national press council," *Columbia Journalism Review,* Fall 1980, pp. 16–26.

25. John C. Merrill, *The Imperative of Freedom* (New York: Hastings House, 1974), p. 92.

26. Alex Kotlowitz, "National News Council: Does It Practice What It Preaches?" *Washington Journalism Review,* p. 27.

27. Ibid.

28. See National News Council Report, " 'Life' criticized for paying accused killer," *Columbia Journalism Review,* May/June 1981, pp. 87–91.

29. Ibid., p. 88.

30. National News Council Report, " 'Voice' article called unfair and reckless," *Columbia Journalism Review,* Sept./Oct. 1981, pp. 85–86. For another viewpoint, see Paul Maccabee's letter to the editor in *Quill,* January 1982, p. 2.

31. Kotlowitz, "National News Council," p. 25.

32. " 'Life' criticized for paying accused killer," p. 91.

33. David Shaw. "Watching the Watchers," *Quill,* December 1981, p. 14.

34. Andrew Radolf, "National News Council folds," *Editor & Publisher,* March 31, 1984, pp. 9, 28–29.

35. Elie Abel, "What killed the council," *Columbia Journalism Review,* July/August 1984, p. 61.

36. "News Council closes, gives files to Minnesota," *Quill,* April 1984, p. 44.

37. Robert Schafer, "The Minnesota News Council: Developing Standards for Press Ethics," *Journalism Quarterly,* Autumn 1981, p. 356.

38. *New York Times,* July 23, 1978, p. 27.

39. Ibid.

40. " '60 Minutes' Putting Itself on the Griddle," *Wall Street Journal,* Sept. 25, 1981, p. 25.

41. Ibid.

42. "Ex-C. E. Relishes Diplomatic Post: The Readers' Man," *Editor & Publisher,* February 5, 1972, p. 30.

43. Suraj Kapoor and Ralph Smith, "The Newspaper Ombudsman—A Progress Report," *Journalism Quarterly,* Spring 1979, pp. 628–631.

44. R. J. Haiman, panel discussion, ASNE convention, April 22, 1981, Washington, D.C.

45. See *Washington Post,* April 19, 1981, pp. 1, 12–15.

46. "L.A. Times' David Shaw, press critic on page one," *Editor & Publisher,* Dec. 25, 1976, p. 13.

47. "Editorial Ombudsman," *Newsweek,* Dec. 14, 1970, p. 72.

48. Lee Brown, *The Reluctant Reformation* (New York: David McKay Co., 1974), pp. 52–53.

49. Cassandra Tate, "What do ombudsmen do?" *Columbia Journalism Review,* May/June 1984, pp. 37–41.

50. Ibid., p. 41.

51. Ibid.

52. News Research Bulletin No. 9, June 3, 1970, including results of research commissioned by the ANPA with William B. Blankenburg, reprinted in Brown, *The Reluctant Reformation.*

53. "Journalism Reviews: Stuck in the Gutter?" *Byline,* Winter 1980, p. 9.

54. See "Publisher's Notes," *Columbia Journalism Review,* March/April 1982, p. 20.

55. Peter Dreier and Steve Weinberg, "Interlocking Directorates," *Columbia Journalism Review,* November/December 1979, pp. 51–68.

56. Edmund B. Lambeth and Robert Ferguson, "The *Columbia Journalism Review* and Scientific Controversy," paper presented to Science Writing Educators' Group, Association for Education in Journalism, Boston, Aug. 10, 1980.

57. "Does the *Progressive* Have a Case?" *Columbia Journalism Review,* May/June 1975, pp. 25–27.

58. Alfred Balk and James Boylan, eds., *Our Troubled Press* (Boston: Little, Brown, 1971), p. xvi.

59. Ibid.

60. "Journalism Reviews: Stuck in the Gutter?" *Byline,* Winter 1980, p. 9.

61. Ron Aldridge, "Marva Collins in the middle of '60 Minutes'—Ch. 2 debate," *Chicago Tribune,* Feb. 25, 1982, pp. 14–15. See also David Smothers, United Press International, "Is Marva Collins real, a myth, or in between?" *Bloomington* (Ind.) *Herald-Telephone,* April 16, 1982, p. 17.

62. See "Conflicts of Interest, Pressures Still Distort Some Papers' Coverage," *Wall Street Journal,* July 25, 1967, p. 1, and "Some Journalists Fear Flashy Reporters Let Color Overwhelm Fact," *Wall Street Journal,* May 14, 1981, p. 1.

63. Lester A. Sobel, ed., *Media Controversies* (New York: Facts on File, Inc., 1981), pp. 69–83.

64. Ernest W. Lefever, *TV and National Defense* (Boston, Va.: Institute for American Strategy, 1974).

65. Leonard J. Theberge, *TV Coverage of the Oil Crises: How Well Was the Public Served?* Vols. I–III (Washington, D.C.: Media Institute, 1982).

66. For an exposition of the rise of the new media monitors, see Lois Breedlove et al, "Media Monitors," *Quill,* June 1984, pp. 17–22.

67. Michael J. Robinson, "Media, Rate Thyselves," *Washington Journalism Review,* December 1983, p. 31.

68. Ibid., p. 33.

69. As a sample, see James W. Carey, "But who will criticize the critics?" *Journalism Studies Review,* 1: 1, Summer 1976, pp. 7–11; Fred Johnson, "The Minnesota Press Council: A Study of Its Effectiveness," *Mass Comm Review,* Vol. 4, No. 1, Winter 1976–77, pp. 13–19; Joseph P. McKearns, Carole L.

McNall and Elisabeth M. Johnson, "Mass Media Criticism: An Annotated Bibliography," *Mass Comm Review,* Vol. 4, No. 1, Winter 1975–76, pp. 9–18.

70. Reprinted in *ids* (Indiana Daily Student) *in review,* compiled by Pat Siddons, publisher, and Barbara Redding, assistant publisher, Vol. X, No. 1, Spring 1982, p. 1.

8. Government and the News Media

1. See "The witness," *Columbia Journalism Review,* Sept.–Oct. 1973, p. 3., a remembrance of Teapot Dome amid the Watergate crisis.

2. Paul Weaver, "The New Journalism and the Old," in John C. Merrill and Ralph D. Barney, eds., *Ethics and the Press* (New York: Hastings House, 1975), p. 92. This article gives an excellent overview of the rise of conflict between the press and government in the 1960s and 1970s.

3. Ibid.

4. The record of deceit in the post–World War II era is amply set forth in David Wise, *The Politics of Lying: Government Deception, Secrecy, and Power* (New York: Vintage Books, 1973).

5. For an excellent summary of the new salience of the news media in politics, see Doris A. Graber, *Mass Media and American Politics* (Washington: Congressional Quarterly Press, 1980).

6. William L. Rivers, *The Adversaries* (Boston: Beacon Press, 1970), p. 8.

7. Twentieth Century Fund, Task Force on the Government and the Press, *Press Freedoms Under Pressure* (New York: Twentieth Century Fund, 1972), p. 55.

8. Ibid.

9. William J. Small, *Political Power and the Press* (New York: W. W. Norton, 1972), p. 395.

10. Stephen Hess, "Fairness and the Media," *Washington Post,* July 31, 1974, p. A–20.

11. In his study of Wisconsin's statehouse press corps, Delmer D. Dunn, *Public Officials and the Press* (Reading, Mass.: Addison-Wesley, 1969), pp. 7–22, finds that reporters see themselves in a number of roles, such as interpreter of government, representative of the public, and more rarely, participant in policy making.

William O. Chittick's role analysis of the U.S. State Department press corps showed reporters' relationships with information officers and interest group leaders were usually cooperative. With policy officials the relationship, measured quantitatively, fell on the borderline between the categories of "more cooperative than antagonistic" on one hand and "both cooperative and antagonistic." See his *State Department, Press and Press Groups* (New York: Wiley-Interscience, 1970), p. 285. See also Robert O. Blanchard, "The Correspondents Describe Their Work," in Blanchard, ed., *Congress and the News Media* (New York: Hastings House, 1974), pp. 180–238. In a survey of self-described role orientations, the most frequently checked category (81%) was "To be an interpreter for the public by putting in understandable terms what Congress is doing and why it is doing it." The next most preferred role self-descriptions (with 64% each) were neutral observer, watchdog against corruption, and checker of the veracity of congressmen's statements.

12. William L. Rivers and Michael J. Nyhan, eds., *Aspen Notebook on Government and the Media* (New York: Praeger, 1973), p. 15.

13. Ibid. Each of the above studies makes the point that, for a variety of reasons, cooperation—however mixed it is, from time to time, with antagonism—is a prevailing characteristic of reporter/official relationships. For example, in ed., *Congress and the News Media,* see Delmer Dunn's "Symbiosis: Congress and the Press," pp. 240–249, and Donald R. Matthews, " 'Covering' the Senate," pp. 253–268.

14. Rivers, *The Adversaries,* p. 48.

15. Ibid., p. 237–253, especially pp. 243–246.

16. Cited in Maurice R. Cullen, Jr., *Mass Media and the First Amendment* (Dubuque, Iowa: William C. Brown, 1981), p. 142.

17. Small *Political Power and the Press,* p. 381.

18. Vincent Blasi, *The Checking Value in First Amendment Theory* (Chicago: American Bar Foundation, 1977), p. 527.

19. Ibid.

20. Celeste Huenergard, "Editors assess warning on excessive press power," *Editor & Publisher,* May 15, 1982.

21. Ibid., pp. 11 and 41.

22. Michael Walzer, "Teaching Morality," *New Republic* June 10, 1978, p. 14.

23. John Stuart Mill, "On Liberty," in William Ebenstein, *Great Political Thinkers* (New York: Holt, Rinehart & Winston, 1969), p. 592.

24. Robert Friedman, "The United States vs. The Progressive," *Columbia Journalism Review,* July/August 1979, p. 31.

25. Telephone interview by the author with Erwin Knoll, October 15, 1982.

26. Philip Taubman, "U.S. abandons effort to prevent publication of hydrogen bomb data," *Louisville Courier-Journal,* Sept. 18, 1979, p. 1.

27. Knoll interview.

28. Ibid.

29. Anon., "Publishers Have Heard This Song Before," and Anthony Lewis, "National Security and the Press: A Riddle Inside a Hard Case," *New York Times,* March 18, 1979, p. 22E.

30. Friedman, "United States vs. The Progressive," pp. 30–31.

31. Samuel H. Day, Jr., "The other nuclear weapons club," *The Progressive,* November 1979, p. 23.

32. Howard Morland, "Errata," ibid., p. 35.

33. Jeremy J. Stone, "Giving Away the Secret of the First Amendment," *Quill,* June 1979, p. 27.

34. Ben Bagdikian, "A Most Insidious Case," ibid., p. 26.

35. Friedman, "United States vs. The Progressive," p. 35.

36. James McCartney, "Vested Interests of the Reporter," in Louis M. Lyons, ed., *Reporting the News* (Cambridge: Harvard University Press, 1965), pp. 97–106.

37. L. D. Hankoff, Letter to the Editor, *New York Times,* January 23, 1975, p. 32. For a detailed discussion of the Wilbur Mills case and the press's responsibilities in such circumstances, see Brit Hume, "Now It Can Be Told . . . Or Can It?" *MORE,* April 1975, pp. 6–11.

38. McCartney "Vested Interests of the Reporter," p. 105.

39. Ibid.

40. Stephen Hess, *The Washington Reporters* (Washington, D.C.: The Brookings Institution, 1981), p. 166.

41. Paul L. Fisher and Ralph L. Lowenstein, eds., *Race and the News Media* (New York: Anti-Defamation League of B'nai B'rith, 1967), p. 14.

42. See Richard E. Neustadt, *Presidential Power: The Politics of Leadership, with Reflections on Johnson and Nixon* (New York: John Wiley & Sons, 1976), p. 18; Rowland Evans and Robert Novak, *Lyndon B. Johnson: The Exercise of Power* (New York: Signet Books, 1968), p. 597; Don Stillman, "Tonkin: What Should Have Been Asked," in Alfred Balk and James Boylan, eds., *Our Troubled Press* (Boston: Little, Brown, 1971), pp. 110–118.

43. A measure of this tardiness is the list of "firsts" registered by Bob Woodward and Carl Bernstein, who then were two unknown reporters. See William L. Rivers, *The Other Government: Power & the Washington Media* (New York: Universe Books, 1982), p. 227.

44. Hess, *The Washington Reporters,* p. 166. Half the Washington reporters surveyed by Hess said lack of coverage of the regulatory agencies was a serious problem.

45. Edmund B. Lambeth and John A. Byrne, "Pipelines from Washington," *Columbia Journalism Review,* May/June 1978, pp. 52–55.

46. Hess, *The Washington Reporters,* p. 166.

47. Ibid.

48. Roger Morris, "Eight Days in April: the press flattens Carter with the neutron bomb," *Columbia Journalism Review,* Nov.–Dec. 1978, p. 25.

49. John D. May, "Goosing the public," *Columbia Journalism Review,* Sept.–Oct. 1978.

50. Paul Janensch, "Who said that," *Louisville Courier-Journal,* Aug. 24, 1980, p. D-3.

51. Speech by Bob Greene, Assistant Managing Editor of *Newsday,* before the Qualitative Studies Division of the Association for Education in Journalism, Athens, Ohio, July 26, 1982. Greene identifies the "enemies of ethical perception" as "expedience, greed, bias, and advantage."

52. "Warehouse Committee," *Nation,* April 17, 1976, p. 454.

53. Harry F. Waters with Tom Joyce, "What Makes Danny Run?" *Newsweek,* Feb. 23, 1976, p. 49.

54. Nora Ephron, "The rain that falls on Daniel Schorr's parade," *Esquire,* June 1976, pp. 50, 52, 54.

55. Lou Cannon, *REPORTING: An Inside View* (Sacramento: California Journal Press, 1977), pp. 48–49.

56. Daniel Schorr, " 'The Daniel Schorr Affair,' a Reply," *Columbia Journalism Review,* July/Aug. 1976, p. 49.

57. Bob Kuttner, "Look Before You Leak," *MORE,* March 1976, p. 6.

58. "Reporters group declines payment for Pike Report," *Editor & Publisher,* Feb. 28, 1976, pp. 11 and 35.

59. Ephron, "Rain that falls on Daniel Schorr's parade," p. 50.

60. Ibid.

61. Kuttner, "Look Before You Leak," p. 6.

62. "Reporters Group declines payment for Pike Report."

63. Jack Landau of the Reporters Committee told Kuttner: "We were thrown into complete confusion. Oh, it was just terrible. Everybody wanted to do the moral thing. But we didn't even know that the *Voice* had Dan's copy. If we confirmed it, we might have been lying; if we denied it, we might have been lying."

64. "Selling Secrets," Editorial page, *New York Times,* Feb. 15, 1976.

65. "Of Secret Documents," Editorial page, *New York Times,* Feb. 22, 1976.

66. "Schorr Under Siege," *Time,* March 1, 1976, p. 42.

67. Ephron, "Rain that falls on Daniel Schorr's parade," p. 52.

68. Harry F. Waters with Nancy Stadtman, *Newsweek*, Oct. 31, 1977, p. 93.

69. Ibid.

70. David Gelman with Jeff B. Copeland, "Defender of the Faith," *Newsweek*, Sept. 17, 1976, p. 85.

71. Thomas Griffith's column, Newswatch: "The Dos and Don'ts of Television News," *Time*, Dec. 5, 1977, p. 114.

72. Ephron, "Rain that falls on Daniel Schorr's parade."

73. Laurence Stern, "The Daniel Schorr Affair," *Columbia Journalism Review*, May–June 1976, pp. 20–25.

74. Schorr, " 'Daniel Schorr Affair,' a Reply."

75. Kuttner, "Look Before You Leak."

76. Ephron, "Rain that Falls on Daniel Schorr's parade."

77. Schorr, " 'Daniel Schorr Affair,' a Reply," p. 48.

78. Stern, "Daniel Schorr Affair," p. 20.

79. Kuttner, "Look Before You Leak," p. 7.

9. Ethics, Investigative Reporting, and the "Tragedy of the Commons"

1. Rowland Evans and Robert Novak, *Lyndon B. Johnson and the Exercise of Power (New York: New American Library, 1968), p. 435.*

2. *Oliver Pilat, Drew Pearson: An Unauthorized Biography* (New York: Harper's Magazine Press, 1973), p. 299.

3. Special issue, "Jerry Landauer," *Wall Street Journal*, March 29, 1981.

4. "Supersnoop," *Time*, Jan. 6, 1975, p. 65.

5. Fred P. Graham, "*Life* Says Wolfson Received and Repaid a Wolfson Fee," *New York Times*, May 5, 1969, p. 1.

6. Clark Mollenhoff's excellent book, *Game Plan for Disaster: An Ombudsman's Report on the Nixon Years* (New York: W. W. Norton Co., 1976), is one of the few accounts of the Watergate scandal that shows its origins in earlier administrations, and also how not only the *Washington Post* but other news media helped in its exposure.

7. See "Pulitzer-winning effort taxed 4-man staff," *Editor & Publisher*, May 21, 1977, p. 41.

8. Paul N. Williams, *Investigative Reporting and Editing* (Englewood Cliffs, N.J.: Prentice-Hall, 1978), p. 193.

9. This account is based largely on Julius Duscha's article, "A Reporter's Committee that Works," *Columbia Journalism Review*, May–June 1973, pp. 26–43.

10. Williams, *Investigative Reporting*, pp. 112–134, 144–45.

11. See *The Best from IRE Conferences*, Indianapolis, 1976, pp. 13–14.

12. See for example Miller's book, a detailed account of injustice in the legal system, *Invitation to Lynching* (New York: Doubleday, 1975).

13. Lenora Williamson, "*Detroit News* wins Pulitzer Gold Medal," *Editor & Publisher*, April 17, 1982, pp. 14–15, 34.

14. Virginius Dabney, "I'm distraught and upset at what I see," *ASNE Bulletin*, November 1982, pp. 30–32. Dabney emphasized his acceptance and approval of the watchdog role and its public benefits, especially by using methods that are "direct, forceful and honorable."

15. Michael O'Neill, "Shop Talk at Thirty," *Editor & Publisher*, May 15, 1982, p. 52.

16. *"N.Y. Times* director hits investigative fad," *Editor & Publisher,* May 22, 1976, p. 12.

17. This survey, suggested by *Chicago Sun-Times* editor Ralph Otwell, was released by the Gallup Poll on Dec. 17, 1981.

18. Barbara F. Luebke, "How the Public Rates Investigative Journalism," *IRE Journal,* Winter 1982, p. 7.

19. Williams, *Investigative Reporting,* pp. 65, 101–102, 162.

20. Ibid., pp. 3, 8, 79, 107.

21. Virginia Dodge Fielder and David Weaver, "Public Opinion in Investigative Reporting," *Newspaper Research Journal,* Vol. 3, No. 2, January 1982, pp. 54–62.

22. William J. Brennan, "Justice Brennan Sprays 'Firestorm of Acrimonious Criticism,' " *ASNE Bulletin,* November 1979, pp. 14–17.

23. For a comparison of recent libel judgments in the United States and Britain, see "The Pound and the Jury," *Washington Journalism Review,* Jan.–Feb. 1983, p. 52.

24. The emergence of this approach is reflected in such articles as "To Deceive or Not to Deceive," *Quill,* December 1981, p. 9, which is a summary and explication of the criteria by Dr. Louis W. Hodges and his colleagues at Washington and Lee University.

25. Edmund B. Lambeth, "Dice, Card Games Played to Aid the Campaign of Merz," *Milwaukee Journal,* Feb. 15, 1960, p. 1.

26. See Gannett Company's *Editorially Speaking,* July/August 1977, p. 1.

27. Ibid., p. 2. For a sensitive and well developed different approach, see Phil Currie, "Sometimes the Ethical Barometer Registers 'Foul,' " Gannett Company, *Editorially Speaking,* July/August 1977, pp. 3–5.

28. Garrett Hardin, "The Tragedy of the Commons," *Science,* 1968, Vol. 162: 1243–1248.

29. Theodore C. Sorenson, *Kennedy* (New York: Harper & Row, 1965), pp. 359–360.

30. Quoted in Charles Fried, *Right and Wrong* (Cambridge, Mass.: Harvard University Press, 1978), p. 60.

31. Ibid.

32. Charles and Bonnie Remsberg, "Investigative Reporter: Ray Brennan," *Writer's Digest,* February 1970, p. 20.

33. Ibid., pp. 21–22.

34. Sissela Bok, *Lying: Moral Choice in Public and Private Life* (New York: Vintage Books, 1979), pp. 77–94.

35. Ibid., p. 25.

36. Ibid., p. 126–127.

37. Ibid., p. 127.

38. Ibid., p. 128.

39. Carl Bernstein and Bob Woodward, *All the President's Men* (New York: Simon & Schuster, 1974), p. 224. At other places, Woodward admits lying to Deep Throat. For Bok's comments, see Bok, *Lying,* pp. 113, 127–128.

40. Immanuel Kant, *Perpetual Peace* (New York: Columbia University Press, 1932), pp. 58–59.

41. John Rawls, *A Theory of Justice* (Cambridge, Mass.: Harvard University Press, 1971), p. 133.

42. Transmittal letter by James Hoge, *Sun-Times* executive vice president and editor-in-chief, Dec. 29, 1978, p. 1.

43. Special Reprint, "The Mirage, A Report on the 'Fix' in Chicago," *Chicago Sun-Times*, 1978.

44. For example, see the numerous differing viewpoints on the *Sun-Times* series in the 1978 publication, "Undercover," a joint project of the *Times* Publishing Co. of St. Petersburg, Fla., and the University of South Florida's Department of Mass Communication.

45. *Columbia Journalism Review*, Jan.–Feb. 1983, p. 52.

46. Quoted in Leonard Downie, *The New Muckrakers* (Washington, D.C.: New Republic Book Co., 1976), p. 256.

47. Ibid., p. 257.

48. Unpublished text of speech by Bagdikian entitled, "A Critical Look at Investigative Reporters," IRE Convention, June 19, 1976, p. 12.

49. John Hughes, "Journalism's next phase: problem solving," *ASNE Bulletin*, Nov.–Dec. 1971, pp. 8–9.

50. Max Ways, "What's Wrong with News? It Isn't New Enough," *Fortune*, October 1969, pp. 110–113, 155–161.

10. Ethics, the Media, and the Law

1. See Don R. Pember, "The 'Pentagon Papers' Decision: More Questions Than Answers," *Journalism Quarterly*, Autumn 1971, pp. 403–411.

2. Ibid., p. 411.

3. Sanford Ungar, *The Papers and the Papers* (New York: E. P. Dutton, 1972), pp. 70–73.

4. Neil Sheehan, Hedrick Smith, E. W. Kenworthy, and Fox Butterfield, *The Pentagon Papers* (New York: Bantam Books, 1971), p. xiii.

5. Ungar, *The Papers and the Papers*, p. 95.

6. Ibid., and p. 204.

7. For a brief summary of the *Time*'s condensation strategy and alternatives considered, see Sheehan et al., *Pentagon Papers*, p. xvii.

8. Ben Bagdikian, "A Most Insidious Case," *Quill*, June 1979, pp. 25–26.

9. Ibid., p. 26.

10. Alexander M. Bickel, *The Morality of Consent* (New Haven and London: Yale University Press, 1975), p. 61.

11. Ibid., p. 60.

12. Herbert Klein, *Making It Perfectly Clear* (New York: Doubleday, 1980), p. 348.

13. Ibid., p. 350.

14. Justice Warren Burger outlined such an approach in giving the majority opinion of the Court. Ibid., p. 347.

15. Ibid., p. 350.

16. Ungar, *The Papers and the Papers*, p. 96.

17. Howard Bray, *The Pillars of the Post* (New York: W.W. Norton, 1980), p. 116.

18. For a critical evaluation of the *Times*'s version of the Pentagon Papers, see Edward J. Epstein, *Between Fact and Fiction: The Problem of Journalism* (New York: Vintage Books, 1975), pp. 78–100.

19. 376 U.S. 254 (1964).

20. *Associated Press* vs. *Walker*, 388 U.S. 130, 134 (1967).

21. See *Rosenbloom* vs. *Metromedia*, 403 U.S. 29 (1971) and *Curtis Publishing Co.* vs. *Butts*, 388 U.S. 130 (1967).

22. 418 U.S. 323, 344 (1974).

23. 434 U.S. 448 (1976).

24. Justice William Rehnquist said even though the public divorce proceedings contained testimony to infidelity, the divorce decree did not actually specify adultery as grounds for divorce.

25. *Washington Post,* July 25, 1982, p. A-3.

26. See "Mobil Chief Sets Up Son in Venture, Management Firm is Used to Operate Oil Company Ships," *Washington Post,* Nov. 30, 1979, pp. 1, 6, 7.

27. See "Four of Six Jurors at First Supported the *Post,*" *Washington Post,* August 7, 1982, A-4.

28. See "SEC Reports No Wrongdoing in Mobil President's Actions," *Washington Post,* July 29, 1981.

29. See "Reporter for *Post* Testifies in Trial of $50 Million Suit," *Washington Post,* July 10, 1982.

30. See "Mobil Oil Company President's Libel Case Against the *Post* Begins," *Washington Post,* July 8, 1982, A-4.

31. See "Hill Employee Says He Gave Documents to *Post* to Get Publicity for Hearings," *Washington Post,* July 20, 1982, A-13.

32. See "Dingell Cites Contradictions in Mobil Statements," *Washington Post,* Dec. 1, 1979, A-3.

33. See "Source for Disputed *Post* Story, Editor, Testify in Mobil President's Libel Suit," *Washington Post,* July 21, 1982, A-4, and "*Post* Reporter Defends His Stories, Describes Sources," *Washington Post,* July 23, 1982, A-15.

34. See "A Chilling Verdict," *Newsweek,* Aug. 9, 1982, p. 46.

35. C. T. Hanson, "On the Libel Front," *Columbia Journalism Review,* Jan./Feb. 1983, p. 36.

36. Ibid., p. 31.

37. "Inside the jury room at the Washington Post trial," *American Lawyer,* Vol. 4, Issue 7, November 1982, p. 2.

38. Mobil Oil Company reprint of advertisement in the *New York Times,* Nov. 18, 1982.

39. "Libel Verdict Reversed For Lack of Evidence," *Editor & Publisher,* May 7, 1983, p. 10; Kenneth Bredmeier, "Panel Reinstates Libel Decision Against the Post," April 10, 1985, p. 1. See also "Fear and loathing of 'holy shit' journalism," *Columbia Journalism Review,* July/August 1985, pp. 27–28.

40. Supreme Court of the United States 1972, 408 U.S. 665, 92 S. Ct. 2646, 33 L. Ed. 2d 626, incorporating in re *Pappas and United States* vs. *Caldwell.*

41. *New York Times* vs. *New Jersey,* 439 U.S. 997 (1978).

42. Matter of Farber, 78 N.J. 259, 394 A. 2d 330 (1978), quoted in Marc A. Franklin, *The First Amendment and the Fourth Estate* (Mineola, N.Y.: Foundation Press, 1979), pp. 25–29.

43. Ibid., p. 135.

44. See Justice Stewart's dissenting opinion in the Branzburg case, Franklin, *First Amendment and the Fourth Estate,* p. 24.

45. Achal Mahra, "Newsmen's Privilege: An Empirical Study," *Journalism Quarterly,* Winter 1982, pp. 560–565.

46. Ibid., p. 565.

47. Alan Bromley, article from unpublished edition of *Juris Doctor,* reprinted in *IRE Journal,* Spring 1981, p. 8.

48. Ibid.

49. Speech before the National Conference of IRE, June 25–27, 1982, Washington D.C.

50. Franklin, 1979, op. cit., p. 137.

51. John Lofton, *Justice and the Press* (Boston: Beacon Press, 1966), p. 102.

52. Ibid., p. 104.

53. Ibid., pp. 104–108.

54. Original research by Kim Jackson, in term paper on the *Courier*'s coverage of the case written for the author's ethics course, 1981.

55. Alfred Friendly and Ronald L. Goldfarb, *Crime and Publicity* (New York: Twentieth Century Fund, 1967), p. 305.

56. Ibid., p. 304.

57. Ibid., pp. 13–20, and 384 U.S. 333, 86 S. Ct. 1507, 16 L. Ed. 2d 600.

58. National News Council, *Protecting Two Vital Freedoms* (New York: National News Council, 1980), p. 5.

59. Ibid., p. 6.

60. *Gannett Co.* vs. *DePasquale,* 99 S. Ct. 2898, 2901–5 (1979).

61. David M. O'Brien, *The Public's Right to Know* (New York: Praeger, 1981), p. 135.

62. Ibid., 139.

63. Ibid.

64. John Rawls, *A Theory of Justice* (Cambridge, Mass.: Harvard University Press, 1971), p. 302.

65. Ibid.

II. Social Science and Journalism Ethics

1. See Lawrence Kohlberg, "Moral Stages and Moralization," in T. Lichona, ed., *Moral Development and Behavior: Theory, Research, and Social Issues* (New York: Holt, Rinehart & Winston, 1976) pp. 31–53.

2. Lawrence Kohlberg, "Stages and Aging in Moral Development: Some Speculations," *Gerontologist,* 1973, Vol. 13, pp. 497–502.

3. Kohlberg, "Moral Stages and Moralization," p. 32.

4. See Benjamin S. Bloom, et al., *Taxonomy of Educational Objectives: The Classification of Educational Goals. Handbook I: Cognitive Domain* (New York: McKay, 1956).

5. The account is based on Seymour M. Hersh, "How I Broke the Mylai 4 Story," *Saturday Review,* July 11, 1970, pp. 46–49.

6. Ibid., p. 49.

7. A possible exception is Leonard Downie, *The New Muckrakers* (Washington, D.C.: New Republic Book Co., 1976).

8. See Hersh, "How I Broke the Mylai 4 Story," p. 48.

9. David Zucchino, "Outtakes for the Defense," *Washington Journalism Review,* January 1985, pp. 41–44.

10. Bob Greene, "Trying to trap the Tylenol Killer: A columnist's conscience," *ASNE Bulletin,* March 1983, pp. 20–22.

11. Bruce DeSilva, "The gang-rape story," *Columbia Journalism Review,* May/June 1984, pp. 42–44.

12. Ibid., p. 42.

13. 1984–1985 Journalism Ethics Report, prepared by the National Ethics Committee, Society of Professional Journalists/Sigma Delta Chi, p. 24.

14. Ibid., p. 34.

15. Ibid., p. 16.

16. Louis D. Boccardi, "Time for us to re-examine some of the basic assumptions," *ASNE Bulletin,* June/July 1984, pp. 6, 13.

17. Philip Meyer, *Editors, Publishers and Newspaper Ethics*, A Report to the American Society of Newspaper Editors (Washington, D.C., 1983), p. 54.

18. Ibid.

19. The study of 1,000 reporters, editors, and writers from all walks of journalism was financed by the Gannett Foundation and conducted at the Indiana University School of Journalism under direction of Professors David Weaver and G. Cleveland Wilhoit, with the assistance of the author and several other faculty members.

20. The objectives of this segment of the chapter have been influenced by Stephen E. Toulmin's *The Place of Reason in Ethics* (New York and London: Cambridge University Press, 1970), especially pp. 130–165.

21. Hersh, "How I Broke the Mylai 4 Story," p. 49.

22. Ibid., pp. 46.

23. Richard Morrill, *Teaching Values in College* (San Francisco, Washington and London: Jossey-Bass Publishers, 1980), p. 67.

24. Ibid.

25. William Perry, *Intellectual and Ethical Development in the College Years* (New York: Holt, Rinehart & Winston, 1970), p. 215.

26. See Clyde A. Parker, ed., *Encouraging Development in College Students* (Minneapolis: University of Minnesota Press, 1978), especially pp. 135–182.

27. Perry, *Intellectual and Ethical Development*, pp. 9–10.

28. Ibid., p. 134–135.

29. Ibid., p. 135.

30. Ibid.

31. Ibid., pp. 177–200.

32. Ibid., p. 131.

33. Ibid., p. 203. Perry, in fact, seems to speak favorably of situation ethics in his footnote 3 on page 203.

12. Toward a Committed Journalism

1. George Gallup, Jr., "Americans favor tougher controls on the press," *Editor & Publisher*, Jan. 19, 1980, p. 7.

2. Milton D. Hunnex, *Philosophies and Philosophers* (San Francisco: Chandler Publishing Co., 1971).

3. George H. Sabine, *A History of Political Theory*, 3rd ed. (New York: Holt, Rinehart & Winston, 1961), p. 81.

4. Ibid., p. 169.

5. William Ebenstein, *Great Political Thinkers* (New York: Holt, Rinehart & Winston, 1969), pp. 66–111.

6. Sabine, *History of Political Theory*, pp. 153–155.

7. Ebenstein, *Great Political Thinkers*, pp. 422–427.

8. Will Durant, *The Story of Philosophy* (New York: Pocket Books, 1955), pp. 4–12.

9. Cited in Irving Brant, *The Bill of Rights*, (Indianapolis: Bobbs-Merrill, 1965), p. 83.

10. Ibid.

11. Ibid.

12. Ibid., Chapter 8, "The Diabolical Art of Printing," pp. 97–112.

13. Ebenstein, *Great Political Thinkers*, pp. 390–421.

14. Ibid., p. 545.

15. Cited by J. C. Rees in "A Re-Reading of Mill on Liberty," from Isaac Kramnick, ed., *Essays in the History of Political Thought* (Englewood Cliffs, N.J.: Prentice-Hall, 1969), p. 357.

16. Reprinted from *On Liberty,* in Ebenstein, *Great Political Thinkers,* p. 592.

17. See Rees, "A Re-Reading of Mill on Liberty," pp. 367–371.

18. Ebenstein, *Great Political Thinkers,* p. 569.

19. See for example Michael Polanyi, *Personal Knowledge* (Chicago: University of Chicago Press, 1958) p. 304.

20. Quoted from *An Enquiry Concerning the Principles of Morals* in Ethel M. Albert, Theodore C. Denise, and Sheldon P. Peterfreund, *Great Traditions in Ethics* (New York: D. Van Nostrand, 1980), p. 214.

21. Durant, *Story of Philosophy,* pp. 258–259.

22. Ibid., p. 277.

23. "Ray Cave on Journalism," Speech at University of Oregon School of Journalism, 1984, pp. 309.

24. Polanyi, *Personal Knowledge,* p. 309.

25. William Perry, *Intellectual and Ethical Development in the College Years* (New York: Holt, Rinehart & Winston, 1970), p. 202.

26. Polanyi, *Personal Knowledge,* p. 315.

27. Theodore Lowi, *The End of Liberalism* (New York: W. W. Norton, 1969).

28. Sabine, *History of Political Theory,* p. 14.

29. Alexander M. Bickel, *The Morality of Consent* (New Haven and London: Yale University Press, 1975), pp. 23–24.

SELECTED BIBLIOGRAPHY

Albert, Ethel M.; Denise, Theodore C.; Peterfreund, Sheldon P. *Great Traditions in Ethics* (New York: D. Van Nostrand, 1980).

Altschull, J. Herbert. *Agents of Power* (New York and London: Longman, 1984).

Baldwin, Donald K., ed. *The Adversary Press* (St. Petersburg: Modern Media Institute, 1983).

Barnes, Jonathan; Schofield, Malcolm; Sorabji, Richard. *Articles on Aristotle* (New York: St. Martin's Press, 1977).

Bay, Christian. *The Structure of Freedom* (Stanford: Stanford University Press, 1970).

Bickel, Alexander M. *The Morality of Consent* (New Haven and London: Yale University Press, 1975).

Bok, Sissela. *Lying: Moral Choice in Public and Private Life* (New York: Vintage Books, 1979).

Cahn, Edmond. *The Moral Decision* (Bloomington: Indiana University Press, 1956).

Chafee, Zechariah, Jr. *Government and Mass Communications,* Vols. 1 & 2; A Report from the Commission on Freedom of the Press (Chicago: Universtiy of Chicago Press, 1947).

Chancellor, John W., and Mears, Walter R. *The News Business* (New York: Harper & Row, 1983).

Christians, Clifford G.; Rotzoll, Kim B.; and Fackler, Mark. *Media Ethics, Cases and Moral Reasoning* (New York and London: Longman, 1983).

Cohen, Bernard C. *The Press and Foreign Policy* (Princeton, N.J.: Princeton University Press, 1963).

Dunn, Delmer D. *Public Officials and the Press* (Reading, Mass.: Addison-Wesley, 1969).

Durant, Will. *The Story of Philosophy* (New York: Pocket Library, 1955).

Ebenstein, William. *Great Political Thinkers* (New York: Holt, Rinehart & Winston, 1969).

Edman, Irwin ed., *The Works of Plato* (New York: Random House, Modern Library, 1928).

Emerson, Thomas I. *The System of Freedom of Expression* (New York: Random House, 1970).

———. *Toward a General Theory of the First Amendment* (New York: Random House, 1966).

Epstein, Edward J. *News from Nowhere* (New York: Random House, 1973).

Fried, Charles. *Right and Wrong* (Cambridge, Mass.: Harvard University Press, 1978).

Friedrich, Carl J. *The Philosophy of Kant* (New York: Random House, 1949).

Feuer, Lewis Samuel. *Spinoza and the Rise of Liberalism* (Boston: Beacon Press, 1958).

Gans, Herbert J. *Deciding What's News* (New York: Vintage Books, 1980).

Gaus, Gerald F. *The Modern Liberal Theory of Man* (New York: St. Martin's Press, 1983).

Gerald, J. Edward. *The Social Responsibility of the Press* (Minneapolis: University of Minnesota Press, 1963).

Goodwin, H. Eugene. *Groping for Ethics in Journalism* (Ames: Iowa State University Press, 1983).

Gustafson, James M. *Can Ethics Be Christian?* (Chicago and London: University of Chicago Press, 1975).

Hardie, W. F. R. *Aristotle's Ethical Theory* (Oxford: Clarendon Press, 1980).

Hardin, Garrett. *The Limits of Altruism: An Ecologist's View of Survival* (Bloomington and London: Indiana University Press, 1977).

Hanno, Hardt. *Social Theories of the Press* (Beverly Hills and London: Sage Publications, 1979).

Harrison, John M. and Stein, Harry H. *Muckraking, Past, Present, and Future* (University Park and London: Pennsylvania State University Press, 1973).

Hartz, Louis. *The Liberal Tradition in America* (New York: Harcourt-Brace, 1955).

Held, Virginia. *The Public Interest and Individual Interests* (New York and London: Basic Books, 1970).

Hocking, William Ernest. *Freedom of the Press: A Framework of Principle* (Chicago: University of Chicago Press, 1947).

Hodges, Louis, ed. *Social Responsiblity: Journalism, Law, Medicine* (Lexington, Va: Washington and Lee University, 1978).

Hohenberg, John. *The Professional Journalist* (New York: Holt, Rinehart & Winston, 1983).

Hulteng, John L. *The Messenger's Motives* (Englewood Cliffs, N.J.: Prentice-Hall, 1976).

Hulteng, John L., and Nelson, Roy Paul. *The Fourth Estate* (New York: Harper & Row, 1971).

Johnstone, John W. C.; Slawski, Edward J.; Bowman, William W. *The News People* (Urbana, Chicago, and London: University of Illinois Press, 1976).

Kelbley, Charles A. *The Value of Justice* (New York: Fordham University Press, 1979).

Kramnick, Isaac, ed. *Essays in the History of Political Thought* (Englewood Cliffs, N.J.: Prentice-Hall, 1969).

Lowi, Theodore J. *The End of Liberalism* (New York: W. W. Norton, 1969).

MacIntyre, Alasdair. *A Short History of Ethics* (New York: Macmillan, 1966).

McCulloch, Frank. *Drawing the Line* (Washington D.C.: American Society of Newspaper Editors, 1984).

Merrill, John C. *Existential Journalism* (New York: Hastings House, 1977).

———. *The Imperative of Freedom: A Philosophy of Journalistic Autonomy* (New York: Hastings House, 1974).

Merrill, John C., and Barney, Ralph D., eds. *Ethics and the Press: Readings in Mass Media Morality* (New York: Hastings House, 1975).

Merrill, John C., and Odell, S. Jack. *Philosophy and Journalism* (New York and London: Longman, 1983).

Meyer, Philip. *Editors, Publishers, and Newspaper Ethics* (Washington, D.C.: American Society of Newspaper Editors, 1983).

Mollenhoff, Clark R. *Game Plan for Disaster* (New York: W. W. Norton, 1976).

Monan, J. Donald. *Moral Knowledge and Its Methodology in Aristotle* (Oxford: Clarendon Press, 1968).

Parker, Clyde A. *Encouraging Development in College Students* (Minneapolis: University of Minnesota Press, 1978).

Perry, William G., Jr. *Intellectual and Ethical Development in the College Years* (New York: Holt, Rinehart and Winston, 1970).

Polanyi, Michael. *Personal Knowledge* (Chicago: University of Chicago Press, 1959).

———. *The Study of Man* (Chicago: University of Chicago Press, 1959).

———. The Tacit Dimension (Garden City, N.Y.: Doubleday, 1966).

Rawls, John. *A Theory of Justice* (Cambridge, Mass.: Harvard University Press, 1971).

Rest, James R. *Development in Judging Moral Issues* (Minneapolis: University of Minnesota Press, 1979).

Rivers, William L., and Schramm, Wilbur. *Responsibility in Mass Communication* (New York: Harper & Row, 1969).

Ross, W. David. *Foundations of Ethics* (Oxford: Clarendon Press, 1939).

———. *The Right and the Good* (Oxford: Clarendon Press, 1930).

Ross, Bernard. *The Nature of Moral Responsibility* (Detroit: Wayne State University Press, 1973).

Sabine, George H. *A History of Political Theory* (New York: Holt, Rinehart & Winston, 1961).

Schaeffer, David Lewis. *Justice or Tyranny? A Critique of John Rawls' Theory of Justice* (Port Washington, N.Y.: Kennikat Press, 1969).

Schiller, Dan. *Objectivity and the News* (Philadelphia: University of Pennsylvania Press, 1981).

Siebert, Fred S.; Peterson, Theodore; and Schramm, Wilbur. *Four Theories of the Press* (Urbana: University of Illinois Press, 1963).

Sigal, Leon V. *Reporters and Officials* (Lexington, Mass.: D.C. Heath, 1973).

Sobel, Lester A. *Media Controversies* (New York: Facts on File, 1981).

Somerville, John, and Santoni, Ronald E., eds. *Social and Political Philosophy* (Garden City, N.Y.: Doubleday, 1963).

Spragens, Thomas A., Jr. *The Irony of Liberal Reason* (Chicago and London: University of Chicago Press, 1981).

Swain, Bruce M. *Reporters' Ethics* (Ames: Iowa State University Press, 1978).

Thayer, Lee. *Ethics, Morality and the Media* (New York: Hastings House, 1980).

Thiroux, Jacques P. *Ethics, Theory and Practice,* 2nd ed. (Encino, Calif.: Glencoe Publishing, 1980).

Tuchman, Gaye. *Making News* (New York: The Free Press, 1978).

The Wilson Quarterly. *News Media in America,* Vol. VI, No. 5, 1982.

INDEX OF NAMES

INDEX OF SUBJECTS

EDMUND B. LAMBETH is Professor and Director of the School of Journalism at the University of Kentucky. He has a Ph.D. in political science from American University and an M.S. in journalism from Northwestern. He has been a practicing journalist, teacher, and scholar.